SACRIFICE IN THE DESERT

A Study of an Egyptian Minority Through the Prism of Coptic Monasticism

Mark Gruber

Edited by M. Michele Ransil
With a Foreword by William Arens

University Press of America,® Inc.
Lanham · New York · Oxford

Copyright © 2003 by
University Press of America,® Inc.
4501 Forbes Boulevard
Suite 200
Lanham, Maryland 20706
UPA Acquisitions Department (301) 459-3366

PO Box 317
Oxford
OX2 9RU, UK

ISBN 0-7618-2539-8 (paperback : alk. ppr.)

To Michelle Gilbert and John Middleton:

The gracious hospitality of their home and marriage inspires their work and enhances their profound contributions to the intellectual project of human self-reflection.

I consider myself to be especially blessed to be the beneficiary of their anthropological discourse and their warm, reverential friendship.

Table of Contents

v

Foreword

In his masterful study, *Nuer Religion*, E. E. Evans-Pritchard concludes in a now famous passage that the religion of these sympathetic people is, ultimately, an interior state externalized in observable rites such as prayer and sacrifice. "Their meaning," he continues, "depends finally on an awareness of God, and that men are dependent on him and must be resigned to his will. At this point, the theologian takes over from the anthropologist" (Evans-Pritchard 1956:322). Perhaps Evans-Pritchard, a firm believer of sorts himself, was offering an invitation to another generation of students of exotic religions to take on the challenge of integrating what he had left asunder. Mark Gruber, O.S.B., and Ph.D., anthropologist and theologian, is well suited to take up the challenge. He does so here with his own admirable study of another, albeit, quite different African religious system with its own focus on sacrifice. In this instance, the sacrifice is a lived and personal one, so befitting a Christian community, and so well presented by its interpreter.

The author, in this instance, is also a believer. At one time, that admission and rare condition would have raised more than a few suspicious, metaphorical eyebrows. Fortunately, we have now come to realize that the anthropological enterprise, especially in the form of a study such as this one, depends for its success primarily on a subjective bent. A deep understanding is called for here, as opposed to a dubious exercise in explanation. Again, there can be no doubt about the success of the present effort.

This study of the desert monks also raises the issue of the possibility of a sympathetic treatment of a world religion, such as Christianity, so prominent in the West and in this country in particular, where religion is a persuasion and a serious commitment, rather than a taken-for-granted sense of identity. As Gruber intimates, and I would make explicit and reaffirm, there is no reason to treat the religious ideas of people such as the Nuer with the utmost respect, and then simultaneously dismiss those closer to home with disdain. This sort of still common, convoluted, academic snobbery is neither acceptable on intellectual nor on logical grounds.

I end in approximation to where I began by noting that Evans-Pritchard once wrote of a pupil that, "We should be grateful for his efforts, for what he did might never be repeated."

William Arens
Professor of Anthropology
Graduate School
Stony Brook University
Stony Brook, New York

Apologia

Author's Preface

> He walks alone across the Sahara sands. Black-robed and be-hooded, he plods slowly onward. Veering now to the right and then to the left, his path is unpremeditated. His bearded face is abstracted, his eyes nearly closed. The Coptic monk is praying, and his prayer perfectly conforms to the setting. The desert purifies him, and he sanctifies the desert.

Nothing in the scene betrays the day or the season. Nothing about the man signifies the age in which he lives. Nothing in his mind seems to reflect the worldview of his century. The monk is attired in garments which transcend the chronology of fashion. His attitude is one of deliverance. He has been delivered *from* the entanglements of this world and, at the same time, he is delivered *up* to the benediction of the other world. The winding path he treads defines not so much a meandering walk in the wilderness as the contours of his interior pilgrimage. To the Copts, he is a living symbol of that which embodies the central mechanism of their survival: sacrifice.

In the following chapters, I have attempted to present the Coptic people through the lens of their central and most treasured institutional communities: their desert monasteries. The Copts have not been studied in the West, both because Orthodox Christian cultures are not of general interest to secular social scientists, and because Middle Eastern studies strongly emphasizes Islam as the essential religion in the region. Moreover, modern Coptic monasticism is an even more remote area of intellectual discourse because ecclesiastical medievalists and Patristic philologists have placed a firm grip on the desert fathers which is strong enough to discourage social scientists from intrusion into their contemporary desert-dwelling descendants.

I have offered this study to provide new resources to fill an academic need and an intellectual lacuna. This work, therefore, is a study of the Coptic community of Egypt, and the critical role of the desert monks in preserving their ethnic integrity down through the ages.

As a Western monk and an anthropologist, I realize that the image of a monk, so inherently charged with significance and meaning, may often obscure the individual behind it. For the West, this romanticizing is often viewed with disdain. Western monks and secular commentators often take undue pleasure in disabusing people of the sacred allusions which continually adhere to monastic lives. But in the Near East, the cultural image of the monk is thought to provide a deeper insight into the essence of the man whose individual personality is only of secondary value. The romanticized description of the monk above serves to reflect the communal perception that the monks enjoy in Coptic society.

Since the purpose of this work is not intended as an exposé, it will not consider how well the monk actually conforms to the traditional pattern of monastic life. Rather, it will explore the role of the monk in its link between the person and its ideal in the spiritual worldview of the Copts. If the thesis below is correct, then the correspondence of the monks' lives to the cultural persona ascribed to them is of critical importance to the viability of that worldview, and hence to the cultural tenacity of the Coptic people. Therefore, some concrete details of monastic life in Egypt must be provided, since the study of any group requires the anchoring of its subjects to temporal and historical contexts. Coptic monks may be esteemed as otherworldly from a moral or spiritual perspective, but for social, scientific purposes, they must also be considered in their earthly moorings, just like any other group.

To the faithful Copts who may be offended by an attempt to subject certain aspects of their religion to cultural analysis, I sincerely apologize. What follows may not please them as a devout interpretation of the religious institution for which they have the deepest respect. But it is not, I hasten to add, a negative interpretation. In fact, I have striven to avoid the false assumptions and biased conclusions that characterize many scientific investigations of religious societies. Instead, I have tried to apply objective, impartial social science criteria in the analysis of the Coptic people and their culture.

Antagonism to the religious orientation of humanity, especially to that of Christians, was probably a necessary position of the secular, scientific mind in post-Enlightenment Europe. Differentiation from a "Mother Church," whether it be social, cultural, or ecclesiastical, involves wrenching punctuations. However, fairness to the interpretation of history requires recognition of the fact that certain cultural circumstances of European Christendom fostered the genesis of science as a likelihood in that particular time and place. But the maturation of a science will eventually permit it to shed the bias of repudiation by which it arose. Anthropologists now stand ready to investigate religious phenomena without the need to project metaphysical judgments about whether or not more ultimate realities may be intuited by a sincerely religious mind.

Something inside even these Western social scientists may actually sigh at the sight of the desert monk walking alone in the distance!

Acknowledgements

This work has been an on-and-off project for over a decade, and the contributors to its present form are too numerous to name. With gratitude to them all, and blame to no one for any limitations found in the text, I am bound to name a certain few of them.

First and foremost, I am grateful to my editor and collaborator, my "shepherdess with staff and rod," Sister M. Michele Ransil, C.D.P., who never allowed me to abandon the task, and always assisted me with bearing so much of its burden. I also extend my appreciation to Miss Kerry Crawford for reading the earlier text, and to Fr. Joseph Linck for proofreading the present version. Their comments have aided me in correcting, revising and refining the work.

The present work has been generated in some large portion from the doctoral dissertation based upon a year of fieldwork among the Coptic people in Egypt. My dissertation acknowledged the many people who contributed to its completion at that time, and they need not be mentioned here. Nevertheless, my primary reader, Dr. William Arens, advised me strongly to pursue a rewriting effort, and my "outside reader," Dr. John Middleton, often encouraged me to find a publisher, and even assisted me in the search. To both of these renowned anthropologists, I offer my sincere gratitude.

I also wish to extend my thanks to Mr. Robert Ellsberg, the Editor in Chief of Orbis Books, who recently published the personal memoirs of my year of ethnographic study in Egypt. Obviously, *Sacrifice in the Desert* covers much of the same material as *Journey Back to Eden*, especially the names of persons and the places I visited, as well as the historical events that affected the Coptic people--although from an anthropological perspective, rather than from a personal one. Mr. Ellsberg has granted us permission to use any of the copyrighted material in this work that may overlap that in the journal.

In 1997, The Institute for Comparative Research in Human Culture in Oslo, Norway, published *Between Desert and City: The Coptic Orthodox Church Today*. The book includes Chapter 4, "Coping with God: Coptic Monasticism in Egyptian Culture," and Chapter 5, "The Monastery as the Nexus of Coptic Cosmology," which are earlier versions of chapters 8 and 9 in this ethnographic study, *Sacrifice in the Desert*. The Chairman of the Board of the Institute has graciously granted us permission to include the copyrighted material in this forthcoming publication, for which I wish to express my sincere gratitude.

Chapter I

Introduction

The metallurgist and the psychologist both realize that the full range of qualities in the subjects of their research will only surface when they are submitted to stress and pressure. "Testing the mettle" is a metaphor for character revelation under trial. Novelists and dramatists also know that the depth of a character is developed and fostered by suffering: "As gold is tested in fire, so is the worthy soul tested in the crucible of humiliation" (Sirach 2:5). Likewise, in social science, the anthropologist understands that culture generates its deepest mechanisms of adaptation and its basic patterns of character formation when societies are subjected to protracted adversity. Certainly, many societies lay claim with varying degrees of validity to the merits which proceed from extended hardship. But what are the strategies employed for communal survival in such circumstances?

Minority status often ranks as one of the chief adversities facing a people who live in a complex state. Minorities must develop strategies for presenting themselves in settings in which their cultural identity is often denigrated by the majority. They must transmit their cultural heritage to their offspring when the larger media of cultural

transmission are often hostile to that process (Yinger 1970:310). The
Copts of Egypt are a people with a long history of minority status
and all the adversity which that entails. They have evolved strategies
for communal survival, public profile, and long-term enculturation
which reveal something of the essential operation of culture itself. In
the unique religious expressions of their society, one might suppose
that Coptic culture has been conditioned by complex historical and
even ecclesiastical forces. But the sheer duration of their marginality,
the intensity of their periodic persecution, and the simplicity of their
response persuade the observer that the Copts have seized upon a
primal cultural agency and have so consistently employed it that it has
become central to their expression of communal sentiment. That cultural agency is sacrifice.

Sacrifice has long been one of the great interests of anthropologists. Its pervasiveness cross-culturally (Bourdillon 1980:1), its extraordinary range of expression (Hubert & Mauss 1964:18), its profound
impact on Western cultures and religions (cf. Robertson Smith 1927:
213-243), and its power to gather people into a unity of act and cult
(Durkheim 1965:389) have made it the most studied phenomenon in
the investigation of religious cults and societies.

The Copts organize their cosmos around sacrifice, as many peoples
do. But beyond that, they have elevated it to such a high level that
it has produced a system of religious specialization totally subordinated to this concept in every aspect of social interaction. That phenomenon is monasticism.

For the Copts, monasticism is the primal, cultic act of human
sacrifice which underlies the foundation of their cultural heritage. It
is the symbolic means by which their adversity of minority status is
transformed into a charter of group validation. The monk, as the
embodiment of sacrifice in the community, personifies the strategy for
Coptic survival. He absorbs into himself the "violence" of his ascetical life, just as his ethnic community must absorb the violence of a
persecuted minority. God is perceived as the arbiter of both fates.
And just as the monk sacrifices his life to save his people, so the
Copts transform their plight into cultural survival in terms of ethnic
pride and solidarity.

In the chapters below, the historical evolution of Coptic society will be explored within a framework in which monasticism is seen to emerge as the *centerpiece* of Coptic culture. This is in contrast to societies in the West where monasteries now exist on the *margins* of culture. The interplay of the Coptic monastic and secular communities will be examined to demonstrate the influence of monastic sacrifice (asceticism) on the wider community.

Some of the best ethnographic monographs have defined one central feature of a society as the means whereby the whole culture can be fairly understood. E. E. Evans-Pritchard saw the role of cattle as the centerpiece of Nuer culture (1940). Potlatch has been presented as the lens through which Northwest Amerindian economies could be viewed (Piddocke 1968:284). Roy Rappaport reports that pig feasts are the organizing principle of certain oceanic aboriginals (cf. 1971:68-82). It may be argued that all of these phenomena are closely related to the exercise of sacrifice, and may even derive their significance from it. The Coptic monk is sacrifice incarnate and, as human sacrifice, his offering is so costly that it must be axial to the community he serves. Monasticism, as the backdrop of the monk's asceticism, is thereby central to Coptic society and informs its unique features.

Human sacrifice is a subject of the greatest fascination. Anthropologists have not been found wanting in their exploration of this phenomenon. Analyzing the ritual slayings of kings is a cottage industry in such circles. The ritual mutilation of Mayan royalty is also of great archaeological interest. The scapegoating and slaughter of prisoners (Girard 1977:274), the execution of criminals (Bourdillon 1980:13-14), the exposure of children to the elements, as well as infanticide (Robertson Smith 1927:407), are all studied under the heading of human sacrifice. The contribution of this work lies, in part, in the presentation of Coptic monasticism in which the various forms of religious asceticism are shown to be a true aspect of human sacrifice. They symbolize what bloody sacrifices symbolize, and they operate within a cultural context just as bloody sacrifices do.

Suzanne Campbell-Jones applied this insight to her study of British nuns (1979:164). In doing so, she relied upon Edmund Leach's reflection on symbolic human killing and sacrifice in a Tongan myth (1972:266). Werner Stark, an American sociologist, translates a passage

from Notker Wurmseer's article, "Von Simm des Mönchtums," as
follows:

> We find in the end that the God-given mission of monasticism
> is the fulfillment of the sacrificial duty of humanity as a whole.
> *The meaning of monkhood is to be humanity's sacrificial offering,*
> a sacrifice in the name of humanity and for the sake of human-
> ity, with all the purposes which sacrifice in its widest conno-
> tation subserves . . . above all, expiation (Stark 1970:225).

Such insights are herein elaborated and applied to Coptic monasticism.

The Monastery as an Enclosed Society

Although Christian monasticism has seldom been the focus of
scholarly investigation[1], the considerable weight of religious and
institutional insight accumulated by the social sciences can be brought
to bear on the subject. As mentioned above, a monastery is a tightly-
bound, small, exclusive society which is conducive to anthropological
study. Erving Goffman classifies such institutions as "total institutions" since they erect a social barrier to the outside world which is
often expressed in such terms as "locked doors, high walls, barbed
wires, cliffs, water, forest, or moors" (1961:4).

The total institution attempts to provide all aspects of a social,
physical, ideological, and organizational life, and may be rather jealous
in its exclusive claims on its members (1961:5-6). Goffman discusses
the total institution in terms of "detention centers, asylums, boarding
schools, and homes for the aged." However, the application of this
concept to the analysis of monasteries, with their cloisters and their
all-embracing internal life, cannot be questioned, as he himself anticipated (Goffman 1961:5). The essential difference between the monastery and these total institutions is that the inhabitants of a monastery
are there voluntarily. They freely choose to enter and remain there,
and deliberately conform their will to that of the communal good
(Asad 1993:125-26).

Monasteries cannot be considered only from their internal institutional aspect as they are a part of the inner workings of a larger reli-

gious and social institution. In Egypt, as in the West, that institution takes the form of a Church which, in this case, is found within the Coptic ethnic minority. Christianity and Coptic ethnicity are so closely connected that should a Copt convert to Islam, he or she ceases, socially speaking, to be a Copt. In the Middle East, Islam and fluency in Arabic are so interrelated that a "convert" will very likely be considered to be an Arab once Christianity has been repudiated. As a result, the Coptic Church has taken, and must continue to take, great precautions so as not to be absorbed into the religious and ethnic majority. Being a Coptic Christian in a nation which declares itself to be "Arab and Islamic" inevitably carries with it the burden of alienation.

Ethnic distinctions between the Moslem and the Copt, whether they be of food, clothing, language, familial roles, customs, or manners, are generally related to their religion. The notable exceptions are in the areas of economics and the general Westward-leaning tendencies of the Copts. Even so, without religious affiliation and the kinship forces tied to it, the Copts would have little trouble integrating themselves into Islamic Egyptian society.

Egypt has not, as yet, formally implemented the *Sha'ria*, the strict code of Koranic justice which would officially reduce non-Moslems to a tolerated second class. However, the government has concrete plans to progressively adopt that system in due time. The very fact that such a legal code is under consideration serves to describe the Copts' increasing lack of acceptance in their own ancestral homeland.

Institutions such as Churches, which have enormous social responsibilities, especially if the survival of the group is in question, must be able to make great demands from their members and representatives. Lewis Coser has observed that celibacy may be a formal requirement of such agents since the institution which they serve has a pressing need of their exclusive, undivided loyalty. These might be called "greedy institutions" insofar as they attempt to reduce competing claims and positions of those they maintain within their boundaries. Their demands on the person are omnivorous (Coser 1974:4). (The Copts would never describe their Church as a "greedy institution." Such a description strikes the ear of the more cynical Western reader as somewhat more acceptable than that of a Copt.)

Monks are enjoined to celibacy both as an expression of the internal discipline of the "total institution" of the monastery, and of the unconditional service required by the larger "greedy institution" of the Church. The celibacy of the monk is thus the axis on which the two roles compete--a tension experienced by monks worldwide, as well as in Egypt. The monastery wishes to subordinate the monk to its internal order; the Church wishes to subordinate him to its external mission. Both employ celibacy as the primary method of subordination; how monks, monasteries, and bishops resolve that tension is largely provisional. The very prominence of celibacy as indispensable to the life of the monastery and to the mission of the Church is something which most people understand, and which Goffman's and Coser's categorical descriptions make comprehensible. At any rate, celibacy figures prominently as the primary element of monastic asceticism as an aspect of human sacrifice.

The Copts in Egypt

The Copts are the Christian, usually Orthodox, descendants of the native Egyptians of antiquity who have tenaciously rejected "conversion" to Islam since the seventh-century Arab invasion. Most contemporary Egyptians would be derived in part from Coptic stock, but are now considered to be Arab due to their Islamic affiliation and long-term association with Arab states. The word "Copt" is an English transliteration of "*Gibt*," the Egyptian word for these people. "Gibt" is derived from the "*gypt*" of the word "Egypt." The Copts are proud of their direct descent from the pharaonic Egyptians and, because of their strict laws against intermarriage outside their religion, claim a unique racial purity of Egyptian stock in counter-distinction to the Arabized blood imputed to Muslim Egyptians.

The Copts comprise perhaps ten percent of the population of Egypt, although that number is strongly debated. Contemporary Copts are no longer restricted to ghetto quarters in the cities of Egypt, but they still tend to cluster in certain neighborhoods. Upper Egypt holds a significantly higher percentage of Copts than does Lower Egypt, that is, the delta region wherein the great majority of Egyptians reside. Some villages in Upper Egypt are entirely Coptic and have been for centuries.

Economically, the Copts have tended to occupy vocational roles not readily exploited by the Moslems. This has often given the Copts a certain financial advantage inasmuch as these occupations have historically been associated with jewelry, medicine, pharmacy, banking and bureaucratic skills. Many of these professions are restricted by the Koran and were the longtime preserve of the Copts until the Nasser era. By democratizing education and nationalizing industries, the late President Nasser was able to successfully urge a wider range of professions on the non-Copt. Coptic representation in these more lucrative professions is now diminishing, and is thereby creating a measure of economic stress for their community.[2] Emigration of professional Copts to the West has consequently become a modern phenomenon which coincides, paradoxically, with the recent resurgence of the Coptic religion and monasticism. The current rise of fundamentalism in the Islamic world has placed another heavy burden on the Copts as they perceive themselves to be subjected to an increase in prejudice and oppression. Their present economic plight is aggravated by a sense of religious persecution which, while not directly government-sponsored, is often at least civilly tolerated.

As might be expected from a religion renowned for tenacity, the Copts have rallied in recent years under the ancient symbols of their Faith. The small tattooed cross, which for years had only been associated with poorer villagers, now appears on the wrists of ever-increasing numbers of young urbanites and professionals. The wrist tattoo is an adamant sign of Coptic affiliation. Since these marks cannot ordinarily be eradicated, the Copt thereby proclaims: "I shall never become a Moslem."

A tatoo presents less of a statement of the religious persona than the white *galabeya* (a flowing, body-enveloping garb) of the more zealous Muslim male. The increase of the Coptic cross tattoo is seen to match the increasing appearance of the traditional Muslim headdress worn by women, now everywhere so noticeable in Egypt. Consistent with the low Coptic social profile, the wrist tattoo symbolizes the Christian affiliation of a soul primarily in one-on-one encounters, whereas Muslim dress is a very public symbol which overtly asserts majority consensus and strength.

The cross is obviously more than decorative. As a traditional symbol, it expresses the profound Coptic belief in the atonement of Christ's Passion, that is, in the efficacy of the human sacrifice of *the* axial Figure. Additionally, the cross is also a symbol of the Copts' understanding of their own ethnic identity. Long persecuted and despised, they feel that they have collectively been crucified throughout history. They display the cross on their person, and property as a sign of their communal solidarity in suffering and as a tacit reminder to their persecutors that they gain no moral advantage in harassing a passive people.

> While the Copts share the cross with the rest of Christianity, with no other group is its presence so obsessive. This ranges from the Patriarch, who holds the cross in front of himself as though it were both a shield and a weapon, to the ragged village children who run after strangers, crude blue tattoos of the cross on the inside of their right wrists and crosses on their necks. . . This fixation is symbolized at baptism when the infant is anointed 36 times [with crosses] all over his body (Wakin 1963:137).

> The cross suits this cruel culture of poverty and persecution, both as an identification and an outlet for the Copts. It is their brand and their balm; it gives a meaning to life when there are only blind nature and inexplicable misfortune. If Western Christianity gives prime glory to Easter, . . . Good Friday is more appropriate psychologically to the Copts (Wakin 1963: 136).

The cross thus embodies the ideal of passive suffering. The Copts evidence a remarkable serenity in the face of oppression. Their impassive face, their stoic silence and patient resignation may be their best strategy, given their limited numbers and the hostile nature of the dominant culture. The cross symbolizes a religious value which, in this instance, expresses the central *motif* of sacrifice.

Coptic monasticism is intimately bound to the cross as its *raison d'etre*. This is clearly evidenced in their liturgical name for a monk, *Shayel Saleeb"* ("cross-carrier"). Any discussion of Coptic or Christian monasticism which attempts to describe a monk's life in terms of merely private fulfillment, self-gratification, or personal evasion or escape, misses its broad social function. The personal asceticism of each monk is considered to be a sacrificial holocaust which intercedes for the society from which he comes.

The monks of Egypt present a vivid portrayal of the culture of their people within the "total institution" of the monastery. Within this context, the monastic life reveals a highly stylized means of institutional adaptation to a pressurized national existence.

How the Egyptian Moslems View the Copts and Their Monks

The relationship of the Moslems to the Copts in Egypt requires some commentary. Civil leaders and religious authorities of the state-supported Islamic establishment encourage toleration and respect between the two communities. The national press and the state-run television, while positively fostering Islamic spirituality, nevertheless criticize sectarian conflict and religious fanaticism. This is all the more evident during periods of violent confrontation which occur rather frequently in Upper Egypt, but also in Cairo.

Coptic religious leaders encourage their followers to exhibit a calm and peaceful demeanor. They soberly realize that their minority status affords them few options against a radical religious majority. At the same time, they sense that the Islamic mood is becoming increasingly fundamentalistic outside of the government-sponsored mosques. The tremendous cynicism regarding Egyptian national politics has undermined the credibility of the loyal sheiks and scholars of the state-operated Azhar University.

More and more Moslems are tending toward a purist Islamicist rhetoric of the student organizations and voluntary political associations which support revolutionary social agendas. In the more extreme view of such popular movements, the Copts are considered to be a dangerous Western and Christian element in Egyptian society. They are said to "corrupt" the purity of the Arab-Islamic character of Egypt and to confuse the people as to the real nature of a properly run

Islamic state. The subjection of the Copts to church bombings, the burning of businesses, the looting of homes, the harassing of students, kidnappings and forced "conversions" (especially of young women) has escalated in recent years. Government denial and the suppression of news make it impossible to quantify these events, but the Coptic people are overwhelmed with apprehension by such tactics.

Given the contemporary Coptic sense of Islamic hostility and social persecution, which is added to their long-standing complaint of educational mistreatment, civil bureaucratic alienation, military under-representation, judicial denigration and economic marginalization, the significant lack of Coptic violence is striking. Some individual Copts do resort to physical force, and their aggression has an anti-Islamic intent. However, these rare occurrences are usually precipitated by local--even kinship--conflicts which spin out of control because no trustworthy mediation of Coptic/Muslim disputes can be found. But there is no national or regional Coptic organization which advocates terrorism or even communal defense as its goal. Coptic youth often meet at night to study chant or to learn their Church's ancient tongue; their cultural sense of survival seems to be sublimated into the symbolic. Searches for stockpiles of arms in Coptic churches invari-ably fail, but Islamic authorities are often surprised by the volume of devotional tracts they find there. While the activity of any militarized Coptic associations or the collective hoarding of arms would bring devastation upon the Copts, should these things be proven, the absence of such pursuits ironically provokes accusations of Coptic cowardice.

Much of what happens between the Coptic and the Muslim sectors of Egypt is nuanced by the social forces of the contemporary Middle East: the general Islamization process; hostility toward Europe for its colonial divisions of the regions which deprive the Moslem of a full sense of *the* "Islamic nation"; the economic forces related to the controlling of oil prices; the cultural forces of the media, especially those which are felt to undermine traditional morality; international banking regulations; and the Western imposition of a Jewish state. Yet in order to appreciate the basis of Coptic/Muslim relations, one must retreat somewhat from the events of the contemporary scene and seek the deeper structures of cultural identity on which the surface layers of conflict and misunderstanding are so predictably laid.

Moslems regard the foundational texts of Christianity and Judaism to be intentionally corrupted. They maintain that the original Judeo-Christian Scriptures plainly anticipated the advent of Mohammed, but the texts were falsified so the Christians could retain their religious beliefs when he appeared. The "real Bible" was lost, although (in their view), it has been restored in the Koran. Hence, while Copts regard the Bible as their religious charter, Moslems do not; they consider the Koran to be the true foundation of Coptic Christianity. Hostility to the Copts, therefore, derives not just from their refusal to accept Koranic revelation and become Moslems (which some regard as blasphemous contempt), but also from the perception of their seeming inability even to be good Christians. One important consequence of this double-bind of intolerance is that, even after all these centuries of co-existence, Moslems have no interest, academic or otherwise, in investigating what the Copts actually do believe or practice. Their perceptions of Christianity are always filtered through the lens of the supposedly corrupted condition of its Scriptures. Not to do so would be an offense against Koranic "truth."

An extraordinary ignorance about the Copts emerges from this situation. The Copts often lament that the Moslems know nothing about their faith. But from the Islamic perspective, a well-read Moslem knows more about the "true" Christian faith than does the Copt. This bifurcation of perceptions has enormous consequences for Coptic/Muslim relations, not the least of which is that the Copts are able to operate out of a symbolic sphere almost invisible to the Moslems. They just do "not get" the significance of the Coptic religion, even after a millennium of physical juxtapositioning. While this is something of an ecumenical tragedy on one level, it permits the Copts a certain subcultural interiority wherein they can assert the values and symbols necessary to reinforce their communal survival. They enjoy a sense of satisfaction that the ignorance of the dominant culture is a vindication of the wisdom of their own subculture, the greatest "secret" of which is monasticism. Its role and significance always seem negligible to the Islamic world, merely an antiquated artifact of a bygone age. But for the Copts, monasticism vivifies their communal order and validates its special character.

Celibacy, from the Islamic perspective, is a nonsensical way of life. Since they believe that having several wives is the ideal of human success and prosperity and that having many sons is a sign of divine good pleasure, the monastic vocation strikes the majority of Egyptians as an oddity of a quixotic religion. Since there is no apparent benefit of such a strange career, Moslems cannot believe that monks are of any importance in Coptic public life. If they see the monk aggrandized by the Copts, they assume that it is a display of meaningless honorifics, not the affirmation of central values. Again, this creates a sphere of influence in which the Coptic monks can operate within the ethnic minority. The few Egyptians who sense something of this influence are unable to locate its exact source. The monks can therefore function with a surprising latitude of religious authority under such a cover.

The Fieldwork

I lived among the desert monks of Egypt for nearly a year. My fieldwork was conducted from October 1986 through August 1987, during which time I visited all the canonically approved Coptic monasteries for men.[3] Since this study required a protracted observation of one site, I was able to pursue my research in one monastery throughout the liturgical cycle of Advent, the Christmas season, Lent and the Easter season, that is, from late November 1986 through April 1987. Additionally, the research involved an investigation of the local Coptic Church and its communities in Cairo and Upper Egypt, including brief visits to seven of the eight monasteries for women. Most of these convents were established in Cairo; however, it should be noted that these foundations have again begun to appear in the desert in recent years, just as they did centuries ago.

I returned to Egypt for a follow-up of this study for almost a month in December 1988 to January 1989, during the same interval in 1993 to 1994, and for several days in May 1997. My interest in comparing the monasteries of Ethiopia with those of Egypt--from which they were founded centuries ago--prompted a trip to Ethiopia in late December 1997 through almost mid-January 1998. The results of this study are appended in the Epilogue.

One sign and measure of my relative success in gaining entrée into Coptic society and its monastic hierarchy was the acceptance by the Coptic Patriarch, Pope Shenouda III, of my invitation to come to my American monastery with his entourage on September 28, 1989, to speak at an ecumenical gathering and receive an honorary doctorate. Anyone who is knowledgeable about the conservative and reclusive nature of Coptic clerics and hierarchs, all of whom are monks, would appreciate how extraordinary this gesture was.

My life as a monk of the Benedictine Order in the Roman Catholic Church can partially account for my long-term access to the Coptic monasteries for men; unfortunately, my gender precluded the same level of access to their monasteries for women. However, a number of the observations which are made about monks in this work may apply to female monastics as well. The situation of the two genders in this regard is not symmetrical, just as they are not fully symmetrical in any other area of social life in this or in any other region. The male-oriented nature of the Coptic religion is such a predictable component of Coptic culture and such a pervasive element of Mediterranean societies that it deserves sustained analysis on its own accord. If this were not the case, if monasticism gave equal and symmetrical voice to both male and female expressions, this unique phenomenon would require special attention.

In preparation for my fieldwork, I studied Arabic intensively for a year prior to my trip to Egypt. Arabic is the language of the Copts, although liturgically they may occasionally employ Coptic, which is a late phase of ancient Egyptian written in modified Greek letters. The manner of the fieldwork was participant-observation, with my dressing, praying, blessing, fasting, and traveling in the manner of an Egyptian monk. I was similarly attired in black robes and a hood, was bearded, and wore a large leather Coptic-style cross suspended from a cord around my neck. In many instances, I was taken to be a Coptic monk by pilgrims to the monasteries, by visiting monks, and by the inhabitants of the Nilotic towns and villages. I lived inside the walls of the monasteries, ate the traditional fare of the monks, and engaged in a number of their labors and pastimes. As a result, the following study contains any number of first-hand insights and analyses not readily apparent to other observers.

The monastery is an ideal subject for a contemporary anthropo-logical study. On the one hand, it represents the exclusive, "minia-ture" society to which ethnographers are traditionally drawn. On the other hand, the monastery exists at the intersection of larger social forces and institutional processes, such as organized religions, popular enthusiasms and the state. Moreover, the cultural and religious ideals of a society find a viable expression in such a setting. In this case, the image of a monk and his monastery still exercises enormous fascina-tion over the secular world, even in the West.

The Egyptian monasteries described here are among the oldest in Christianity. Although they are central to the Christian remnant of Egypt, they have not been the object of sustained study, nor have monasteries generally engendered such interest among anthropologists in either the East or the West. The well-known reluctance of Western social science to investigate its own religious heritage and institutions is slowly diminishing, and it might be expected that monasteries will become the subject of greater interest in the future. The Egyptian monastery, at once non-Western and yet the antecedent of Western monasticism, appears to be an excellent subject for consideration.

Chapter II

Sacrifice in a Historical Perspective

The frequent consideration of sacrifice in this work requires a survey of the historical treatment of the subject over the past century. Anthropologists have dealt with the religious phenomenon of sacrifice from a plurality of social insights and methods. The earliest treatments have been oriented toward understanding the Judeo-Christian and Greek experiences of sacrifice.

A survey of the first three chapters of Leviticus, as well as a review of other sacrificial narratives of the Bible establish a ready-made example of sacrificial activity for the Hebrew model.[1] Such a review may be useful as a point of contrast and comparison with Coptic monastic sacrifice for several reasons. Structurally, the mechanisms of sacrifice should be recognizably similar anywhere, if the category of sacrifice has validity. Culturally and historically, the Hebrew model of sacrifice derives, in part, from Egyptian antecedents in particular, and from a desert Mediterranean milieu in general, as does the Coptic model. Religiously, the Hebrew model has had a direct impact on the religious formation of Coptic Egypt inasmuch as Coptic orthodoxy looks to the Bible as its basis.

The treatment of animal sacrifices in the Bible can be fairly reduced to six operations:

1.

The animal selected was to be pure. It was to be unblemished, whole, healthy, and strong. The animal was to represent a significant loss or else it was not sacrifice (Deuteronomy 15:21). Later Old Testament prophets would rail against sacrifiers who brought inferior beasts to the temple, not so much because God minded a lesser specimen, as because it represented a lesser priority for God in the one who offered it.

2.

The animal was to be taken to a special place, often outside the settlement, or to a consecrated place apart from daily routines where the sacrifice was to be prepared and performed. This separated the animal from the rest for its sacred purpose and kept a particular moment of divine commerce from disturbing the mundane order (cf. Genesis 31:54; Exodus 3:18; 5:3; 8:4,21,23).

This was especially clear when the Jews consecrated the so-called "scapegoat" on the Day of Atonement. The high priest laid his hands upon the goat's head and invested it with the sins of the people, implying that the priest himself either already carried them, or was a conduit of them. Since the goat was to carry off these iniquities to an isolated region, it had to be sent away into the desert (Leviticus 16: 21-22).

The ideal location of sacrifice is not a humanly controlled space, but a divinely ordained one. The desert, "no man's land," is precisely God's land and is ideal for sacrifice. Later, the development of cultic life in Israel would make the temple site the desert heart of an urban and agricultural people. Indeed, the temple's Holy of Holies retained a tent-like character, reminiscent of the desert exodus dwelling of God (2 Chronicles 5-6). Moreover, the priests who offered the sacrifice were likewise initiated into this office by a period of social isolation (Leviticus 9).

3.

Violence was inflicted on the animal. It had to be restrained or tied; it was then cut in such a way as to produce the blood which was used in post-sacrificial rites (Leviticus 5:8,9).

4.

Since fire was to be used to offer up the sacrifice to God, the fire of the temple had to be kept burning continually (Leviticus 6:6), and daily sacrifices had to be laid upon its flames. But fire was the general means of offering up sacrifices everywhere; hence, this type of animal sacrifice was called a "holocaust" (Exodus 10:25; 40:26-29; Leviticus 4:7). Moreover, fire was also seen as God's act of accepting the sacrifice.

5.

Incense and smoke were interpreted as signs of the success of sacrifice, for as they ascended to heaven, so did the prayer of the priests and the people. It is generally held that Abel's sacrifice of a lamb was favored over Cain's sacrifice of the first fruits because the fat of an animal burns better and provides more smoke than vegetables which smolder.

6.

The fruits of animal sacrifice were varied. God was appeased, evil was expelled, sin was forgiven, people were reconciled, unity was re-established, fertility was guaranteed and wars were won. Many of these themes can be gleaned from Solomon's dedication speech of the temple (1 Kings 8:14-61). Hence, the sacrifice signified wide-ranging sociological functions.

These six activities associated with sacrifice in the Hebrew Canon represent well-grounded procedures and attitudes of the temple period and have abundant scriptural support.

Non-Western Rituals

Later ethnographic analyses have largely been concerned with non-

Western rituals. This has resulted in an evolutionary development in the understanding of sacrifice, one which admits of diverse approaches and is open to new applications.

In his seminal work, *Primitive Culture*, Edward Tylor proposed the "gift theory" of sacrifice which was prevalent in anthropological circles for many years. This approach held that sacrifice is primarily an attempt to give a gift to a deity which will more readily reach the god if it is offered in the form of smoke. Although this is by no means the only way, burning sacrificial gifts has often occurred in the religious rituals of various peoples in various times over the course of time. The purpose of giving a gift to a god mirrors the purpose of gift-giving on the social plane; it implicates the giver and receiver in a relationship of mutual obligations. Tylor claimed that people engaged in sacrificial gift-giving because they mistakenly believed that gifts would be returned from heaven (1958b:461-62).

Tylor's theory provided two enduring theories in the understanding of religion and sacrifice. First, he subordinated the understanding of religious practice to the general dynamics of social behavior. Seeing sacrifice within the networking of exchange made a supposedly questionable act intelligible without reference to any religious dimension of human nature. Second, Tylor fostered an understanding of religious rites which fundamentally doubted their inherent efficacy. He believed that sacrifice does not succeed in anything so much as in indicating the ignorance of the religious practitioner. While later anthropologists would differ with his position, its attitudinal influence remains.

Following Tylor, William Robertson Smith dealt with sacrifice at great length in his analysis of Semitic society. He asserted that "the origin and meaning of sacrifice constitute the central problem of ancient religion" (1927:27). T. O. Beidelman points out that Robertson Smith's assertion was echoed by Loisy, Evans-Pritchard, Hubert and Mauss and Durkheim and, therefore, by most modern anthropologists. But unlike Tylor, Robertson Smith was concerned precisely with the efficacy of the social dimension of sacrifice (Beidelman 1974:53).

For Robertson Smith, sacrifice was originally a ritual through which a communion of souls was effected in its offering to a transcendent being. Communion, i.e., social integration, was achieved by the joyful celebration of the sacrifice and by the riveting act of destroying the sacred animal, which Robertson Smith mistakenly argued would have been the totem animal of the Semitic tribe (1927:239-40,244-45). Sacrifice, then, reaffirmed the reunion of a society and gave that union a powerful and positive character.

In discussing the origin of Semitic sacrifice, Robertson Smith was also attempting to explain the underlying structure and function of all sacrificial rites. Solemn cultic sacrifices offered for atonement, for instance, were for him at variance from the early joyful ideal, but still retained something of their power for social affirmation. Later Biblical and Semitic experts would dispute Robertson Smith's version of the origin of sacrifice in the Near East, seeing expiation as more primal and central (Beidelman 1974:55). As such, the power of sacrifice to bind a community together would remain an insight of considerable power.

Robertson Smith raised sacrifice above the level of analysis centered on economic exchange. He held that sacrifice embodies a feature of society which is proper to a religious dimension of human behavior and is not totally reducible to an economic level. Sacrifice externalizes the moral state of a society because certain spiritual relations are not operative until they are ritually enacted. The dependence upon material objects in ritual behavior and social expression binds a society to its environment symbolically, just as it is bound physically (Robertson Smith 1927:437).

Finally, Robertson Smith applied his theories of sacrifice to the slaying of the divine king practiced by certain Semitic peoples before the rise of Israel. He wished to integrate the slaying of Christ into his communion theory of sacrifice and to show that the Christian rite of sacrifice had risen from a primitive material level to a superior ethical level (Beidelman 1974:57). Robertson Smith, as a Protestant minister and seminary professor, had religious as well as anthropological interests in the associations of Christ's Passion. Nevertheless, in analyzing the Christian practice and understanding of sacrifice, his ideas are relevant, for they show that Christianity attempts to interpret the Passion of Christ as the perfect fulfillment of all former rites: human sacrifice, the sacrifice *par excellence*.

Emile Durkheim would accept Robertson Smith's teaching that the act of ritual sacrifice, more than moral teaching or doctrinal belief, integrated a society and embodied its ideals. Nevertheless, for Durkheim, sacrifice could not be interpreted independently of a society's cultural and valuational systems. Moreover, communion could be regarded as its significance as readily as expiation or oblation. Communion sacrifice, enhanced by a social fellowship and an expiational interpretation of the sacrifice, subordinated that fellowship to an orderly ideal (Durkheim 1965:378). For both Robertson Smith and Durkheim, then, society's recurring need for ritual sacrifice indicated the instability of individuals and their social systems, which had to continually reaffirm themselves by their participation in such behavior. Sacrifice is thus viewed as a primary means of addressing the supposed precariousness of human relations (Durkheim 1965:474-475). The more unstable the society, the more its need of sacrifice. An institution of sacrificial relations and symbols, such as a monastery, would then appear to be exactly what a beleaguered minority needs. The alleviation of guilt, the expiation of sin, the offering of gifts, as well as the communion of the faithful, are all means of symbolizing the benefits bestowed on a community from the sacrificial work of such an institution.

Durkheim's view of sacrifice depends largely on the research of his colleagues, Henri Hubert and Marcel Mauss. These two scholars considered the nature and function of sacrifice largely from the Greco-Roman, Semitic, and Vedic traditions, although the implication of their analysis was clearly intended to be much broader (1964:8). Hubert and Mauss considered sacrifice in terms of its accomplished social transformation. A sacrifice transforms an object or a person from a secular realm into a sacred state. "Sacrifice is a religious act which, through the consecration of a victim, modifies the condition of the moral person who accomplishes it" (1964:13). Concerning themselves primarily with bloody sacrifices, they noted that they had arbitrarily limited their discussion by that focus. For them, any offering to the gods could be deemed a sacrifice, although the intensity and efficacy of the rituals could vary.

Hubert and Mauss also abandoned the effort to locate the original rite of sacrifice in human societies. Moreover, they perceived that all of the various intentions which had been ascribed to sacrifice actually overlap one another in the practice of a sacrificial rite. Expiation, thanksgiving, petition and gift-giving are not different types of sacrifice, but various aspects of it which receive varying degrees of emphasis (Hubert & Mauss 1964:14).

Stressing the social efficacy of the sacrifice, Hubert and Mauss continually referred to the subject, i.e., the "sacrifier," who obtains the benefits of the sacrifice (1964:10). In order to become capable of receiving these benefits, the sacrifier must become worthy of divine commerce; he must therefore be isolated from the impurity of secular associations and mundane attachments. The diet, dress, grooming, and speech of the sacrifier are changed so that worldly ties are stripped away (1964:20). Such behavior is especially evident in societies with strong and extensive categories of clean and unclean. Hubert and Mauss chose, therefore, to discuss these rituals as performed by the practitioners of the Hindu religion.

Like the sacrifier, the one who makes the sacrifice stands at the threshold of heaven. This one is the "sacrificer." The sacrificer is more often a religious professional, a priest who lives closer to the divine realm than most others because of the frequent necessity to commute to the sacred (1964:23). The sacrificer must not only be competent in the exercise of ritual, but must also be a person of exceptional sanctity. To some extent, a sacrificer's role often overlaps with that of the sacrifier, for both obtain benefit from the ritual of sacrifice. The sacrificer, moreover, can even take on some of the qualities of the sacrificial victim, inasmuch as the priest may bear guilt and sin, and therefore positions himself between heaven and society, much as the victim is so positioned (1964:24-25). This overlapping of roles is to be expected. How else could the sacrificial victim, for instance, find itself caught up in the divine drama of a people, unless someone else could negotiate that dramatic engagement along with it?

Hubert and Mauss make much of the geographical location of sacrifice. It should be a place specified by the divine, not by mortals. Often the site would become a shrine or a temple where sacrifices could be continued. It had to be a pure place, not in the midst of secular or mundane defilements (1964:25-26). The victim of a sacrifice, likewise, had to possess a character stipulated by the deity; i.e., it had to be healthy and without defect or blemish. Its age, sex, size, and other features were also laid down, and the victim had to be isolated from its kind and reserved for sacred use, just like the sacrifier and sacrificer (1964:28-29).

Curiously, the animal victim of a sacrifice had to be placated. The beast would be addressed as though it were a moral agent. It would be praised, calmed, and adorned; forgiveness for the violence of the sacrifice would be sought. Human victims of sacrifice would be made drunk so as to make them passive recipients of the rite (1964:30). The reason for the address of the victim, the authors argue, was to anticipate the release of the victim's spirit after its bodily destruction. The religious practitioners expected that the act of sacrifice liberated a spirit, one which had to be carefully affirmed (1964:30). The liberated spirit entered the sacrifier who now possessed a new vitality which was absorbed from the victim just destroyed (1964:39).

Hubert and Mauss called the new vitality "redemption." They claimed that there is no sacrifice into which some idea of redemption does not enter (1964:99). This characterization makes sense in their general scheme, for if sacrifice establishes a medium of communication between the sacred and the profane, it will entail the blessing of, or the consecration unto, a saving benefit (1964:97-98). The sacrifier and sacrificer do not enter directly into the divine milieu so much as stand at its threshold. The victim is sent in by them, and it bears the burden of direct contact with the divine. It is thereby altered, or even destroyed, on behalf of the sacrifier who wishes the blessing of the divine presence without the danger of it.

The paradox of divine beneficence co-joined with danger is commonly appreciated by many societies. Franz Steiner would observe that monotheistic religions make their god absorb all taboos so that much of the deity's power would consist in the possession of such an awful potential (1956:66). To enter into the divine presence would be to risk the danger of defilement as much as to court the benefit of blessing. Conversely, a properly offered sacrifice could produce the effect of eliminating an evil, discharging it into the ambivalent divine milieu (Hubert & Mauss 1964:6). Mary Douglas would later argue that each society must have its own notions of danger and defilement in relationship to its understanding of the divine (Douglas

1978:159). For Hubert and Mauss, the ambivalence of the divine, of blessing and of danger, played a great role in the rite of sacrifice. This ambivalence granted the possibility of substituting a victim for the more delicate sacrifier.

Finally, Hubert and Mauss, like Robertson Smith, applied their theoretical methods to the sacrifice of Christianity. They, too, would see an ethical superiority of the Catholic Mass over all other sacrificial rituals because the transformation effected by the Mass is moral and, they supposed, is not intended to regenerate the material universe, as did other rites (1964:93). Robertson Smith's concern was with the sacrifice of Christ's Cross since he was a Protestant and was naturally interested in the finality of Christ's saving death. This work, already completed in the Biblical past, may now be the subject of homiletic discourse. Hubert and Mauss, however, discussed the sacrifice of Christ in terms of the Mass, as would any devout French believer, even a lapsed Catholic. The need to give preference to the sacrificial system of one's own group is evident, even among social scientists. How much more might this be expected of religious practitioners!

The influence of Hubert and Mauss on anthropologists has been profound. Durkheim drew upon them as fellow members of the French sociological school, and through him they would come to influence Radcliff-Brown, Evans-Pritchard, and a great number of British and American anthropologists. Some social scientists, like Edward Westermarck, would still attempt to reduce sacrifice to one of its basic functions and claim that function to be the historical origin of the rite (Westermarck 1924,1:65-66). But for most scholars, the wider view of sacrifice would prevail without reference to any alleged origins. Additionally, the followers of Hubert and Mauss, as Robertson Smith before them, would explain sacrifice in terms of the social or psychological efficacy of the rite over the explanation provided by the participants (Bourdillon 1980:6).

Emphasis on the ritual aspect of sacrifice did not preclude interest in the participants' explanation of it (Hubert & Mauss 1964:28). Victor Turner states that symbols and gestures in sacrificial rites often function on layers of social interaction and cultural meaning which may partly elude even the participants and their conscious explanations. He is quite explicit about this in his analysis of the Ndembu

(Turner 1967:26), but he is by no means alone. Rene Girard has commented that the primary social efficacy of sacrifice obtains precisely on those levels of cultural perceptions which do *not* intuit its essential operations. He considers vicarious substitution to be a mystifying process essential to sacrifice, but from which the mind must be momentarily distracted (by the drama in the sacrificial act) in order to effectively credit it (Girard 1977:82).[2] In cultic sacrifice, the drama occurs in the shedding of blood.

Evans-Pritchard's interest in sacrifice, as that of Hubert and Mauss, chiefly concerned the rite which centered on the killing or immolation of a victim (1962:197). This arbitrary focus reflects a fairly continuous tradition in anthropology--one which may be conditioned by the cultural background of Western academicians who have been enculturated on stories of the Passover and Calvary. It is therefore not surprising that anthropologists keep returning to the primary moments of Western religious practice with renewed insight from their ethnographic analyses. The rather surprising phenomenon of anthropologists converting to Catholicism in certain circles may be better understood from this perspective.

The four-part division of Nuer sacrifice of the presentation of the victim, the process of consecration, the invocation, and the immolation (cf. Evans-Pritchard 1962:197-230) closely resembles the divisions of sacrifice suggested by Hubert and Mauss (cf. 1964:19-49). Evans-Pritchard perceives a rich ritual life among the Nuer as he portrays the subtle, spiritual mind of the Nilotic people. The Nuer exercise a wide range of overlapping intentions when they offer sacrifice, including communion, purification, homage, expiation and propitiation. He concludes with this observation:

> If we have to sum up the meaning of Nuer sacrifice in a single word or idea, I would say that it is a substitution, *vita pro vita*. Substitution, a common enough interpretation of sacrifice, is the central meaning of the rites (Evans-Pritchard 1962:281-82).

The notion of substitution is not only thematic to Nuer sacrifice, but recurs in the analysis of most sacrificial rituals. How can an animal or another human being embody the sacrifier before a deity? How can an animal or another human absorb the impurity or guilt of the sacrifier and completely discharge it through suffering or immolation?

The notion of substitution implies the radical blurring of categories which distinguish one entity from another and one moral state from another. Edmond Leach offers an insight to this problem by suggesting that sacred rituals are performed in a context in which principles of causality and identity no longer apply. For Leach, sacrifice occurs in an ambiguous boundary which blends this world of temporal experience with the other world of "experience-reversed" (1976:81-93). Leach suggests that the sacred realm exhibits profound reversals of the sense and values of the secular realm, and that the medial zone between the two realms will necessarily blur normal distinctions. Sacrificial substitution becomes the normal activity of this medial zone. The desert has the power of such a realm for many Near-Easterners, especially the Copts.

Substitution, once admitted, provides an inexhaustible source of elaboration in the process of sacrifice. An ox substitutes for a man in a sacrifice among the Nuer; but when this is not feasible, a wild cucumber can be substituted for the ox (Evans-Pritchard 1962:197). That an ox may substitute for a person seems remotely possible, if for no other reason than this religious logic is familiar to the secular Western reader. But that a cucumber can be substituted for an ox substituting for a person, provides an extension of that concept beyond ready understanding of the Western mind. Yet that arrangement is little different than bread and wine, as species preselected for the Eucharist, substituting for the body and blood of Christ substituting for humanity. This daily sacrificial ritual of traditional Catholic religion reflects the same sense of ritual substitution found among the Nuer, as Suzanne Campbell-Jones notes (1980:90).

Not only are distinctions of identity and causality blurred in sacrifice, but distinctions of time are also obscured. Leach observes that the continuous flow of normal secular time is interrupted by ritual intervals of sacred timelessness (1976:34). In the medial zone at the threshold of the divine, events which shape a community and symbolically anchor a society are ever present. These basic events are subject to being reentered or re-presented in the drama of ritual acts, communal sacred meals, and religious sacrifice (Turner 1968:5). Hence, a community engaged in certain sacrifices can collectively participate in its own epic of origin, in the saga of its founding heroes and memorable ancestors, and in the great successes of its forebears.

Against a backdrop of the disintegration-integration of common-sense categories, sacrifice can be better viewed as it takes on ethical and ascetical dimensions. Hubert and Mauss thought the Christianity of their culture had "purified" the process of sacrifice by transferring the intention of efficacy "from the physical world to the moral" (1964:93). But "transferral" and "transformation" are terms which register fairly clear meanings, implying the change of one state to another. However, Christian sacrifice, as it is performed in the Catholic Mass (the rite to which Hubert and Mauss referred), retains its physical and communal intentionality even as it takes on a moral dimension. The pattern revealed and re-enacted in the Mass is Christ's death and resurrection, but it is also the hidden rhythm of creation as much as the atonement of sin, and the model of the moral-ethical life of suffering service as the source of world transformation. The multiplicity of applications speaks not so much of a "purification" of the Christian rite, as an extension of the capacity of sacrifice to blur distinctions and overlap categories cross-culturally, across centuries.

Sacrifice achieves its efficacy in a zone of experience where the logic of substitution knows no bounds except those which are ritualized. What the benefits of sacrifice may be, who may perform it, and what form it may take, are questions left to the religious imagination or to revelation. Evans-Pritchard notes that the Nuer are ultimately identifying themselves with their sacrifice (1962:281), for the objects offered are precious enough to hold a claim over them.

Campbell-Jones observes that, by extension, the same logic defines the kind of sacrifice proper to the ascetical lives of nuns in a Catholic convent (1980:93). Asceticism, like ritual, when performed in a cul-turally religious context for religious reasons, moves one toward the sacred sphere and, therefore, resembles sacrifice in its most critical elements. As Raymond Firth comments:

> [in] . . . the ideology of the symbolic equivalent of things which
> may be offered in sacrifice, . . . the greatest surrogate of all is the
> sacrifice of the mind and heart, the abnegation of individual

judgement and desire in favour of devotion to more general moral ends (Firth 1963:21).

It is the application of sacrifice to the realm of religious asceticism which will be demonstrated throughout this work.

Sacrifice has a ritual form which Rodney Needham would define in terms of "polythetic classification." That is to say, the variety of sacrifices which exist, the levels of their intentions, efficacies, substitutions, and moral applications are too diverse to be grouped under a "monothetic" term (Needham 1985:156). The logic of substitution, the blurring of categories, and the application of sacrifice to an ascetic self-donation indicate that there is a family resemblance of references which are named "sacrifice," but the pattern of classification remains a mode of behavior open to virtually inexhaustible analyses.

Leach and Aycock summed up the situation well when they reported that sacrifice obscures distinctions between the victim and the believers and confuses the boundaries of heaven and earth (1983:123). They also noted that this blurring of distinctions applies to the Christian understanding of sacrifice as well.

Biblical/Coptic Sacrifice

Although, in their treatment of sacrifice, anthropologists have continuously built on the non-Western foundations laid by Robertson Smith and Hubert and Mauss, Coptic monasticism has largely evolved from the Biblical model. As shown below, the sacrificial operation and activities of Coptic monasticism reflect the same structure of sacrifice as that of the Hebrews.

1.

Just as animals selected for sacrifice were to be pure, whole, and strong, the candidates for monasticism were noted in their hagiography to be noble, aristocratic, prosperous and intelligent. Most of them were regarded as virginal. Just as the Biblical record indicates that ancient Israel fell into the temptation of sacrificing inferior specimens to God (Leviticus 27:11; Deuteronomy 15:21),

so, too, the Coptic record notes that, in certain periods, monasteries held mostly the marginal members of society. From the
point of view of religious purism, this was unacceptable. In both
cases, reform was necessary.

Today, the Copts note with special pride the presence of professional,
educated and formerly prosperous men as monks in the *adiora* (monasteries). The designation of doctor or engineer is especially regarded as
a prime value for a monk in Egypt. These careers are the most esteemed professions, and have the highest personal status among the
Copts. They therefore embody the fullest substance of sacrificial
quality.

2.

Just as the Biblical sacrifice belonged in a setting removed from
mundane events, the Coptic monk must live out his vocation
apart from the world. Like the scapegoat, he is led into the
desert where he must deal with the presence of divine holiness as
a representative of sinful humanity. Or conversely, he resembles
the priests dedicated by the High Priest, Aaron, who were separated from all social commerce for one week prior to assuming
their sacrificial roles.

Like the high priests of Aaron, it is left to the monk to absorb the
dread of God's immanence by the appeasement of self-oblation which
is more perfect than that of the religious society he represents.

The cultic priest of the Coptic Church who lives in a *deir* (monastery) has a remnant of the desert zone of God's presence in the *haikal*
(sanctuary) of the church. This is analogous to the desert encounter
with God in the tent of the Holy of Holies of the Solomonic temple.
But for the monk who is also a priest, the sense of separation from
the world can be doubly intensified in the monastic sanctuary. Indeed, all the monks (priests or non-priests) are invited into the inner
sanctuary during the *Kodes* (Eucharistic Liturgy), since by their monastic life they are thought to be more intimately bound up in the
liturgical sacrifice of Christ on the altar. This is decidedly not the
case with the laity.

The liturgical intensification of the priest-monk's sacrificial role, however, presents some problems in the framework of the Coptic Church. The sacrifice of a monk's life is seen as moral and ascetic, whereas the liturgical sacrifice is formal and symbolic. The monk's separation from the world is idealized as silence and solitude; the liturgy idealizes community and public worship. The Kodes is the public presentation of the institutional Church's formal structure, order, and hierarchy. The monastic sacrifice derives its force from the informality of charismatic and personal example.

The uneasiness of the interrelationship of priesthood and monk-hood is fairly widespread in Christian apostolic Churches. Both strive after a recapitulation and re-presentation of a primal sacrifice, but both do so from different directions which are difficult to reconcile. This is especially evident when the two extremes of both types are con-trasted: the indulgent and worldly cleric versus the hermit who es-chews sacramental participation due to his preferred isolation. The former presents a sacramental sacrifice without asceticism; the latter, a sacrificial asceticism without a sacrament. Coptic hagiography passes over the conflict of these two types in silence. Since no reconciliation is possible, any reference to them would only serve to weaken the del-icate apparatus of the sacrificial system at work. An analogous, unre-solved tension also runs through Old Testament reflections on the relationship between cultic efficacy and ethical purity (Rogerson 1980:52).

Before Michael Jackson or Edmund Leach used the term "limi-nality," Arnold Van Gennep introduced its concept as a means of describing the medial stage of a rite of passage whereby the initiate is suspended outside the commerce of mundane affairs in order to be transformed. Much as the desert locale itself is a medial state between God's domain and the secular realm with its own inverted social grammar, the rules which govern secular or ordinary culture are suspended or reversed (Van Gennep 1960:10-11). Victor Turner elabo-rated this view at length by suggesting that liminality is part of the process of genuine human creativity whereby, in certain moments of intense affect, boundaries (structures) of the mind disintegrate and new connections are forged with other people or with nature and comprise a short-lived phenomenon called "communitas" (Turner 1969:136).

But as the initiate must re-integrate into the society, the liminal soul must return, although altered, to the ordinary structures of society (Turner 1969:153).

Van Gennep's sense of the liminal nature of initiates in rites of passage conforms well to the status of the sacrifier and victim in the analysis of Hubert and Mauss:

> Their condition must be changed. To do this, rites are necessary
> to introduce them into the sacred world, and involve them in it,
> more or less profoundly . . ." (1964:20).

The reversal of mundane customs, as in grooming, has already been noted as part of this altered condition.

What the monastery affords is the possibility of sustained liminality whose "end" is not the re-integration of monks into secular society, but the continuous infusion of that society with their renewed religious symbol and value. Van Reidhead argues that monasticism can foster a condition of permanent liminality (1993:9), a condition which is analogous to the continuous sacrifice offered in religious rites cross-culturally (cf. Hubert & Mauss 1964:74-76). The case of the perpetual ordinance of the burning oil lamps in the Hebrew temple, linguistically and structurally linked to sacrifice, is likewise an allusion to at least one level of cultic activity possessing the sign value of permanent liminality (Exodus 27:20,21; Leviticus 24:1-4). Given the association of Coptic monks with fire in their holiness and prayer, their inclusion in the role of permanent liminality seems better warranted than any other.

3.

As violence is inflicted on the sacrificial animal, the monk is perceived as beset by the rigors of mortification and asceticism.

In the ancient church of Deir el Suriani, a cave is shown to all pilgrims where the great Anba Bishoi prayed day and night. Hanging from the ceiling of the cave is a long wire which, the tour-guide monk informs the pilgrims, was used by the saint to tie his long hair so that whenever he should begin to doze off from his vigil and tilt to one side, his head would be rudely jerked. Invariably the pilgrims rejoice at the story if they are Copts. Foreign tourists, on the other hand, have recoiled, doubted, or disapproved of the story when told. However, the latter do not perceive themselves as beneficiaries of the act, nor in need of such acts, whereas the former perceive both, and are edified.

Celibacy must also be seen as an act of human violence for the monks. The pleasures of sex, the role of reproduction, the status of marriage, and the importance of family can hardly be overestimated sociologically. The monastic repudiation of these comforts is more than deprivation; on the level of the social and communal imperative, it is total self-abandonment. Moreover, celibacy is a further separation of the monk from the world, for he disowns his former family by his "monastic death" and takes on no new family in his solitary life. He become "kinless" which, in most traditional societies, is death itself, or a powerful isolated mode of life.

In his analysis of sexual renunciation in early Egyptian monasticism, Peter Brown notes that the body of a monk is a "landmark" on the cultural map of a society (1988:243). His ongoing denial of sexual activity separates him from the world and at the same time makes him a representative of the world to heaven. The asceticism of a monk reveals him as a mediator placed between the divine and the human. His prayers are believed to affect nature, the rise of the Nile, and the course of the Empire (Brown 1988:257).

Special note should also be made here concerning the monastic practices of the Coptic Holy Week, the yearly week-long ritual celebration of Christ's Passion and death which the monks call the "Week of Suffering." During this week, the monks eat only bread and salt. Bread was the food eaten by the Hebrews during their exodus; salt is the mineral which renews the pain of a wound. (The wounds are at once the ascetic commitment of the monk and the Passion of Christ in which the former resides.) Daily liturgical rites, which are conducted while the monks remain standing, exceed twelve hours in length. The pain and difficulties associated with these services, in which the moment-by-moment events of Christ's last days are recapitulated, are so significant that the monks are permitted to use special wooden poles on which to prop themselves up. The wood of

the Cross comes to mind. Friday of this week requires a total fast
from all food and water, and finds the monk in church without
interruption almost the whole day. Real physical distress often results
from the mortifications of the week, which also include increased
numbers of full-body prostrations and decreased sleep. As much as
morally possible, the monks attempt to share in the violence inflicted
upon Christ at the moment of his Messianic sacrifice. Along these
lines, Gertrud van Loon quotes two tenth-eleventh century Syrian
texts describing the rite of monastic initiation in the Wadi Natroun in
which the candidate tellingly hands a pair of scissors to the *kommos*
(spiritual father or abbot) and says three times: "I want to offer myself
to God" (1990:49).

4.

The role of fire as an image of monastic sacrifice has already been
introduced. Fire is the proper medium of converting an animal
sacrifice into a gift to heaven. God consumes a sacrifice by fire
(1 Kings 18:36-39).

In addition to the hagiographical and linguistic references to the fire
of monastic sacrifice, the whole aspect of a desert locale should not be
overlooked in this respect. The Saharan monastery is popularly perceived to fry in the desert sun. The monks are pitied for being baked
in a waterless, treeless, sunburned sandscape. This suffering also
enhances their mission.

Again, Van Loon notes a monastic rite described in a manuscript
dating from the ninth-tenth centuries in which the candidate is led to
the church door as if he were a burnt offering. He is thereafter called
"thy servant who is offered as a whole burnt sacrifice" (1990:49-50).

5.

Smoke and incense are aspects of fiery sacrifice clearly associated
with the monks. Throughout the Kodes, the monks are incensed
along with the sacramental gifts.

Certainly, the laity are also incensed in the Coptic liturgy, but their
incensation is more a formality compared to the incensation of the

consecrated monks. Smoke is blown into their faces and crossed over
them. During their extra-liturgical prayers, incense is burned in large
amounts to waft to heaven with the monks' prayers. The consecration of a monk requires that his prostrate body and his monastic garb
be incensed repeatedly. "A monk is a man who smells of incense,"
according to many Copts. The expression carries no derogation since
a sacrifice ought to be sweet smelling (Genesis 8:21; Exodus 29:18;
Sirach 39:14). God is expected to be pleased by the fragrance, for it
conjoins with the odor of the monk's oblation of self.

6.

Finally, the various functions of monastic sacrifice reflect the
same range of benefits accrued from animal holocausts.

The monastery is a place where the single come to seek the blessing
of a spouse; the infertile seek the blessing of conception; and the
pregnant seek the blessing of bearing a son in safety. Parents seek the
blessing of a baptism for their child, the sick seek the blessing of
healing, the oppressed seek the blessing of deliverance from evil. The
sinful seek the blessing of mercy, and the confused seek the blessing
of wisdom. The discouraged seek the blessing of exemplary encouragement, and the lukewarm community seeks the blessing of dedication and consecration. The broken community seeks the blessing of
a transcendent vision of their solidarity, and the grieving seek the
blessing of the consolation of spiritual reunion with the dead.

These blessings cannot be bought. In fact, the attempt to purchase
them on the level of the natural economy would be considered
ludicrous. Such blessings can only come from the renunciation of the
world's economy so that a space can be set aside for a new divine
order, the kingdom of God. The desert is such a place for the monk,
and for the community which gathers around the blessings which the
monk obtains.

Chapter III

Desert Spirituality and Its Symbolic Location

I am concerned about you and about the way you are being treated in Egypt; so I have decided to lead you up out of the misery of Egypt into the land . . . flowing with milk and honey. . . . Then you and the elders of Israel shall go to the king of Egypt and say to him: "The Lord, the God of the Hebrews, has sent us word. Permit us, then, to go a three days' journey in the desert, that we may offer sacrifice to the Lord our God."

Exodus 3:16-18

Monasticism is a life of crucifixion. The monk unites himself by his asceticism to the paschal sacrifice of Christ. He does not labor in any service for the Church because his very being is a work of self-offering to God on behalf of his people. The desert has always been the location of this sacrifice, for there the offering is purified, and there the world will make no claim on the gift which the monk makes to God (Shenouda III, Coptic Patriarch of Alexandria. Address presented to the Benedictine monks of St. Vincent Archabbey of Latrobe, Pennsylvania, during an ecumenical gathering on September 28, 1989.)

Judging from the citation of Exodus 3 quoted above, Moses' first commission from God was not only to lead Israel to the "promised land," but to institute a cultic life of sacrifice through a three days' journey deep into the desert terrain. Moses would eventually accomplish this mission in the forty-year trek into Sinai, but the preference for a desert locale for sacrifice is never clearly explained. Perhaps, as a kind of "no man's land," beyond the province of Egypt's idols, the desert is indeed "God's country." Moses introduces later generations of Israel (and by extension, the Christian Copts) to a special regard for desert places and divine initiatives.

Popular representations of Moses portray him, after learning of his Hebrew origins, as wandering about alone in desert wastes. The faithful are told that Moses was purified in the heat, thirst, and pain of the desert and that, through this process, he was brought to a resignation of life and will, which would later prepare him to become an instrument of Divine Providence in the liberation of his people. Actually, the biblical text mentions no such purgative experience for Moses at that time, but there are enough other desert accounts associated with him to justify the extra-Biblical accounts.

The desert is a powerful biblical and Egyptian pan-religious *motif*. Israel was wooed into a forty-year desert retreat with God (Hosea 2:16). David prepared for kingship by a desert flight (1 Samuel 23:14). The prophets Elijah and Elisha found their inspiration in remote desert hideaways (1 Kings 19:3-15). John the Baptist preached and baptized in the desert (Mark 1:3-4). Jesus began his public life by a forty-day desert fast (Matthew 4:1-2) and retired to the desert at certain intervals for prayer (Mark 1:35; 6:32). Paul of Tarsus went to Arabia after his conversion for several years of spiritual development in the desert, and cited this experience as credentials for his ministry (Galatians 1:17).

The association of the desert with a spiritual mission is so frequent in the Bible and across so many genres and literary periods that it is not difficult to believe that the desert-holy-man theme is broader than the biblical *motif*. Desert ascetics may be found on vision quests, on supernatural fasts, and in commerce with the divine in the New World and in Asia. Indeed, the concept of the desert as a proving ground for religious leaders and as the place of privileged divine encounters seems to be secure as an archetype in the universal mind (Cirlot 1991:79).

One reason why this is so, is that the desert inflicts suffering upon its inhabitants. Some human suffering, after all, is unavoidable in every life and community, and the great religions of the world consider that it may be either voluntarily and fruitfully embraced, or that it may be imposed on a victim unwillingly. The desert affords special opportunities for accepting and enduring suffering, as it did for Moses in the popular account, or as a place for offering up expiatory sacrifice. Israel's scapegoat carried the sins of the nation on its head, and was led out into the desert to discharge the guilt of the nation by its abandonment and death (Leviticus 16:20-28). Michael Jackson would call the desert a "liminal" zone, for the desert exists at the limits of human activity, transitional between the present social world and the next world (1982:9-10, 71-72). The desert is intimately associated with holiness, nearer in some respects to heaven than the secular world. Desert dwellers hold a hallowed place in the popular imagination which is legitimated by their ascetical lives. Such suffering provides the strongest credentials for spiritual leadership in Egypt, as well as elsewhere, cross-culturally.

The monks described in this work are voluntary desert dwellers. They do not merely visit the desert from time to time, nor initiate their religious ministries by a desert retreat, although Coptic pilgrims often do. Rather, they have chosen to live out their adult lives without interruption in the arid wilderness of the Egyptian Sahara, after taking perpetual leave of their secular lives in the valley or the delta of the Nile.

Since desert regions are places where the ordinary calculations of human, secular life are confounded, the Egyptian desert provides the ideal setting for the Coptic monasteries of Egypt. Therein, forces in the dominant society which oppress the ethnic minority, e.g., advantage-seeking, violent need-assertion, and economic absorption are overcome. The desert monk undermines the wholly relative value of popular secular goals by sacrificing himself.

Upon interview, numerous Coptic monks and laymen agreed to this analysis of desert asceticism, although quite a few said that it presents a somewhat novel view of the matter. To the Coptic reader, it is surely unlike any of his perceptions of monastic life, but it is hoped that sufficient evidence can be produced to make this case.   An anthropological analysis of religion does not simply present the surface features of theological or spiritual doctrines. It does account for popular religious sentiments, but it also seeks to understand how religious behavior is integrated into the larger complex whole of the culture.

Anthropological interest in the Copts' own explanation of monastic mediation can partly be served by referring to Coptic hagiography. These texts were written from the desert about desert ascetics. The nature of the writings are varied, owing to their great volume, but this almost exclusively desert-monk narrative is more than a record of historical attitudes toward the monastic life; it is also a good barometer of present sentiments. These desert-monk stories, maxims and exhortations are still very much the folk interest and popular wisdom of the Copts, and form part of the living, spiritual framework of the desert monastery, as well as of Coptic social life and culture.

The Copts believe that monks in the desert are superior to virtuous men in the world. Even the novice monk is believed to surpass the virtuous man in righteousness. Ancient desert wisdom holds:

> It is well known and manifest that the men, who are in the world and who are exceedingly excellent in their conduct, are not equal to the monks in their labours; for our Lord Jesus Christ surnamed the monks "sons of light," and those who are in the world, "sons of the world." Now the monks with their members, and with their thoughts, and with their bodies, and with their conduct, serve God perfectly with stern labours and afflictions, and they offer themselves up to God as a living, and rational, and holy sacrifice, with rational and spiritual service, and they are crucified unto the world, and the world is crucified unto them. (Budge 1972,2:285)

The Monasteries in the Desert

The desert is a seamless expanse of space and time; its emptiness invites an atemporal perspective. Egypt is the one nation which lies completely within the Sahara Desert. All the Coptic monasteries for men lay claim to desert locations; the degree of aridity proximate to most of them is severe. However, the desert is much more than a geographical zone to the Copts. This arena is the site of privileged encounters with the divine, and the spiritual testing ground of the condition of human integrity and purity. For the Copts, the desert is the religious heartland. Hence, the desert of the Wadi Natroun is rendered in Coptic as *Shiet* and Latinized as *Scete*, or *Scetes*, meaning "the measure of the heart," or "the scales of the heart." Both translations imply the testing of the mettle which living in the desert affords. For the Copts, a desert location legitimates the spiritual experiences which occur there; in fact, they tend to focus on such occurrences. This has been true since Christian monasticism first emerged in Egypt as a Coptic reaction to the hostile administrations of Egypt's varied occupiers.

Geographers and hagiographers alike make their pronouncements about the significance and consequences of the desert in human experience. Their observations are variously accurate and illuminating, but cannot substitute for the actual encounter of a great desert terrain. The desert is properly its own class of a locational phenomenon, a vivid and profound engagement of sense and affect, of body and soul. To visit the desert with any degree of openness to its essence is a baptismal moment, a true immersion into a bath of paradoxical values.

The Ancients considered the Sahara to be the analogue of the sea, a "red-brown" or "rusty" sea (the etymology of the word "Sah-rah") into which the traveler is plunged. Although the Sahara can be crossed, the traveler must respect its vastness and dangers. The "sea-lanes" of the caravan routes cover only the smallest fraction of its endless expanse. To leave the familiar path is to invite death. The pilgrim realizes this at once when he visits the Sahara; his realization is visceral. To live in the desert causes almost continuous terrestrial disorientation, a kind of geographical vertigo. Blinding sunlight and reflecting sand; biting winds and their treacherous dust storms; the eye-numbing monotony of barren aridity; an infinity of relentless featurelessness; death stalking in every seamless vista: such are the impressions which recur daily.

The desert monk knows this experience; this is his milieu. Just as importantly, he is known by this reference. His life is radically defined by the desert. It provides a framework for the values and images espoused by the Copts and embodied by their monks. God in his goodness; the world in its dangers; the soul in its torturous convolutions and the devil in his deceits--all these come together in the experience of the desert baptism. Angels lead monks out to the desert; demons attack them ceaselessly once they arrive. Isolation is their goal; pilgrims are their constant burden. Asceticism is their way of life, but every need and desire of the human imagination is stirred in the wilderness. Personal sanctification is their hope, but constant intercession for others is their prayer. Only the desert is vast enough to encompass all these paradoxes.

Thomas Merton, one of the great monastic figures of the twentieth century Western Church expressed the matter well:

> He [the monk] withdraws from [the world] in order to place himself more intensely at the divine source from which the forces that drive the world onwards originate, and to understand in this light the great designs of mankind. For it is in the desert that the soul most often receives its deepest inspirations. It was in the desert that God fashioned his people. It was to the desert he brought his people back after their sin. . . . It was in the desert, too, that the Lord Jesus, after he had overcome the devil, displayed all his power and foreshadowed the victory of his Passover (Merton 1977:175).

Merton understood just how fully the desert ascetic is integrated into the heart of the Church. From this position, the monk has the symbolic authority to challenge the values and operations of the non-Christian society.

> Peace exists where men who have the power to be enemies are, instead, friends, by reason of the sacrifices they have made in order to meet one another on a higher level where the differences between them are no longer a source of conflict. These things need to be said . . . about life in a contemplative monastery (Merton 1977:41).

For Merton, the peace-making ability of the monk derives from his location in the monastery, beyond the world, and in "the victory of his Passover," i.e., in his capacity for self-sacrifice. The desert monks exhibit a manner of intra-monastic relationships quite different from the competitive relationships of the secular world. This ability enables them to resolve conflicts which arise in the society and threaten the ethnic Church. "The monk belongs to the world, but the world belongs to him insofar as he has dedicated himself totally to liberation from it in order to liberate it" (Merton 1973:341).

Such a notion of monasticism perceives the monk as "outside" the world only to the degree that he has attained the symbolic authority to act without the compromise of vested interests in the world. For these reasons, it remains important for the monasteries of Egypt to claim desert habitations even if, geographically, that claim is not shared equally by all the monastic sites.

Some adiora in Egypt are still relatively remote; visiting them requires a whole day or, more likely, a weekend. Other monasteries, such as those of the Wadi Natroun, while totally surrounded by the Sahara, are nevertheless conveniently located off a major traffic artery between Cairo and Alexandria. They can now be visited en route to a family gathering or a vacation at the seashore. Some monasteries, especially those of Upper Egypt, are actually located on the edge of river-based agricultural zones. However, they attempt to maintain a "desert-face" with one or more of their sides still facing outward toward the wilderness beyond.

Except for these latter sites, the monasteries of Egypt were almost inaccessible until recent years. Few Copts had the time or inclination to visit them, owing to their cloistered status and the burden of desert travel. However, the construction of highways across the Sahara and the building of private roads have lately provided access to the monasteries as potential sites of pilgrimage. The Coptic Church, moreover, has recently fostered the shrine status of the adiora, making the once forbidden cloister a place of welcome for Egypt's Christian population.

The location of each monastery is a matter of greater temporal consequence today. The proximity of the site to population clusters and good roadways affects the kind and number of pilgrims who visit. This, in turn, determines the income for the deir to a considerable

degree. Its location is also dependent upon other economic consider-
ations such as fresh water and, nowadays, electricity. Some monasteries must import these resources; others have sufficient wells and
generators of their own. Those of the Wadi Natroun, for instance, are
situated directly on the line of the great electrical cables which
connect Alexandria with the hydroelectric power of the Aswan High
Dam.

Finally, the location of a monastery is associated with its own
symbolic and hagiographical heritage. Each deir has its own saints,
relics, holy places and evocative history. These associations contribute
to its individual character and to the nature of each shrine in which
its saints are venerated.

Unlike the shrines of the Nansa Valley of Northern Spain, the
monasteries of Egypt do not exist simply to service holy places
(Christian 1972:51). People come there not merely to "take blessings"
from the saints' bones, but just as much to see the living saints
themselves. The monks dispense *barakah* (blessings) to the pilgrims;
they constitute much of what makes Coptic desert shrines holy.

Even so, William Christian's analysis of shrines and pilgrimages in
Spain offers some important insights into the operation and location
of holy places--insights which can help make the Egyptian experience
more comprehensible both by comparison and by contrast. For
instance, Christian sees that better means of transportation in the
modern era can result in the nationalization of shrines which were
previously only regional (1972:66). Likewise, devotion to holy places
increases with greater popular mobility (1972:65). Both of these
insights apply to Coptic monasteries.

However, Christian also maintains that the Spanish shrines are not
sources of popular devotion in themselves, and their distance from
population centers is fairly arbitrary.

> In other words, the shrines themselves do not seem to stimulate
> devotion or religiosity; rather, they are providing a focus or an
> object for an already extant devotion; or perhaps they are provid-
> ing a needed service, as a gas station or a drugstore might. Gas
> stations come and go, depending on the fortunes of their owners,
> but there always tends to be one around--not necessarily in the

same place, but within the same range. The "hidden hand" of
the market takes care of that. (Christian 1972:64)

Coptic monasteries differ from the Spanish shrines on two points.
First, while a few old or ruined adiora may have been pilgrim sites for
centuries in Egypt, most of them were not the object of popular
visitation until quite recently. Greater mobility of the Coptic population and the construction of new roads do not fully explain their
sudden popularity. Nor is the location of a deir a matter of chance.
A Coptic patriarch or a charismatic monk cannot convert a conve-
nient desert tract into a future monastic site or a pilgrim center as the
land is still under the control of the Islamic state in Egypt. The
Coptic Church would meet significant bureaucratic resistance to
claiming new land for religious use. Rather, a patriarch would have
to utilize ancient or ruined adiora, that is, he would have to find land
with a precedent of holiness, such as an earlier monastic site, in order
to establish "new" shrines. Catholic Spain would hardly impose such
restrictions.

Second, the monasteries were never established arbitrarily in their
place at any time in Coptic history. Putting aside the religious explanations for their location, e.g., the leading of angels, the visit of the
Holy Family,[1] or the site of the founders' ascetical perfection, most of
the early adiora were well placed on caravan routes, by bountiful
wells, or close to inhabited Nilotic regions. At the same time, if some
of them are still relatively difficult to reach, difficult access is often
deemed a prized ascetic value to the pilgrim. At any rate, the lack of
opportunity to create "new" shrines, the long history and rich heritage
of the old monasteries, and the discomfort associated with a desert
pilgrimage all contribute to the fixed location of each deir.

The reclamation of earlier monastic sites has occurred several
times. When Abuna Matta el-Meskeen led his maverick following of
desert ascetics from the established monastery of Deir el Suriani in the
Wadi Natroun to the "inner desert" for greater isolation and solitude
during the 1950s, he chose the Wadi Rayan, south of the Fayum, for
his eremitical experiment. The Wadi Rayan had already figured quite
prominently in early Coptic history as a place of profound monastic
retreat for those monks who transcended the ascetic life in a common,

walled monastery. Similarly, when Pope Kyrillos VI founded a monastery in the 1960s, he actually refounded a long-abandoned monastery,
Deir Mari Mina. The present great success of this pilgrim site is due
to the popularity of the cult of St. Mina, the presence of a vital
monastic community, and the tomb of its refounder, Pope Kyrillos,
now also widely regarded as a great saint. Fortunately for the Copts,
the number of early monasteries in Egypt must have been impressive.
Rather telling is the fact that many of the original deir were built on
older pre-Christian holy sites, even pharaonic tombs. Hence, there is
no danger of exhausting potential sites of reinhabitation.

　　　William Christian makes one other reference to monasticism in his
analysis of Spanish shrines. He notes that the ascetic practices associated with pilgrimages are colored by monastic tradition. Pilgrims
take on a bit of monastic identity by their spiritual and geographical
journey (1972:126-27). This is even more the case in Egypt. Presence
to, and interchange with the monks grant a kind of monastic aura,
blessing, and purity to the pilgrims by association. When they return
to their families, the pilgrims are often told that they carry back the
afterglow of their brush with holiness. Hence, Coptic monastic
shrines are more than just the focus of an already extant devotion.
They actually generate devotional life and religious solidarity among
the Copts, and are the driving force behind their religious renewal.

　　　The details highlighted above are not meant to portray the
prominent characteristics of any particular deir. Rather, they present
both a sense of the many facets of the monasteries, as well as provide
a cumulative impression of the overall monastic scene. Thus, while
all the monasteries for men are located in, or adjacent to, the desert,
their particular ecological settings are subject to considerable variation.
This affects the physical constitution of the adiora, and ultimately
influences their internal life and cultural function.[2]

Where Angels Led Them

A proper perspective of monastic behavior and an overall picture of
the history of monastic foundations in Egypt must be considered in
relationship to their geographical context. All the sources agree,

although many clearly exaggerate, that the number of hermitages or *laurae* and monasteries in the region of Scete was initially quite high. When the social pressures weighing upon Egypt found their most direct resolution in monastic reactionism, the Wadi Natroun came to be the thriving religious center and ethnic focus described in contemporary records of the period. The eventual reduction of such originally large numbers to four monasteries may be seen as a result of what is conventionally called a "selection process."

In the heyday of early Coptic monasticism, nearly 1,700 years ago, the ecology of the Wadi Natroun would have been somewhat more supportive of human habitation than it is now (Gabriel 1969:16). The Sahara's hold on North Africa has been tightening, but ground water was fresher and closer to the surface a few thousand years ago. Consequently, the first monks, even in the thousands, were able to procure sufficient well water for their simple needs. Relatively high numbers remained in the Wadi Natroun for several centuries, as the complex combinations of religious and worldly social conditions always seemed to reinforce the countercultural institution of monasticism. The early monks tended to live in diffused, small settlements throughout the region rather than in large compounds.

However, the number of monastic centers in the Wadi Natroun fell intermittently, and sometimes dramatically, even in the initial centuries of monastic success. The actual social conditions of the monks, unlike an abstract monastic ideal, adapted to ever-changing external conditions according to their own evolutionary needs. The ethnic church-society, ever more estranged politically from the international world-church, came to depend more and more practically upon its own monastic leadership. The political utilization of these monks by the society fostered the natural process of consolidating eremitical cells into monastic communities, requiring that some sites be abandoned. Also, the number of candidates often failed to sustain the monasteries, causing many of them to close. The monasteries that survived across the Wadi desert were those with enough water to support the concentrated numbers of monks. The sites which provided constant water supplies and large wells had an advantage over those whose water sources proved to be inconstant or progressively saline.

Many archaeological sites of abandoned adiora in the Wadi Natroun have been found to be at a distance from the changing subterranean water courses which still underlie other monasteries. It should come as no surprise that the four surviving monasteries of the Wadi Natroun are situated on the best water reserves of much of the Libyan Desert.

Just how the monasteries of the Wadi Natroun and, by extension, many of the other monasteries of the Egyptian Sahara came to rest above the best water reserves of the desert is explained by the Copts in terms of their hagiography. They claim that the great monastic founders, in commerce with heaven as they were, were directed by angels to the most favorable spots. A desert waste with sweet water just below the surface is a marvelous sign of the paradox of Coptic ethnic life: they are an oppressed people with a secret source of life. They are vindicated by God. The angelic assistance of the founding monks reinforces the divine validation of the beleaguered minority. Both groups must traverse a certain desert milieu, searching for rest.

Desert Asceticism

Many of the functions attributed to sacrifice in the social sciences are relevant to the study of Coptic monasticism. The renewed consolidation of a community occurs around the monks. The Copts have found in the monks a symbol of suffering which ennobles their cause and canonizes their ethnic aspiration. Moreover, the monastery is the single most celebrated site of Coptic ethnicity today, as demonstrated by the thousands of pilgrims who regularly congregate there. The joyous convergence of these groups around their religious symbols corresponds closely to Robertson Smith's sense of sacrifice.

An analysis of Coptic history will also reveal a precariously positioned ethnic group, which required affirmation on a transcendent order to symbolically counterbalance political and economic repression. The powerful religious icon of the desert holy man who lives in constant battle with dark forces on behalf of his own people was, and is, a sacrifice which reinforces an ethnic social order (Durkheim 1965:474-75).

Anba Gregorius, Bishop for Higher Studies of Coptic Culture, says this about the desert monk:

> On the whole, then, the monk is given wholly unto God: his mind, his heart, his emotions, his sentiments, his sensations, his consciousness and his perceptions are in God and for God. God is incessantly within the center of his consciousness (all else being aside); every thing and every person that does not aid him in his relationship with God becomes pale, lusterless, without incitement and without magnetism. For the monk is indeed a man of Religion. He hungers and thirsts for Religion. He breathes by it, for it, and because of it. He is a complete burnt offering unto God and for Religion. He is totally offered unto God, his worship and his service. The sacrifice of the burnt offering is special. It is burned, entirely, on the altar of God. No one else has a share in it, not the poor, nor the priest, nor the one who offered it. All is for God. (Classroom lectures, Patriarchate, Cairo, 1988)

When the Coptic prelate asserts that "no one else has a share" in the monastic self-sacrifice, he means that the monk's life has no pragmatic value for the secular world. However, precisely because the monastic life is regarded as temporally impractical, it is spiritually efficacious for many as a manner of sacrifice.

"He is a monk who does violence to himself in everything" (Ward 1975:58). This short statement quoted from an ancient desert father, aptly condenses numerous aphorisms of desert lore into a basic declaration of the essence of monastic asceticism in Egypt. No systematic attempt was made in Coptic hagiography to reconcile the Greek notion of moderation or harmony into the monastic life. Greek dualism may have given credibility to the idea that the body should be diminished, but the Coptic understanding of the body's role in religion is at once more forceful and more positive. The body is not to be merely deprived or sequestered, but violated. It is to be damaged, however, not because it is harmful to the spirit, but because it is beneficial enough to be a respectable sacrifice. Another desert saying has it: "If the spirit does not sing with the body, labour is in vain" (Ward 1975:61).

In this same sense, numerous hagiographical passages liken
monastic prayer and asceticism to fire, the medium of sacrifice. "Abu
Maqar said: 'Man purifies his soul in the fear of God [*raheb*], and the
fear of God burns up his body'" (Ward 1975:110).   Another monk
said: "'If I had one of Anba Antony's thoughts, I should become all
flame'" (Ward 1975:179).   Again it was said: "You cannot be a monk
unless you become like a consuming fire" (Ward 1975:88).   Likewise,
the prayers of monks were portrayed as "ascending to the presence of
God like fire" (Ward 1975:59).   A certain monk claimed that during
a priest-monk's Kodes, "'I saw the angel of the Lord descend from
heaven and place his hand on the priest's head, and he became like a
pillar of fire'" (Ward 1975:128).   A monk who escaped martyrdom at
the hands of heretics was, nevertheless, considered to be a martyr, for
"he offered himself as a holocaust to Christ" by his monastic life
(Ward 1975:41).

The self-offering of a monk is truly considered to be a holocaust
with a sacrificial value for the larger community. Coptic hagiography
bears out this contemporary view when it compares a desert monk to
a man who stands on the rooftop of a burning house, preferring to
burn there in sacrifice for the benefit of all to see, rather than to burn
with lust for women in the secrecy of the bedroom below (cf. Budge
1972,2:302). Or again, an old monk said, "'Knowest thou not that the
labour of a monk is fire, and wheresoever it entereth, it consumeth?'"
(Budge 1972,2:211).

The work of fire is to immolate and destroy the sacrifice, to offer
up its object to God so that nothing is left. Offerings which fail to
be fully consumed by violence or flame are considered to be lesser
kinds of sacrifice. According to this logic, the spiritual offerings,
prayers, fasts, obedience, and good works of the Coptic laity are less
sacrificial and are therefore termed *dahiah*. Still, one can apply the
works of dahiah to profit, comfort, or social control. The ideal of
monasticism suggests, however, that the monk has no self-will or
self-gain remaining after his daily self-sacrifice. This kind of sacrifice
is termed *zabihah*, a word which is only otherwise used to denote the
object of an offering on an altar.

Abba Timothy said unto a certain brother, "How art thou?"
The brother said unto him, "I destroy my days, O Father." And
the old man said unto him, "My son, my days are also destroyed
and I give thanks" (Budge 1972,2:255).

The fruit of this destructive consummation is the pardon and blessing
of the people. "Find a man who lives according to righteousness, and
I [the Lord] will pardon the whole people" (cf. Jeremiah 5:1 in Ward
1975:50). In this respect, the name of the Coptic monastery near
Assiut in Upper Egypt is significant. "Deir el Muharraq" has the
literal meaning: "The monastery of the burning holocaust." The
monks of this House are puzzled over the application of its name.
They suggest a variety of origins, e.g., that it is taken from its barley
fields which are yearly burned, or it may derive from the oblations
offered by pilgrims. However, the connotation on the cultural level
cannot be missed: the monks are "a burning sacrifice" of asceticism
offered for the blessing of their people.

Hence, while ordinary virtue and moderation are acceptable for
the average Christian, the Copts greatly esteem the more extraordinary
acts of self-immolation offered by their monks. In the English translation of *The Paradise of the Holy Fathers*, these acts are seen to be
efficacious for the broader society. Prayers merit forgiveness, not only
for the monks, but also for the community (cf. Budge 1972,2:79,89,95).

Asceticism is seen as operative, not for the private gain of the
monk, but within a great moral economy of souls united by spiritual
bonds and edified by material sacrifice (cf. Budge 1972,2:90,93-94).
Indeed, the dramatic evidence of such costly and personal sacrifices,
including lifelong celibacy, exhaustive fasting, fatiguing rituals, harsh
mortifications, and silence, grants strong legitimacy to the reality of
such a moral economy. Socially speaking, it is hard to argue with the
presence of monks who dedicate their lives as a sacrifice offered on
behalf of their people. Monastic sacrifice, perhaps like so much in
religion, operates on levels which may be enhanced by assent, but
need not be hampered by intellectual dissent.[3] One need only be
impressed.

Copts may occasionally express serious reservations about the
rationale of religion. Nowadays, the monastic life, in particular, may

be rejected by many as nonproductive. But when these Copts are in the presence of a monk, there is usually an immediate acknowledgement of his significance which exceeds all requirements of ordinary respect. His hands are kissed; his words are approved and re-echoed, no matter how banal. He is the focal point of intense attention; all eyes, all comments, are directed toward him. In public, the monk unquestionably presides. His role is unassailable.

For the Copts, sacrifice may be interpreted as an inversion of secular economic forces. The latter is at least geared toward reciprocity on the level of kinship exchange or, more likely, toward purposeful gain, whereas the former creates an appearance of needless and sometimes dramatic loss. Indeed, one of the great stresses on markets based on reciprocity in the kinship network of secular life is the likelihood that some members will attempt to profit unduly, or at least be perceived to do so (cf. Polanyi 1971:148-55). Even in Western economies, great tension can be created when disproportionate wealth accumulates in the hands of the few who know best how to manipulate the economy. Societal focus on this universal problem can eventually be destructive, yet little else in a society commands such interest as this problem.

Sacrifice, and especially human or self-sacrifice, by its arcaneness and ambiguity, and especially by its graphic violence, may be a drama of greater social interest than the pettier matters of profit and self-promotion. At least, sacrifice may dramatically punctuate the secular economic concerns of a group. For the Copts, monastic sacrifice inverts a somewhat hostile secular economy in a spiritual realm where the concerns of the majority, its secular system, temporal values, and ambitions are excluded. That realm is the desert, a zone largely rejected, where a submerged anti-economy can still function.

The subversive influence of monasticism on worldly values is no longer so apparent in the West. The long association of ecclesiastical and secular institutions eventually afforded the latter the opportunity to enlist monastic sacrifice in endorsing contemporary culture. But monasteries, even in the West, still possess certain theological restraints which may place them in opposition to the secular establishment from time to time. This is the case of the quasi-monastic institutions of celibates in Central America, South America, Eastern

Europe, as well as in Tibet, India, and Southeast Asia. Who can forget the self-sacrifice and human immolation of the Buddhist monks who burned themselves alive to protest the war in Vietnam?

When the desert serves the function of cultural and economic inversion, the interrelations of the desert dwellers must bear witness to this operation. Hence, these relationships must represent at least a symbolic opposition to the prevailing custom of personal gain in social contacts. A monk must sacrifice the objective of personal advantage, or at least the appearance of it, in all his relationships. His behavior reverses the standards of self-promotion in the secular society. Monastic modesty and humility provide a context for a new kind of social decorum which grants the monk the credibility of the otherworldly. The Coptic monks, therefore, evidence a studied self-deprecation in their inter-monastic relations, as will be seen below. Monks in other monasteries outside of Egypt may evidence something of the same behavior; however, the intensity of the Coptic example is more profound and more closely corresponds to the social function of monasticism among the Copts than does monastic practice elsewhere.

The history of this people and their monks will involve the reading of two texts: (1) the hagiography of the faithful remnant; and (2) a survey of the secular pressures of politics, ecology and economics to which they were subjected. Therefore, some discussion about monastic origins may help to explain the contemporary dimensions of Coptic culture, as well as provide a thread of the historical development of the Coptic people.

Chapter IV

The Origins of Coptic Monasticism

Religious literature dealing with the early history of monasticism in Egypt is extensive. Most of the academic interest in the subject has been generated by the realization that Western monasticism, a critical link in historical sequences leading to the modern era, is grounded in models and inspiration from the first desert monks. Western treatment of Egyptian monasticism tends to provide enough information to make it the first point on the historical curve. Once monasticism spread westward, most notably in the Benedictine tradition, interest in and literature about later Coptic monasticism diminished.

For the long middle centuries of their existence, no systematic records can be found about the conditions of the desert monasteries, only the occasional impressionistic reports of travelers. Western disinterest in the monasteries of Egypt was compounded by the country's isolation from the European community after the Arab invasions. The Coptic Church's long-term estrangement from Roman and Byzantine ecclesiastical institutions contributed to the swift and complete isolation of Egypt by the beginning of the eighth century. It is possible to read later Western treatments of Coptic monasticism

without any hint that this ascetic institution has continued to exist
from the fourth century into the present era.

Derwas Chitty's carefully researched history is typical of this
genre. As such, his text ends with the Arab invasions suppressing
Christianity throughout the Near East, supporting the view that further history of the religion needs to be sought elsewhere (cf. 1966:179).
Even before the first Arab invasion, the monastic movements which
sprang away from Egypt had already claimed his attention.

Jacques Lacarrière's well-received text, *Men Possessed by God* (1964)
evidences the same treatment. In an epilogue, Lacarriére notes that
some few monasteries still exist in Egypt, but his assessment of their
significance seems to be limited to their small numbers in contrast to
former times, and by their qualitative inferiority to the bygone golden
age of their founders (cf. 1964:217). In his brief enumeration of exis-
tent adiora, Lacarriére appears to be unaware of the fact that the
monastery of el Muharraq still stands! His omission of the longest-
thriving, most continuous, and the strongest monastery of Egypt at
the time of his writing, only makes sense when the reader recognizes
the selectivity of his interest. Deir el Muharraq led the monastic
movement of Egypt after the monasteries of the Wadi Natroun and
the Eastern Desert had exerted their formative influence on the West.
Western historical interests are not concerned with the internal relations of monasticism to Coptic affairs, but only with the relationship
of Coptic monasticism to outside religious movements. About this
latter concern, much has been written; about the former, very little.

Talal Asad criticizes not only Western academic interests in
general, but anthropologists in particular for dismissing as unimpor-
tant the latter-day analysis of non-Muslim communities in the Middle
East:

> Although Christianity and Judaism are also indigenous to the
> region, it is only Muslim belief and practice that Western anthro-
> pologists appear to be interested in. In effect, for most Western
> anthropologists, Sephardic Judaism and Eastern Christianity are
> conceptually marginalized and represented as minor branches in
> the Middle East of a history that develops elsewhere--in Europe,
> and at the roots of Western civilization (Asad 1996:3).

Social anthropologists must be careful not to repeat the religious prejudices of their sources as cultural facts. Western literature dealing with Coptic monasticism and the Coptic Church is filled with biased observations which find their way into non-religious discussions. It is not the province of social scientists to determine that a religious ethnic group, or its institutions, is "decadent," nor to report that certain ritual practices are "backward," or on the verge of extinction. Nor should a whole society be regarded "leaden," "grave," or "bankrupt." As a social anthropologist, Edward Wakin's otherwise helpful sociological reflection on the Copts (1963) is permeated with such negative value judgments, but he is hardly alone among Western commentators.

Islamic sources naturally have no difficulty in maintaining that the Christians on their lands are inferior, and substantiate their view by quoting the judgments of Western political observers (cf. Kepel 1985). Erroneous statements of British observers are also quoted. Stanley Lane-Poole (1968) is the most articulate. Such descriptions suggest that the Copts are not evaluated in terms of their unique historical circumstances but, rather, in terms of other religious movements in different and more unthreatened environments.

Monasticism in Egypt does not merely *survive*. The maintenance of a monastically oriented Church, with the heroic efforts and commitments which desert monasticism entails, must surely be a phenomenon in its own right, warranting serious anthropological study. In a similar vein, its history must surely be worthy of an assessment unsubordinated to Islamic apologetics, Western social developments and ecclesiastical concerns. In the latter regard, an enormous body of ecclesiastical literature exists about the "desert fathers," about Christological controversies and the earliest ecumenical councils, about the monophysite schism[1] and the catechetical School of Alexandria. But most of this literature treats the Coptic ethnic question as peripheral; it is conditioned by theological agendas in the Christian West. In any case, a contemporary, social scientific treatment of Coptic culture and its central religious symbol will gain little from the arcane "classical" literature of medievalists and philologists.

The most important modern forays into the complete history of Coptic monasticism were essentially a by-product of archaeological expeditions that were conducted in the Wadi Natroun in the 1920s. Hugh Evelyn White visited the region several times with a team of archaeologists, and he documented several huge volumes on the antiquities and history of the monasteries of Scete, even for the many centuries which other historians generally ignored (1973). The ancient texts and archaeological records from which he drew have never been so well correlated either before or since. Nevertheless, his work, voluminous as it is (495 folio pages, plus plates), is more of a chronicle than a history. More recently, in 1989, Otto Meinardus updated and expanded his 1961 study of *Monks and Monasteries of the Egyptian Deserts* which compiles most of the relevant sources of several languages on the subject of monastic history. While social forces which influenced Coptic monasticism may be gleaned from these texts, no social functions of the adiora are discussed during the time of their long histories.

Byzantine Exploitation and the Emergence of Desert Monks

The brief historical review of Coptic monasticism which follows emphasizes its development in the Wadi Natroun, if for no other reason than the documentation is sufficient only there. For the origins of Coptic Christianity, the reader is referred to Pearson and Goehring's *The Roots of Egyptian Christianity* (1986). It provides a history of Coptic monasticism after the Arab invasion which challenges the view of its being a mere decline of a once impressive institution. A "decline" of an institution which covers a thirteen-hundred-year period, and still continues, should indicate, even to the casual observer, that something aside from the process of disintegration must be at work!

A study of Egyptian monasticism is presented here primarily against the backdrop of the singular circumstances of Coptic Egypt, rather than simply in the broad religious framework of Mediterranean Christianity. To properly appreciate its specifically Egyptian expression, early monasticism cannot be seen just as a pan-imperial phenomenon which simply happened to spring up first in Egypt. Monasticism *was born* in Egypt; it was formed by forces peculiar to Egypt, and has continued to exist, and sometimes flourish, in its deserts, even after the region severed ties with Europe. What then are its formative influences and social consequences?

Of special interest in this study is the movement from anchoritic or eremitical monasticism to cenobitic or communal monasticism. The movement partially occurred already within the first generation of monks in Egypt, but it took centuries before communal monastic life gained full ascendancy. The historical and social forces which fostered this change deserve special attention.

The origins of monasticism in Egypt are obscure. As with so much of the ecclesiastical literature from the period, history and hagiography largely overlap. The volume of hagiography is enormous, since Egypt was something of an ecclesiastical hub immediately following the first great monastic expansions. Accounts and reflections about desert asceticism were widely available in fourth century Gaul, Italy, North Africa, Syria, and Mesopotamia. Traveling theologians, bishops, merchants, nobles, politicians, and pilgrims passed through Egypt and visited the earliest monks. Word of their rigor and wisdom filled the Roman Empire. Unfortunately, reports from religious enthusiasts about religious enthusiasts often fail to answer questions that are of interest to the social historian. In this case, the Greco-Latin perception of so many historical reporters of the time often obscures important aspects of events conditioned by the circumstances and sentiments of a people more marginal to the Empire.

All this is not to say that hagiography is only of value to the student of mythology. In the case of Western monastic studies, those who turn their attention in that direction are deeply indebted to ecclesiastical historians of the last century who have produced an enormous amount of critical, literary, and hermeneutical studies on the subject, gleaning great insight from ancient religious records. Literary critical methods, and the very word "hermeneutics," had a long history in liberal Biblical and patristic studies before being adopted by philosophers and social scientists. Even in this case, however, the interests of the authors could fairly be termed "Eurocentric," as they were neglectful of the unique Egyptian context of monastic origins, preferring to interpret them in the larger Byzantine milieu. As noted in *RB 1980*,[2] "the literature of the monastic movement includes biographies, collections of sayings, letters and homilies of various monks, *ex professo* treatments of the ascetic and monastic life, such as those of Basil, Evagrius and Cassian, and finally the works of historians" (Benedict 1981:11).

The most influential and one of the earliest monastic texts is *The Life of Saint Antony*. The *Vita*, so called, was said to be produced by Athanasius, patriarch of Alexandria, shortly after the death of St. Antony, the man most often credited with being the father of all Christian monasticism. Paradoxically, Athanasius (fourth century), one of the most prolific and preoccupied churchmen of his era, chose to write the biography of the most retiring man of his day! *The Life of Saint Antony* became the model for all later vitae of Christian saints, and created a genre of hagiography still influential today. A helpful bibliography of religious literature about the period of monastic origins can be found in Evelyn White's aforementioned *The Histories of the Monasteries of Nitria and Scetis* (1973). However, the multiple volumes of hagiography form more a body of cultural artifacts than historical records.

No one is certain about when the first Christian monks migrated to the Egyptian deserts on the fringes of civilization. If the date could be determined, then the exact social and political factors involved with monastic origins would be better appreciated. Still, it is generally understood that hundreds, perhaps even thousands, of Egyptian Christians fled to the desert during the sporadic but violent persecutions under Emperors Decius, Valerian, and Diocletian (from A.D. 250 to A.D. 305). Surely the majority of these refugees returned home, but many undoubtedly lingered there, making a spiritual virtue out of practical necessity. It is recorded that a certain Pola lived as a hermit from A.D. 250 until A.D. 341 in the Eastern Desert, and that he met St. Antony, the revered father of monasticism, just before his death (Evelyn White 1973:12).

If St. Pola had not been unique, but an example of a wider eremitical phenomenon, then the origins of monasticism in Egypt were rooted in the period of Egyptian history which directly followed the great persecutions. After A.D. 313, Christianity was tolerated, then became the official religion of the Roman Empire. However, the genesis of monasticism in this era of peace for the Church was not as uneventful as might be expected.

Egypt's role in the family of nations of the Roman Empire was not enviable. The nation's long-term servitude as a granary for Rome often left it scarcely able to feed its own peasant population (Little 1958:37). Poor administration of the levies and canals of the Nile over a protracted period of time reduced the harvest, even as agricultural demands increased. The leading city of Egypt, Alexandria, was populated by foreign merchants, military personnel, colonial officials, and Greek and Jewish academicians. Native Egyptians could hardly have considered Alexandria as *their* cultural capital, even though they had no other city of similar significance which could claim that distinction. When Christianity was introduced into Egypt, its first appeal may have been as an Oriental religious alternative to the Greek and Roman *Pax Deorum*[3] which was promulgated by the Empire and enlisted in the cult of the Caesars.

Paradoxically, in Alexandria, the new religion had some adherents among the upper classes, as well as among the populous Jewish Diaspora. The trend injected a fresh idealism into a Roman religious and moral system which was too obviously subordinated to political and economic ends. These classes attained a certain prestige by claiming to possess a religious system superior to the political administrators of the Empire who granted them their status in Egypt. Alexandrian philosophers consciously and thoroughly translated Christian symbols and beliefs into Hellenized terms, leaving the nation with two Christian traditions developing at once. The Alexandrian tradition was literary, academic, and Hellenized and belonged to the upper classes. The other tradition, called "Coptic," was popular, initially non-literary, and poor.

When Christianity became the imperial religion after A.D. 313, Egypt did not experience the collective liberation or colonial relaxation which the Coptic peasantry had hoped for. The newly emerging Christian Byzantine province of the Empire proved to be as oppressive as that of the old pagan Roman regime. Alexandria was able to play a leading role in ecclesiastical affairs, especially in the first ecumenical councils, but only because the Byzantine world saw the city as a Greek transplant more than as an Egyptian capital. Political leadership was still in foreign hands.

These events engendered a growing sense of ethnic and cultural alienation in Egypt. The frustration of the Copts was doubled because the religious system they had initially adopted as an expression of provincial independence was co-opted by foreign nationals in Alexandria and in the imperial state. Even some of the Alexandrian Christians had to re-examine their loyalties, as Roman and Byzantine episcopal sees conspired to subordinate the Alexandrian patriarchy to their religious authority. With a universal Church now made legal and powerful, the matter of a visible central authority became more important. The philosophically trained and theologically articulate leaders of the School of Alexandria were not prepared to accept an inferior religious role parallel to the political and economic plight of the Copts. In the end, a mood of Egyptian cultural and religious differentiation would attract many, though not all, of the Hellenized Alexandrians, but not until the Copts had already expressed their ethnic solidarity by the circuitous means still left them, that is, by the institution of monasticism.

It would be precipitous to suggest that the Coptic, communal alienation and aspiration was a true form of "nationalism." Such an assumption would represent the reading of future ethnic development into an earlier strata of Coptic history. Nevertheless, the eventual recrudescence of an indigenous national movement was already anticipated by the rise of Coptic monasticism.

Already in pre-Constantinian times, the Copts had mounted revolts. Under Marcus Aurelius, in the second century A.D., the upper Egyptian conscripts in Caesar's colonial army broke ranks and fought the Bucolic Wars. They were defeated, but rebellion flared again toward the end of the third century (cf. Little 1958:38). Diocletian's entrance into Egypt at that juncture of history appears as particularly ruthless. Coptic hagiography records massive persecutions and martyrdoms on an unparalleled scale. Christianity seems to have been equated with the rebellion, and hundreds of thousands of Christians fell victim to Diocletian's purge. Quite notably, the Coptic calendar is not calculated from the date of Christ's birth, as is the Roman calendar. Rather, the Copts consider the beginning of Diocletian's reign as the first year of their calendar; i.e., the 29th of August, A.D. 284, the so-called "Year of the Martyrs" (Meinardus 1965:4). The attention focused on martyrdom had great consequences on the interpretation of monastic life in Egypt.

The earliest role of monasticism in this setting may well be introduced by an illustration. Sir Henry Morton Stanley's reputed remark, "Mr. Livingston, I presume?" has become famous for reasons other than its rhetorical grace. The phrase, half artificial inquiry and all understatement, summed up a social commentary which was a symbolic, tactical coup. Coming after months of painstaking search in the bush of "darkest Africa," the comment captured something of the ideal of British imperialism in the Victorian Age. British manners, British style, British decorum and, therefore, British civilization were deemed superior to the hostile elements, the forces of nature, and the "foreign" cultures of other races. The insistence on a foreign etiquette, like the conventional politeness and restraint of Stanley's remark, is symbolically powerful. When behavior which only makes sense in a very special setting is exhibited elsewhere, it can be a social challenge to the prevailing context. Stanley was, in a very real (although symbolic) sense, extending the borders of the British Empire by his statement as if to say: "Even here, British custom prevails."

In a similar way, when St. Antony met St. Pola in the Eastern Desert, the recorded remark, often repeated, puts monasticism in Egypt in its proper social perspective. According to St. Jerome, St. Antony, who thought himself to be the first lifelong hermit, was led in his old age by God even deeper into the desert in order to find an anchorite more advanced in holiness than himself (Waddell 1936:44). After several days' search, he met St. Pola in his simple cave. Pola had become a hermit in the desert long before Antony, in the mid-third century, having fled persecution in his youth. He had seen no mortal for nearly a century, and had had no contact with the world for the same period. St. Antony was duly humbled to meet a more seasoned anchorite than himself and, as many disciples had required of him, he attempted to elicit a God-inspired word of advice or encouragement from the hermit. But it was Pola who made the memorable observation, showing, indeed, that a hundred years of isolation intensifies rather than dulls social interest.

Behold him whom thou hast sought with so much labour, a
shaggy white head and limbs worn out with age. Behold, thou
lookest on a man that is soon to be dust. Yet, because love
endureth all things, tell me, I pray thee, how fares the human
race: if new roofs be risen in the ancient cities, whose empire is
it that now sways the world; and if any still survive, snared in
the error of the demons (Waddell 1936:47-48).

St. Pola had so positioned himself that he alone of all the rational
souls in four centuries of history in the Mediterranean Basin could
meaningfully ask, "Whose empire is it that now sways the world?"
How striking the question must have been to a civilization which had
been under Roman occupation for centuries! The very inquiry invites
the possibility of another perspective, no less compelling in that time
than the astronaut's photograph of an "earthrise" to the nationalism
of contemporary times. If Stanley's remark was mildly provocative,
Pola's rhetorical question was subversive; it generated an intense social
enthusiasm for monasticism in an Egyptian nation long wearied with
foreign oppression. The monastic experience of Antony, Pola, and
their thousands of followers manifested a new perspective, one which
had the force of establishing an entirely new culture. The former culture, by Pola's question, was equated to the devil's snares.

Based upon the scanty historical resources available for the contemporary reader, St. Antony may well be better associated with the
northern Egyptian and Hellenized Church of the imperial see of
Alexandria. The diptych of him beside St. Pola as presented in the
hagiographical account above may contain a remembrance of the
contrast between the Antonian ideal of an Egypt immersed in a layer
of ecclesiastical unity (of which St. Athanasius would write) versus the
humbler, repressed, unwritten ideal of older Coptic piety represented
by the almost forgotten and decrepit St. Pola.

In any case, at the intersection of the two traditions above, stands
the monk who stepped out of the economic system of the Empire and
the kinship structure of a society ensnared by the Empire. Childless,
the monk had no hostages to the well-being or favor of the Empire.
He did not eat the food of the Empire, nor sit at the table of those
enmeshed in its agriculture. He did not live on lands protected by its

armies or administered by its civil servants. When the Empire was pagan, he was Christian; when the Empire became Catholic, he was Coptic Orthodox. The symbolic presence of an outside and hostile force was nowhere more radical than the one in the desert, and it was from the desert that a continual stream of subversive literature filtered back into a state whose unhappy natives were often starved for signs of ethnic power and solidarity. The monks led the popular revolt against paganism when paganism was the imperial style. The monks turned their immense symbolic credibility against imperial Christianity when that religion came into fashion (Little 1958:39).

Herein, then, is the social dynamism which gave rise to Egyptian monasticism, and has sustained its function throughout the long ages of Coptic oppression until the present. Others more religious in their interests may wish to consider whether any more ultimate spiritual impulse underlies this dynamic, but even if one is discovered, it would still dovetail with this countercultural ethnic aspiration.

The fact that monasticism was adapted to other regions and diffused rapidly after its Egyptian origins is no discredit to this perspective. The areas which first adopted monastic models were all regions which suffered similar kinds of political and economic oppression in the Roman or Byzantine empires. Monasteries flourished in Palestine, Syria, and Armenia, as well as in Egypt. In each instance, ethnic dissatisfaction with foreign administration remained great (Betts 1978:6). When monasticism finally entered into regions traditionally at peace with imperial controls, it often did so only when the Empire was in full collapse. Thus, rejecting the imperial system was at one with repudiating its weakness and demise--something that a son of a patrician (such as St. Benedict) might do in Italy, just as an Egyptian national might, as he made his way into the wilderness.

"Flee the world!" is the universal maxim of monasticism. But the world is always its secular embodiment. For the desert monks, the world was the "Evil Empire" of Rome. Outside Egypt, that same world would learn how to co-opt the powerful counter-secular symbol of monasticism as a means of civil legitimation. But for the Copts, the monasteries remain what they started out to be, simply because the Copts have remained an alienated ethnic community in their own country for centuries. The monasteries retained a sign value of protest, non-acceptance, and of ethnic confidence. They represented a hidden, unbreakable strength for the Copts from Roman and Byzantine times, through Persian, Arab, Fatamid, Turkish, French, British, nationalist and Islamic periods. Even when their monasteries hardly lived up to the ideals ascribed to them, the Copts still maintained an identification with those standards by the strong influence of the inspiring hagiography shared among them.

Max Weber's central insight into the cultural role of religion can easily be enlisted to support this view of the social, historical rationale of monasticism:

> Religious ethics penetrate into social institutions in very different ways. The decisive aspect of the religious ethic is not the intensity of its attachment to magic and ritual, or the destructive character of the religion generally, but is rather its theoretical attitude toward the world. . . . Indeed, the very tension which the religious ethic introduces into the human relationships toward the world becomes a strongly dynamic factor in social evolution (Weber 1963:209-10).

Few religious institutions have such antagonistic attitudes toward the world as sharply delimited as traditional monasticism. The social evolution of the West, whose monastic institutions maintain a collective proximity to worldly events while, ideally, their individual monks evidence a strong disinterest in worldly associations (the latter perhaps counter-balancing the former), was at one time decisively influenced by monasticism. The Copts in Egypt were no less influenced by the institution, though in greatly varying ways throughout their history.

Monasticism erupted on the Egyptian scene in the mid-fourth century. The few earlier anchorites and hermits who initiated desert-based solitary asceticism became, in their older age, magnets for the literally thousands who followed (Wellard 1970:55). Desert centers for monasticism flourished in various places. The Eastern Desert around Mount Colzoum near the Red Sea attracted candidates more desirous of individual solitude. Here St. Antony's model of monasticism prevailed. Near the broad loop of the Nile north of Thebes, in the region called "Thebaid," another tradition of monasticism was established, following the rule and example of St. Pachom. These monasteries were more communal, stressing an asceticism of collective labor and common prayer. They were located closer to the inhabited Nile Valley than any other, and seemed to interact with native populations in a way resembling the relationship of Western monasteries to their surrounding societies.

With St. Pachom and his monks, Egypt witnessed the genesis of communal (cenobitic) monasticism. St. Pachom did not establish his communities from an eremitical base, although he enlisted eremitical monks to join his movement. Rather, he founded a unique form of monasticism with no earlier monastic precedent, one which was patterned on the social model of the military. He had formerly been an Egyptian officer in a Roman garrison and was imprisoned during his service. He converted to Christianity when he was released, but was disillusioned with the imperial fashion of that religion. He sought out a desert spiritual director to help him find his destiny; this eventually led him to the monastic life (cf. J. Kamil 1987:39).

This cenobitic form of monasticism coexisted for centuries in Egypt with the eremitical form founded by St. Antony. Ultimately, communal monasticism prevailed on a practical level, but the eremitical form was, and continues to be, considered as the ideal. Communal monastic structures admit of greater possibilities of institutionalization and continuity. They are more easily enlisted by the Church and can more easily negotiate their interests with outside society. As Max Weber saw it, the charisma of a single religious master tends toward "routinization" in future generations (cf. 1947:363-73). Weber defined charisma as:

> . . . a certain quality of an individual personality by virtue of which he is set apart from ordinary men and treated as endowed with supernatural, superhuman, or at least specific exceptional powers or qualities. These are such as are not accessible to the ordinary person but are regarded as of divine origin or as exemplary, and on the basis of them the individual concerned is treated as a leader (Weber 1947:358-59).

The original desert fathers possessed such a charisma in abundance (Pearson & Goehring 1986:241). Whether or not they intended to develop communal monasticism, the "routinization" of their ideal into communal institutions was built into their spiritual activities. Even beyond the process of consolidation inherent in the eremitical project, the ecclesiastical and ethnic demands of the Copts over the centuries contributed further to the development of the "total, greedy institutions" of Church and monastery.

The desert of Scete or the Wadi Natroun dominated the monastic scene in Lower Egypt. In addition, at one time, a strip of desert closer to the western edge of the Delta, called the *kellia*, housed thousands of monks in individual cells. Lower Egyptian monasteries exhibited a wider range of monastic styles, from the solitary, to the dyadic, to the communal. From the very beginning, all monastic forms in Egypt stressed the absolute importance of the relationship of each monk to his *hegoumenos* (spiritual father), who was often the abbot of a monastery, or a spiritual director among a group of monks in a local region, who were living alone.

The relationship of the monks to their hegoumenos exceeded in importance all other influences on the manner of life which the monks led, including rules and church regulations. This feature of monastic evolution gave the Coptic monks a surprising latitude of possible responses to the world they had repudiated, but had not ceased to affect. The charisma of the founders and their followers made it difficult to subordinate their manner of life to civil or ecclesiastical decree. The physical consolidation of monks around central spiritual leaders was a natural process in the evolution of discrete monasteries. This process was hastened by the frequency of Bedouin raids on unprotected isolated cells (Wakin 1963:125). Nevertheless, Coptic monasteries, even the most communal or cenobitical, never exhibited the kind of uniformity which typifies monastic formation in the West. The Coptic monk retained a sense of solitariness even in the consolidated deir.

Victor Turner's analysis of solitariness and community bears some relevance on the centralization of Coptic monasteries. He considered the paradox of how the enthusiasms of radical individuals tend to resolve into corporate movements. Some idealists, he maintains, may exhibit remarkably sustained energy for leading intensive ascetical lives because they have locked into certain deeply embedded cultural models of behavior which, even if not consciously grasped, provide them with an integrity of intentionality which grants special purpose and power to their behavior. Such models of behavior are most often religious in nature; Turner calls them "root paradigms" (1974:64).

Root paradigms, because they are often only unconsciously employed, may be considered by the enthusiast as a private and unique vocation. The idealist may believe that God has infused in him or her a special election for a life to be lived quite apart from the common culture. But in reality, the ideals espoused by the individual may have been inspired by a strong but submerged cultural current into which the person had lately tapped.

As a result of the cultural origin of the root paradigm, the enthusiast's life has an immediate reference to the broader society. Ultimately, its social religious significance will prevail over the private spiritual goal.

> Root paradigms are shown in behavior which appears freely chosen but resolves at length into a total pattern. They go beyond the cognitive, and even beyond the moral, to the existential domain, and in so doing become clothed with allusiveness, implicitness and metaphor (Turner 1979:148).

Turner's root paradigms are a useful tool in understanding the relationship of the private monastic calling to the total monastic institution and the ecclesiastical exploitation of monasticism in the Coptic Church.

Coptic Monasticism as Cultural Opposition

The social position which the first monks held in Egyptian society is not hard to determine. In the last years of Rome's pagan emperors, insurrections in Egypt were associated with Coptic Christianity. The casualties of war in Upper Egypt were regarded not only as national heroes, but also as religious martyrs. Martyrdom became the self-ascribed virtue of the Coptic Church (cf. M. Kamil 1968:32-35). The fact that, overnight, the same Empire which exploited and slaughtered Christian Egyptians should subsequently not only profess Christianity, but proclaim itself the dominant voice of Christianity was completely incomprehensible to the Copts. But as Church politics proceeded into the fourth century, that state of affairs gained international credibility. With absolute refusal to be seduced by an Empire which seemed to co-opt its colony's best standard of opposition, religious figures in Egypt turned away from ecclesiastical roles which were becoming subordinated to the Empire's religious establishment. They sought a religious identity which even more intimately identified itself with native religious sentiments and indicted the claims of a so-called "universal" Church.

The religious and ethnic identity of the Copts was not, therefore, absorbed into the emerging imperial Church. If martyrdom was the price for ethnic solidarity before the Edict of Milan and the Christianization of Rome, then a special refinement of martyrdom would animate the heroes of the resurging Coptic religion against what they perceived as a debased Western Church state. The new martyrs, the new heroes of Egypt and of her true ethnic religion were, as all the contemporary witnesses declared, the monks in the desert (Benedict 1981:15). This is not to say that the immensely rich and profound tradition of early monasticism can entirely be reduced to an ethnic protestation, no more than the Reformation can be entirely reduced to the emergence of German nationalism. However, the religious significance of the movement, which usually exhausts the literature on the subject, does not well address the social function and cultural contributions of monasticism.

The first monks explicitly avoided structured organization and codification as they were, after all, asserting something of an anti-institutionalism. The firm hold of charismatic leadership, over and against institutional persona, would begin to mark a structural feature of the Coptic Church even after its routinization. Although the traditional offices of bishop and patriarch could not be jettisoned, so firmly had they taken hold of the popular understanding of church, the Coptic monks would no longer recognize the episcopal plants of the Byzantine Province after the Council of Chalcedon in A.D. 451. For the greater part of their history, the Copts would choose their episcopal and patriarchal candidates from among their anti-clerical (or at least non-clerical) desert monks, and not from the professional ecclesiastics of populated areas of the Empire. This custom became a sacred canon of the Coptic Church. To show the Coptic distaste for what they perceived as the power-mongering of the foreign Church, their candidates for ecclesiastical position were ceremoniously fettered in iron when they were retrieved from the desert and consecrated (Burmester 1960:55). In all of this, the Copts perceived themselves as exhibiting a piety superior to the imperial Church which, after becoming licit, then became lax (cf. Benedict 1981:15).

The famous ecumenical Council of Chalcedon is usually considered to be the moment of the decisive breach between the Egyptian and universal Churches. Certainly at this time, the Byzantine leadership attempted to suppress the Coptic leaders in the Egyptian Church, and the Coptic rejection of this decision forever sealed the division (Malaty 1987:61). But other events, earlier ones, fostered the tension of Coptic relations with the imperial religion, and these events, which emanated from the desert, set Egypt on its separate path.

Greek notions of spirituality, at variance with the sentiments of the native Copts, were heavily inbred with imperial philosophical traditions. The Roman-Byzantine Church recognized Alexandria as the perfect port of dissemination for the Hellenized model of Christianity which was expected to integrate all contrasting ideological movements by the prestige of its philosophical superstructure. Hence, the School of Alexandria became a powerful ideological agency of the Christian voice of the Empire. Generations of Western scholars would read about Coptic monasticism as a practical extension of the ascetic and dualistic principles outlined by Greco-Alexandrian masters such as Origen and St. Clement.

The School of Alexandria emerged in this early period of Church history as an intellectual phenomenon which was more Platonic than Coptic. The rank and file desert ascetic felt little kinship with it. However, the monks were of interest to the Hellenistic scholars, some of whom assumed their desert ascetic life style, and thereby obtained their charisma and credibility. Moreover, the Coptic patriarch of Alexandria knew that the popular Coptic Church was deeply rooted in its monastic institutions, so he likewise desired to blend the mentality of Alexandria's famous school with the spirituality of the desert. Today, Coptic historical revisionists dismiss the Greek character of the Alexandrian school, and claim it as a native intellectual phenomenon (cf. Malaty 1986b:3,9,17,72,93).

Native Egyptian monasticism did not spring from the intellectual theories of Alexandrian theologians, nor did Coptic ethnic revitalists establish the Greek theological school of that city. Certain spiritual subtleties were no doubt received by the native Egyptian Church from the colonial port city, and certain Copts from the wealthier families were no doubt educated there, but as the political situation worsened, Alexandrian intellectual refinements became more and more distasteful to the Copts, who were already drawing their ethnic spiritual inspiration from the desert, rather than from their capital.

The tension between the Alexandrian Greek party and the native monastic party is well illustrated by the theological crisis which raged in Egypt over half a century before the Council of Chalcedon. Greek notions of spiritual contemplation rested on the strong anti-materialist bias of Platonic dualism. Hence, Greek ascetics claimed that their method of the contemplation of God was superior, as it conceived no images of physical realities in the mind. Coptic monks, however, resented the implication that their richly imaged folk meditations were somehow inferior to the contemplation of the Greek ascetics. The Greeks accused the Coptic monks of a heresy which reduced God to a pictorial and corporeal nature, while the Copts accused the Alexandrian party of following the dualistic philosophy of the great master of the Alexandrian theological school, Origen, to the detriment of revealed truths. It is not hard to read the larger problem of Coptic nationalism into the dispute (cf. Benedict 1981:40).

In A.D. 399, the crisis came to a head when an angry mob of monks emerged from their desert retreat and entered the city of Alexandria with the intention of burning the patriarch's residence for his supposed collusion with the Origenists. When the patriarch intercepted them and evidenced loyalty to their position with the words, "I behold you as the face of God," they demanded his condemnation of the foreign intellectual pollution which came from the Empire. Even though the patriarch agreed to do so, the monks continued to riot in Alexandria and in the desert, purging their own ranks of unsupportive foreign elements. In A.D. 400, with the conflict still intense, three hundred Greek-speaking monks, who had insinuated themselves into the Coptic monastic movement, were forced to leave Egypt. Included among the exiles were native bishops, scholars, and foreign ecclesiastical journalists. John Cassian and Germanus were part of the exodus, and they carried a Greco-Coptic variation of monasticism to the West (Sozomen 1855:377-78). Benedictine monasticism would eventually emerge in the Western Church as a result of this dispersion.

Because this diaspora is the basic Western source of monasticism, and because Westerners are so uninformed or prejudiced regarding the simple Coptic character of the Egyptian Church, they cannot conceive of Coptic monasticism without thinking it to be a product of Greek spirituality. Hence, when the Greek party fled Egypt, Coptic monasticism seemed to detach itself from the spiritual currents of the universal Church (cf. Benedict 1981:41). However, this was not the case. Coptic monasticism was not detaching itself from its spiritual heritage with the expulsion of the Origenists. The Coptic monks were precluding the absorption of their original ethnic religious institutions into imperial religious structures. The same process would recur on a grander scale in the Chalcedonian Schism.

At the Council of Chalcedon, the theological issue which exacerbated long-standing political, ethnic, and economical tensions was a subtle difference over the human and divine aspects of the person of Jesus Christ. Although the arguments were well beyond the comprehension of many of the participants in the Council, as well as the laity they represented, the Christological question clearly presented the possibility for deep ecclesiastical division. At stake was the conclusion that one side possessed Christ through its orthodoxy, while the other side did not. Legitimation for a Christian Church rests on its sole possession of Christ. Christological argumentation at ecumenical councils is a sign that the Church, meeting together, has factions deep enough for schism and, therefore, the nations which foster national churches are seeking greater autonomy.

When the Council was convened, Dioscorus, the Alexandrian patriarch, was scrutinized from its very beginning. Dioscorus, it seems, more than earlier patriarchs, only too well represented the aspirations of his see rather than the agenda of the larger Church. Alexandrian patriarchs were quite successful in consolidating local

powers to themselves. Dioscorus was called the "pope" of ten metropolitan sees and 101 bishoprics. He was the proprietor of countless
estates and a naval commander who controlled the country's trade.
Coptic patriarchs were at times governors of the region, commanders
of the military, and distributors of national resources. In these
capacities, they had inherited offices, titles and prestige which had
accumulated from Roman procurators, Ptolemaic regents, and ultimately from pharaonic rulers. In these capacities, Dioscorus was
accused of conspiring with militant monks in intimidating bishops of
colonial sees to join the doctrinal positions at odds with Greek and
Roman ideology. He was, moreover, accused of withholding grain
shipments from the Delta to the Empire.

Dioscorus refused to buckle under the international pressure and
was relieved of his office and exiled. A new and submissive governor-
patriarch was dispatched to Alexandria. The Copts did not accept this
imposition for one moment. With rioting, they attacked and killed
the new bishop (Evelyn White 1973:220). They proclaimed a monk
to be their own new patriarch, and since he could not sit in the
imperial port of Alexandria, he reigned from the desert monastic
outposts. The desert monasteries, after all, were far better symbolic
centers for Coptic rule than a regional, imperial capital.

The Copts called the foreign elements of Christianity in Egypt
Melkites (the king's people) for their association with the Church of
Rome. The Melkites retained a separate foreign-supported patriarch
in Alexandria, and possessed their own church institutions. The
Copts had a parallel Church which operated clandestinely out of the
adiora. There was seldom any real peace between the two Churches,
and imperial efforts to crush the schism were never quite successful.
The Copts were tenacious, and by the fifth and sixth centuries, the
weakening Empire was without either the internal resources or the
resolve to further subordinate Egypt (Little 1958:41). Popular Coptic
patriarchs were pursued, arrested, or exiled with some regularity
(Malaty 1987:71), but the number of monks and monasteries steadily
increased.

During these turbulent years of national resistance, the monasteries attracted such significant numbers of candidates as to give
commentators occasion to ponder the demographic consequence.

Monks were so numerous as to be likened to armies. The Coptic patriarch was said to have a "standing army" of five thousand men in Nitria alone (Butcher 1897,1:273). Jerusalem, a capital city of a region similarly in revolt against the Empire, was said to be "occupied" by an army of monks (Wellard 1970:120). Since Pachom's rule was established on a military model of collective discipline, ten thousand monks were said to "swarm" in the region where his rule prevailed. The sheer numbers of celibate monks has more than once occasioned Western observers to wonder if the nation was not opting to discontinue reproducing rather than produce slaves (King 1947,1:343).

Celibacy is an unusual social option by definition. While second sons of landed families in Catholic medieval Europe may have had celibacy as a distinctive choice, for the popular level of society, it seldom represented anything serious enough to dramatically influence population levels. Even when clerics did not marry, their choice did not necessarily amount to a commitment to celibacy. More often, it seems that marriage delays, prolonged nursing periods, contraceptive techniques, abortion, and infanticide were the usual ways of world cultures to reduce family size or a population if, indeed, that was desired. But massive celibacy is obviously rarer. And yet, within a few generations after its inception, monastic celibacy was a hugely popular option in the backwaters of the Empire, and nowhere more so than in Egypt. Butcher's *Story of the Church of Egypt* titles the chapter on the rise of monasticism, "Suicide of the Egyptian Nation," with clear reference to the demographic consequence of widespread celibacy (1897,1:191).

Imperial domination of Egypt had already led to unusual social and familial behavior among the Copts before the time of the first monks. Documentation exists which demonstrates that during this period some members of Egypt's middle classes were choosing brother-sister marriage arrangements (Arens 1986:120). This does not, in itself, prove brother-sister incest or procreation, but it does provide a *social appearance* of marital relations for all practical purposes. No comparable seemingly incestuous, societal behavior is known to have existed on the scale of the phenomenon evidenced in Byzantine and Roman Egypt. W. Arens notes a study of Keith Hopkins who opines that these alliances were apparently self-serving marital strategies of siblings to protect inheritances and family estates, and to evade heavier taxation (Arens 1986:9). As such, these strategies constitute a kind of social adaptation proper to sociological analysis (Arens 1986:120); they "appear to have been a transitory response to foreign domination" (Arens 1986:10).

Celibacy, another alternative to traditional marriage, results from the same kinds of social pressures, although its appeal was far wider than that of the middle class. Conjoining the themes of sibling marriage and monastic celibacy, the historical record of the desert fathers often reflects on the role of their sisters in the discernment of their vocation as is seen in the case of St. Antony, St. Amoun, and others. Benedictinism, the immediate successor of desert monasticism in the Western Church, emulates this pattern in the historical account of its founder, St. Benedict, as his twin sister, St. Scholastica, also founded a monastery of women near that of her brother.

Celibacy and institutionally implied incest emerged as two novel responses to the conditions of Egypt in the first centuries of the Christian era, and they argue well to the extremity of the social stress of the times. However, monasticism was to have a more lasting impact on Coptic society than the formality of sibling marriage; the latter disappeared in the early Middle Ages. One is tempted to reflect that the Copts possessed a heritage from pharaonic times which might have made such social choices more comprehensible. The phenomenon of brother-sister marriage was a renowned pharaonic prerogative, whereas, in contrast, chaste and otherworldly religious enthusiasts called "Therapeutae"[4] are described by Philo as living near Alexandria already in the first century of the Christian era (cf. Evelyn White 1973:7,11). Perhaps remote precedents, by virtue of their niche in the culture of the folk, had a certain conditioning or formative influence on social choices in this period of history.

Byzantine control in Egypt was not unrelieved oppression. When economic and political pressure failed to subdue resistance, some emperors turned toward policies of appeasement. In A.D. 482, Emperor Zeno issued the decree, Henoticon, which called on all Eastern episcopal sees to return to ecclesiastical unity even without a consensus about the theological terminology of Chalcedon. Since the unity which Constantinople desired was the establishment of an

Oriental counterbalance to the authority of Rome, the Byzantine Empire was willing to permit a limited autonomy to Egypt in return for its cooperation. Egypt cooperated; its patriarch signed the Henoticon, and the emperor handsomely endowed the Coptic Church and her monasteries (Malaty 1987:74). Coptic hagiography explains the strange beneficence of a Byzantine emperor by a story of a woman who successfully disguised herself as a desert monk for many years in Egypt only to be revealed as Zeno's long-lost daughter (Malaty 1987:74). The fact that the emperor should discover his daughter in a desert monastery is a strong testimony of the paternal position assumed by Zeno over the adiora. His desire to enlist them in the order of the Empire witnesses to the social strength of monasticism in Egypt. He rebuilt monasteries, fortified them, and lavishly supplied them.

Zeno's policy of appeasement of the Copts continued during the reign of the next Byzantine emperor, Anastasius. In A.D. 519, however, Justinian became emperor, and the policy changed. Rome had become more an opportunity for military expansion than an ecclesiastical problem by then; Byzantium required less cooperation from its colonies and sought more conformity. The Melkite patriarchs once again forced the Coptic patriarch underground and, quite literally, out into the desert (Malaty 1987:78).

The centuries of oppression which the Copts experienced under the Byzantine Empire have forever conditioned the Coptic view of the West, or at least their view of the Western and Orthodox Churches. These formative years of monastic genesis and development, of an ecumenical council and ecclesiastical intrigue, of violent persecutions, of desert mystics and exiled patriarchs, comprise an era of Coptic history from which all generations of future Copts would derive the symbols and sentiments of their ethnic and religious solidarity. If, as it has often been said, the Muslim world ponders the Crusades as though they were recent history, the Copts ponder their even earlier estrangement from the West as a factor which continues to give rise to their special status in the world. The turning of Egypt away from its mooring in the European stage was in no small way influenced by the Copts' disaffection with Byzantium. The rapid and almost effortless advance of Islam over Egypt was aided by this breach in the wall of Christendom.

In A.D. 640, an army of no more than ten thousand Arabs stood at the gates of the fortress city of Alexandria. Within the city were over fifty thousand troops of the Empire's African garrison. The navy was present and intact in its protected harbor. Nevertheless, the city surrendered in a short time. Although the Emperor Constans would briefly retake the Egyptian capital in three years, it fell again shortly thereafter, and was forever lost to the West. According to Western interpretation, it was the Coptic patriarch, elected by desert monks, who enjoined the populace to offer no resistance to the invaders (Little 1958:43), making the Arab occupation possible. Modern Copts, however, dispute this scenario and maintain that it was the Melkite patriarch of Alexandria who handed over the city. Nonetheless:

> Egypt chose, more than thirteen centuries ago, to mortify its suffering flesh in the arms of Asia. It has never, in so far as the true Egyptian is concerned, changed its mind. . . .
> The failure of Greece, Rome and Byzantium is the dividing line, for before the Arab conquest, there was nothing to show that Egypt would turn to the East and, after it, no sign that it would ever turn back to the West (Little 1958:40-41).

Chapter V

Monasticism in Egypt's Modern Era

From the time of the Arab invasions, Egypt became progressively Islamicized. This was accomplished by tax incentives for "conversion," and by recurring waves of persecution and proselytizing efforts. The Coptic population became a minority after several centuries, and its language gave way to Arabic. The political stage of Egypt passed from one external power to another: Saudi Arabia, the Ottoman Empire and the Fatamid and Abayyid dynasties which were followed by the Mameluks.[1] However, the Coptic situation remained much the same. The Copts were persecuted or barely tolerated, and their monasteries remained what they were when they were founded: out-posts of an alienated people, a frontier where ethnic aspiration was not yet subjugated; a silent, symbolic center at the margins of the temporal realm.

The armies of Napoleon invaded Egypt in 1798. The Middle East was becoming more important in the arena of European trade and politics, and more military entanglements would follow. However, Egypt resisted Napoleon's efforts to build a North African empire at every step with riots, revolts and a retreat into economic chaos (Little

1958:55). Nevertheless, the four brief years of the French occupation of Egypt led to profound changes.

The French introduced an adapted form of Napoleonic law and political organization which survives in some form even today. Academicians were brought into Egypt ostensibly to study its culture, but with the more important, unintended, effect of exposing Egyptians to Western learning. European parochial schools were opened, and new generations of Moslems and Copts now became aware of another world and other religious views.

In 1805, an Albanian Mameluk rebel, Mohammed Ali, swept into power, replacing the Mameluk Ottoman pasha and the French emperor. His efficiency in governing and his openness to reform enabled Egypt to assume its modern role in international affairs. He despised the Copts, but had the sense to employ experts of any minority for the smooth operation of his government (cf. Little 1958:59,65). He retained much of the French organizational machinery and turned Egypt westward for modernization. This orientation would profoundly affect the Coptic Church and the desert monasteries.

For the first time since the Arab invasion, the Copts in Egypt had to deal with the sustained proselytizing presence of Western Christian missionaries. Catholic schools were built which offered superior training to the young which, at the same time, suggested the benefits of ecclesiastical subordination to Rome. Jesuits and members of other religious orders visited the monasteries, consciously aware that Roman retrieval of the Copts depended upon the moral persuasion of the monks (Sicard 1780:17). The weakened position of the adiora at this time did not dissuade the missionaries from focusing upon them as the key to the whole ethnic group. Catholicism had learned long before to co-opt monastic foundations in order to secure ecclesiastical unity.

Protestant missionaries also moved into Egypt. They were initially interested in converting Moslems to Christianity, but when that failed in the face of massive Islamic resistance, they turned to the Copts whose liturgical rites, sacramental piety, Mariology, relics, and ecclesiastical structures reeked to them of a decadence they associated with Rome. Numerous churches, hospitals, universities, and schools were built, and they made many converts.

The influence of the Protestant missionaries, especially of the

Evangelical type, is difficult to calculate. Intuitively, one would suspect that the theological, devotional, and liturgical practices of Evangelicals would be so foreign to Coptic Orthodox sensibilities that the popular response to it would be indifference, or even hostility. But perhaps because it represented a decisive alternative to the more familiar and, therefore, attractive Catholic presence, which, if repudiated, could absorb the whole Coptic Church intact, the Evangelical presence was allowed to exercise a paradoxical influence over the Orthodox Egyptian mind. To allow this helped keep the Orthodox Church quite separate from Roman ecclesiastical influence. Till today, one marvels that Coptic Orthodoxy often employs spiritual, congregational, political, and exegetical categories more proper to Evangelical Protestantism than to European Orthodoxy.

In 1853, Pope Kyrillos V, a Coptic patriarch of a prominent house with a Westernized education, established the first modern Coptic grade schools in Egypt, including the first school for girls. He purchased a printing press for ecclesiastical use and authorized the opening of secondary and technical schools all over the country (Karas 1986:43). In 1875, a theological school was established in Cairo for the preparation of pastors. Annexed to the school was the Didymus Institute, founded to train blind boys to become cantors in Coptic worship (Karas 1986:44).[2]

The opening of Egypt to the West presented significant challenges to the Coptic Church. Not only were rival religious views a threat, but Western secularism and materialism were introduced into the arena of Egyptian social relations and economics. Notions of democracy led a number of lay Copts to seek greater participation and partnership in the management of church properties and affairs. By 1873, these Copts had persuaded ecclesiastical officials, through appeals to government interests, to modify the old Ottoman Millet system in order to make it more democratic.

Theoretically, the Millet system instituted by the Ottomans was the framework of a Coptic "nation" within Egypt. In every town and city of the country, the Copts had small units of self-government (*Millets*) which supervised matters of education, marriage, social welfare, and church maintenance. The basis for such a subsystem of minority self-regulation is found in the Koran, but the Turks formalized the arrangement. Until 1873, the Millets were firmly under the control of the Church, but in that year, Butros Pasha Ghali, a leading Copt from a great family (ancestor to the former United Nations General Secretary), who was involved in high state politics, engineered the passage of a government decree which changed the status of the Millets. They were now established as the *Maglis Milli* or Community Councils, to be managed jointly by the clergy and the laity. The Maglis Milli were created to assign pastoral care to the clergy and to delegate administration of the *waqf* (religious endowments of land, buildings, and monies) to the expertise of the laity (Wakin 1963:147). Understandably, many of the bishops who formed the Holy Synod and who had assisted the patriarch in ruling the Millets, were not pleased with these developments, and they began to look for alternate solutions.

Acting in concert under the patriarch, the bishops prevented the Maglis Milli from assuming its decreed authority. The Holy Synod accomplished this obstructionist agenda by securing the cooperation of the desert monks, who held a very considerable proportion of the waqf which the Maglis Milli hoped to administrate. The charter of the Maglis Milli only called upon the monks and bishops to voluntarily share the trusts of these estates. This redistribution of land administration was not forthcoming, especially since the monasteries depended upon their delta- and valley-based farm endowments for subsistence and economic survival. In question were six thousand *feddan*[3] of valuable farmland owned by the monasteries, and three thousand feddan controlled by the bishops or the patriarch (Wakin 1963:150). These numbers do not seem to be very significant in terms of Western agricultural estates, but in terms of the circumscribed, rich land along the Nile, they were quite significant.

The Coptic hierarchy of bishops became more closely allied with and influential over the leadership of the monasteries by these events, making them an issue of even greater ecclesiastical concern. Not only was the symbolic authority of the adiora now more and more preempted by the bishops, but so was their real estate. This becomes clearer when it is recalled that, in most cases, heads of monasteries had also become the bishops who sat on the Holy Synod.

The new alliance of Church and monastery might appear, at first, to have been wholly dominated by the hierarchy. This may have been true initially, but once the rule of a monastery was assumed as an episcopal privilege, it exacted from the bishop-abbot certain responsibilities. Bishops who enjoyed the privilege of administering monastic estates could be called upon by the monks to rebuild abandoned sites and to aid in monastic maintenance. At the same time, bishops could enhance their ecclesiastical standing by promoting the well-being and growth of their monasteries. The deir could become a source of clerical formation and a site of renewed interest for pilgrimages and devotional restoration for the laity.

British Influence

British forces invaded and conquered Egypt in September 1882. Claiming to be saving the nation from internal political anarchy and to be protecting European interests at risk, the British were actually attempting to gain complete control of the Suez Canal and to consolidate their African empire (Milner 1970). This military expedition would begin a period of direct British occupation of Egypt for forty years, and an indirect military and economic control lasting into the mid-1950s.

British relations with the Copts were seldom positive. The Copts complained that they fared better in attaining bureaucratic positions under Mohammed Ali and his line, rather than under Christian England (Mikhail 1911:12-13). British policy, in fact, seemed intent on appeasing the Islamic majority as a means of keeping the nation pacified. Islamic perception that a foreign Christian power was elevating a domestic Christian minority might have caused serious reactions. As Moslems, Mohammed Ali and his successors could make concessions to the Copts without being accused that they were favoring their own kind (Wakin 1963:15). But as Egypt was exposed more and more to Western influences, the charge that the Copts were spiritually aligned with foreign interests would be voiced again and again by some of the Muslim leaders.

Toward the end of the nineteenth century, there were clear signs of a small monastic revival. Within a few decades, the monasteries became active forces within the Church once again, engaging the hierarchy and the laity from positions of strength which had not been enjoyed since before the medieval plagues brought them down. Popular catechetical movements, no doubt a response to the proselytism of foreign churches, took root in the Coptic Church through the work of the laity. The rediscovery of the Coptic heritage also provided a cultural, formational preparation for later monastic vocations.

Other social forces coalesced to raise the monasteries of Egypt from their marginal status. In 1909, Butros Pasha Ghali, the Copt responsible for the formation of the Maglis Milli, was appointed prime minister of Egypt. The British, in a departure from their norms, appointed Ghali because he was considered an unobjectionable elder statesman, even though a Copt. Some political cooperation had begun to occur with the foundation of the Wafd Party, composed of liberal Moslems and Copts. The "Cross and Crescent" movement was also begun, urging new nationalistic cooperation between the two religions. However, Ghali was assassinated by an Islamic extremist in 1910.

The Wafd Party and the Cross and Crescent movement were by no means derailed by the assassination, but history would later show the event to be a portent of future political and social conflict. Sir Eldon Gorst, the British High Commissioner, opined in 1911 that:

> In Upper Egypt, at the present time, the Copt is prosperous but not popular. Were he to be placed in a high executive post, in addition to his lack of natural aptitude for it [i.e., of being in charge of Moslems], he would find a majority of the population animated by antagonistic feelings toward him, and he could not count on ready obedience and cooperation (Wakin 1963:16).

Concurrent with the rise of ecumenical movements in Egypt, fundamentalist Islamic movements also became popular. The Copts, already impatient with the British policy of appeasing Muslim prejudice, began to make more formal protests. In opposition to patriarchal admonition, a Coptic Congress was held from March 6 to 8, 1911, by leading lay Copts, many of whom were frustrated members of the Maglis Milli. It was convened in Assiut, a city in which patriarchal power was compromised by the proximity of the Upper Egyptian monastic and ecclesiastical binary capital, Deir el Muharraq. According to Kyriakos Mikhail, the Congress published five grievances:

1. As a Christian body of people, the Copts are forced to violate the commandments of their religion by Sunday labor. . . .

2. A large number of administrative posts in the government service are entirely closed to Copts, and it is felt that in general they are not promoted in accordance with their capabilities and merit. . . .

3. Under the existing electoral system in Egypt, they are left unrepresented on the Provincial Councils. . . .

4. The Copts have no equal right to take advantage of the educational facilities provided by the new Provincial Councils.

5. The Copts claim that Government Grants should be bestowed on deserving institutions without an invidious distinction of race or creed (cf. Mikhail 1911:28-30).

The Coptic sense of minority alienation in a Westward-leaning state was aggravated by a fundamentalist Islamic revival. On March 8, 1911, an Islamic Congress was held to counter the Coptic Congress in Assiut. Its response is summarized as follows:

1. Egypt is an Islamic country and cannot honor the Christian day of rest.

2. Copts are disproportionately represented in lower civil service posts and, therefore, are not entitled to equality in higher government positions.

3. No financial aid should be given to Coptic schools or charitable organizations.

4. Provincial Councils ought to reflect the Islamic character of Egypt, and not have Coptic members.

5. Coptic domestic courts [part of the Millet] should receive no
   tax income [although the Millet raise tax revenues] (cf. Karas
   1986:19).

The Muslim Brotherhood formed in Egypt in April 1929 was to have
an enormous impact on Egypt and on the whole Middle East from
that time on. Its reaction against the West was bound to include a
violent repudiation of Christianity which would naturally ill-affect the
Copts (Wakin 1963:74).

Hence, when Gamal Abdel Nasser, a former member of the
Brotherhood, led Egypt to complete independence in the 1950s, the
Copts had considerably less reason to celebrate than the Moslems. No
Copts were involved in Nasser's military coup and, initially, he
appointed none of them in his new government. When the Copts
were finally admitted to their disproportionately small place in the
government, it was perceived as sheer tokenism. Deprived of direct
ways of expressing ethnic interests, and inhibited from taking a high
profile reactionary posture in a land where they were a precarious
minority, the Copts once again found themselves in need of subtler
and more convoluted ways to represent their ethnic identity and their
sense of protest. Historically, monasticism had served the Copts as
such before, and armed with their hagiographical lore, it would do so
again.

Contemporary Monastic Revival

The immediate antecedents to the present revival of monasticism in
Egypt involve a complex set of relations among all of the adiora, the
patriarchate and the laity. The modern monastic revival proves to be
an interesting narrative which illustrates to some degree how these
bodies interact. The full story is impossible to document, if only
because the most important players, many still living, have remarkably
divergent views of some of the significant events. Nevertheless, the
following account has been compiled from a series of widely ranging
interviews.

An Ethiopian monk named Abuna Abd el-Masiha lived in Deir el
Baramous after the turn of the twentieth century. The relationship of
the Coptic and Ethiopian Churches has always been close, and Ethio-

pian monks have always been represented in Coptic adiora. Abuna
Abd el-Masiha was the only Ethiopian monk left in Deir el Baramous, and he lived apart. His ascetic practices were known to be
severe, and after five years of mortification within the walls of the
monastery, he graduated to living in a hand-hewn cave some three
miles away. The "charisma," or symbolic credibility with which Coptic culture would revere such a life would be enormous, and anyone
who associated with Abuna Abd el-Masiha would share in this symbolically powerful prestige. James Wellard was aware of this, then
very aged monk, on his visit to Deir el Baramous, but apparently
knew of no association between him and the later monastic reforms
(cf. Wellard 1970:31,36,38,198).

In 1927, a young man of twenty-five years entered Deir el Baramous and took the name Mina. Abuna Mina was from a prosperous
old family in the Delta and was well known to the patriarch, Pope
Kyrillos V, who gave him permission to enter Deir el Baramous, his
own monastery of episcopal origin.

Pope Kyrillos V, before his death in 1927, had arranged for a
school for monastic studies to be opened in Helwan in 1928. It was
not intended to educate all monastic candidates, but only those designated by their hegoumenos (Karas 1986:44). It was expected that
future episcopal and patriarchal candidates would come from that
school. As the Helwan School never had the obvious trappings of an
educational institution, it is difficult to gauge its activities, or to know
for certain how long it existed. It closed within a few years after its
opening, but not before Abuna Mina had passed through it, early in
his monastic career. Not long after his return to Deir el Baramous,
Abuna Mina was said to fall under the influence of Abuna Abd el-
Masiha and took to a cave about a mile from the deir.

Thus far, Abuna Mina had accumulated a number of the characteristics deemed typical of holiness which lead to important Church
leadership. He was from a prominent family and possessed a fine job
which he ostensibly repudiated in becoming a monk, gaining inverse
spiritual capital in the process. Moreover, he was sent to his monastery by a reigning patriarch, the very thing which hagiography was
expected to recall. He was a student of the latest educational establishment of his Church and, while still young, had become a solitary

cave dweller, following the example of an esoteric Abyssinian holy man.

All this foreshadowed the rise of Abuna Mina to greatness in his Church. The pattern of hagiography, not only in Egypt, but universally, often has the saint emerge from an aristocratic son who turns purposefully toward holy poverty (as St. Francis of Assisi). A poor man is poor, but not necessarily by virtuous choice, whereas the rich son's holiness can be gauged by the extent of what he has renounced. Moreover, the later ecclesiastical elevation of the dispossessed rich man is made more certain by the associations which his former wealth and active family provide.

However, the collateral attained by renunciation cannot be redeemed too quickly. Haste will expose the translation of material wealth to spiritual power as no renunciation at all; the translation only succeeds when it appears unintended.

Haste was Abuna Mina's greatest obstacle in the classical ascent of the holy man to that of church leader. In 1936, after nine years as a monk, the majority of which were spent either outside the deir, in schools, or travels, or in desert solitude outside the normal monastic routine, Abuna Mina sought permission to head his own monastery. He hoped to rebuild the ancient ruin of Deir Mari Mina in the desert near Alexandria, the monastery after which he took his name. However, his request was refused.

After a series of quarrels with the abbot of Deir el Baramous, Abuna Mina left the monastery and settled in an abandoned windmill in Old Cairo. The charisma of his conspicuous anchoritic life style and his appearance in a densely populated Christian quarter caused a sensation. Abuna Mina demonstrated that he was a master of the monastic symbol by convincingly exhibiting it under public scrutiny for years on end. Great crowds hemmed him in for blessings, and innumerable miracles are ascribed to this period of his life.

During World War II, Abuna Mina was expelled from the windmill by British forces, who were concerned that he might be a security risk or even a spy (Wakin 1963:111). He moved to a local church where he continued his public ministry. Throughout this time, Abuna Mina cultivated a special following among the Coptic graduate students in Cairo. He encouraged them to fully familiarize themselves with Coptic hagiography and monastic wisdom, and he prepared many of the students to become monks.

In 1944, Abuna Mina obtained his monastery, but it was not Deir Mari Mina. Instead, Church authorities granted him Deir Anba Samwil, the most desolate, remote and primitive of all of Egypt's monasteries. The site had only been reinhabited by a few monks since the last century and, as of yet, had evidenced no sign of long-term promise. Perhaps this was considered to be a means of placating the charismatic monk, while distancing him from the public upon whom he had such an impact. If so, the plan failed.

Shortly after his installation as hegoumenos of Deir Anba Samwil, great crowds of pilgrims descended upon the monastery. Within a few years, the deir attracted significant numbers of new vocations, once again freeing Abuna Mina to travel. He was soon back in Cairo rebuilding a church (St. Mina's!) and educating graduate students on the monastic life. Many of these he sent to Deir el Suriani in the Wadi Natroun, the other "strong" monastery of the region, rather than to Deir el Baramous, his monastic roots.

The abbot of Deir el Suriani, Anba Tafilos, had expanded the agricultural base of his monastery, installing new water pumps and rebuilding many cells. He esteemed education, and was thus a natural leader to whom graduate student candidates could be sent. By filling Deir el Suriani with new monks, Abuna Mina gained an acceptance in the Wadi Natroun where he had not been highly regarded after he left Deir el Baramous.

The number of monks nominated in patriarchal elections from this region had been growing in importance in the twentieth century, and by the mid-1950s, Abuna Mina was the candidate of at least two adiora, Deir Anba Samwil and Deir el Suriani, as well as the populace of Cairo and several leading families in the Delta.

The elder patriarch who led the Copts into the Nasser Era was Anba Yusab II. A monk only briefly, and originally from Deir Anba Antonius, he had become archbishop of Guergueh in Upper Egypt in 1920, and was acting patriarch for the sick and weak Pope Macarius III from 1942 to 1944. Breaking Coptic canon law, Anba Yusab became pope in 1946. (Coptic canons forbid a territorial bishop from becoming patriarch; only a monk is eligible for the office.) Anba

Yusab was a career ecclesiastic, however, and maneuvered his way onto the ballots.

As patriarch, Anba Yusab II at once became extremely unpopular. No less than sixteen episcopacies were said to have been bought from the pope. In Sohag, his valet was preparing a lawsuit against a bishop who refused his promised simoniacal payments. Rumors of corruption and scandals shook the Church. The monasteries reflected on the mistake of elevating diocesan bishops to the patriarchate, when simple monks would less likely be so corrupt or appear to be so reckless.

In 1954, a short-lived militant group born out of Coptic frustration, the *Umma Coptya* (Coptic Nation), overpowered the police guard of Anba Yusab and kidnapped him! Umma Coptya was the tentative Coptic answer to the Muslim Brotherhood, although it never had comparable popular appeal or organizational resources. Anba Yusab was taxied to a convent in Old Cairo where he was forced to sign documents of resignation. Within a short time, however, the police arrested the leaders of the Umma Coptya, and liberated Anba Yusab II. Interestingly, the one great illegality of a Coptic protest movement was directed against a Coptic patriarch, rather than a Moslem or a national leader!

Coptic militant groups have seldom risen in Egypt, although the social forces necessary for such a development are prevalent. However, many of the leading Copts hold privileged economic positions in Egypt, and have too many hostages to fortune to participate in political resistance. Moreover, the Copts are the only minority of any size in an otherwise homogenous Islamic state. Even a full-force resistance would ultimately be overcome by the majority, and any lesser displays of unrest would incite militant reactions of fundamentalist factions against the entire Coptic community (Wakin 1963:97).

Nevertheless, the embarrassing abduction of Anba Yusab served to focus official scrutiny on his office. In 1955, the Holy Synod of Coptic Bishops relieved Anba Yusab II of his patriarchal powers, although canon law required that he remain nominal pope until his death. With government approval, Anba Yusab II was retired to Deir el Muharraq, where he died two years later.

During the interregnum, the Holy Synod attempted to assert a more dynamic leadership of the Church. In response to civil legal changes which had made it easier for Copts to obtain a divorce through conversion to Islam, the bishops threatened to cancel Christmas celebrations in Egypt in 1955. Christmas and Easter are the two Christian holidays recognized by the state as observable by the Copts. On these days, the president of Egypt and many Islamic officials on all government levels customarily visit the churches to offer formal greetings to the Copts and their leaders. These greetings have evolved into occasions whereby the political offices of Egypt are legitimated in the Coptic community, and as opportunities for Arab leaders to be seen by the foreign press as accepted by the Christian minority. To cancel the Christmas celebration is a sacrifice to be sure, but one that approximates symbolic revolt. The act declared, in effect, that Islamic officialdom would not be recognized or respected that year.

The bishops resolved that should the cancellation of the celebration fail to gain them a hearing, they would leave their dioceses and return to their monasteries of origin to pray. They calculated that little would increase their authority more than an apparent renunciation of episcopal power. For the Copts, it was an act of daring! President Nasser sent his Minister of Justice to meet with the bishops to persuade them to allow government officials to attend church services for Christmas. He succeeded by making promises of legal changes--promises which were never kept--but the bishops were never able to act so concertedly again.

The diaconate includes several degrees in the Coptic Church; the minor orders are open to boys. In 1959, a five-year-old deacon, Rafik Bassili, pulled a slip of paper from a container, thereby selecting the new patriarch of Alexandria. This random selection process made elections possible without consensus, something difficult for the Copts to achieve. The name inscribed on the paper chosen by the boy was Abuna Mina el Muttawahad el Baramousi, Father Mina, the Solitary from the Monastery of the Romans. Within the hour, large pictures of the new patriarch--with his new name, Pope Kyrillos VI--were plastered all over Cairo!

The speed of the printers in supplying the posters caused some to wonder if the name on all three slips in the container was that of Abuna Mina (Wakin 1963:104). Nevertheless, a fractious election pro-

cedure, which had initially exposed many monks and bishops as patriarchal hopefuls, was over. The other two final candidates were monks
from Deir el Muharraq, a monastery whose wealth and strength of
numbers had seemed to be sufficient to carry the election. But the
Church of Lower Egypt could never accept ecclesiastical dominance
from Upper Egypt for long.

In 1959, Pope Kyrillos VI laid the cornerstone for a new monastery to be built next to the ruins of the ancient monastery, Deir Mari
Mina. The project was one he had hoped to begin twenty-five years
earlier on the site which had been abandoned for a thousand years.
This effort occupied much of the pope's time and attention. Wakin
lamented the patriarch's obsession in these words:

> In some ways, the incident symbolizes the reign of the new
> Patriarch: religious grandeur demonstrated by a charismatic
> leader suffering what the politically-oriented regard as withdrawal
> symptoms. The community was besieged, the minority anxious,
> the hierarchy, clergy and monks in disarray, the Church woun-
> ded by turmoil, and the Patriarch lays a foundation stone in a
> desert place for another monastery (Wakin 1963:112).

James Wellard, a British travel journalist, pondered the same matter:

> One other monastery struck me in particular as typifying the
> decline of the Egyptian Church. . . . I am referring to the new
> Coptic cathedral and monastery being built on the outskirts of
> the ancient City of St. Menas. This project, I was told, was dear
> to the heart of the present patriarch, Kyrillos VI, and is to be his
> monument for all time. It will certainly be an enormous ceno-
> taph, but who, one wonders will visit it. Who needs it? It is
> too far away from the populated centres of Alexandria and Cairo
> to be reached by commuting worshippers. . . . Christians, I dis-
> covered, were more interested in leaving their unhappy country
> altogether than in building another great cathedral in the middle
> of nowhere. Who, then, is to fill the cells and cloisters of this
> new convent when the ancient sites are almost empty, and would
> be empty if it were not for a few old men who regard them as
> places of retirement? (Wellard 1970:198-99)

Wakin and Wellard, for all their careful study, completely over-looked the basic intuition of Coptic monasticism. Direct, effective action is the one means the Copts cannot take to defend their ethnic or cultural aspirations. Indeed, whenever they have unified into a politically coherent and pro-active course, they have met with perse-cution. The appearance of divisiveness and collective incompetence in the management of internal affairs, while certainly a genuine social feature, may well be a highly evolved means of cultural posturing, which has little to do with accomplishing anything, so much as exhibiting a harmlessness to an ever-leery majority. The Copts, whose very religious affiliation is incendiary and whose economic position is provocative, need an ecclesiastical apparatus which is apparently dys-functional in order to exist in peace. However, Coptic monasticism is not simply the dysfunctional institution it first appears to be, as it operates on a cultural level beyond the maintenance of temporal church affairs. What it lacks in Western efficiency and foresight, it more than compensates for in its cultural value.

Pope Kyrillos VI was reviving monasticism. In so doing, he was tapping into the disintegrating force of Coptic emigration from Egypt which Wellard notes as afflicting the minority and, instead, turned it to a specialized religious withdrawal. This sort of withdrawal ulti-mately endorsed the Coptic society from which the monks took their leave. Today, Deir Mari Mina, contrary to Wellard's expectation, is thriving with monks, and besieged with pilgrims.

It so happened that the graduate students whom Pope Kyrillos VI inspired from his windmill in Cairo, became the core of a new gener-ation of monks. One of them, Abuna Matta el-Meskeen, eventually led a group of monks from Deir el Suriani deeper into the desert for the purpose of recovering a pristine monastic experience. Abuna Matta's disciples were so numerous and so popular, that Pope Kyrillos VI ordered them back to the monastery in the early 1960s. To weak-en Abuna Matta's following, Pope Kyrillos consecrated a number of these disciples as bishops, and thereby drew them into his own charismatic, yet institutional, fold. Among these bishops were Abuna Antonius el Suriani (who later became Pope Shenouda III), and Anba Samwil, who was killed with Sadat in 1981.

Interestingly, the new bishops of Pope Kyrillos VI were not

territorial or diocesan prelates. Hence, canonically, they were permitted to assume the patriarchy if elected. Abuna Matta, on the other
hand, refused to return to a monastery that he did not direct, and was
canonically adrift until the nearly collapsed Deir Abu Maqar was
offered to him in 1969. He was not consecrated as bishop of that
monastery, in view of his unbridled charismatic history but, as hegoumenos of the deir, he very rapidly reversed its fortunes.

Pope Shenouda III, likewise, took a nearly vacant monastery, Deir
Anba Bishoi, and like Pope Kyrillos VI at Deir Mari Mina, he emptied
much of the patriarchal treasury into restoring it. At the same time,
he began to rebuild Deir el Baramous. He also took direct control of
Deir Anba Antonius and Deir Anba Pola, reforming their houses and
horariums (daily schedules). Taking as his model the habits of other
oriental churches, Pope Shenouda changed the hooded apparel of all
the monks of Egypt. Only the monks of Deir Abu Maqar refused to
comply with the patriarchal directive, indicating their distance from
his authority. Finally, Pope Shenouda approved the reinhabitation of
the ancient monastic ruins in Upper Egypt, which by now are in
readiness to become "autonomous" adiora.

The monasteries of Egypt became the institutional heart of the
Coptic Church almost overnight. Hagiographically, of course, they
always were, but not for centuries had they been so crucial institutionally. Their rise would not have been predicted by ordinary sociological analysis, but they are now dynamic agents in Coptic affairs.

The Patriarch Enthroned in Exile

Western commentators have not been alone in misunderstanding the
significance of the adiora. In September 1981, reacting to Pope Shenouda's assertive voice in Coptic advocacy, President Anwar Sadat
attempted to silence the patriarch. As part of a general crackdown on
religious extremism specifically designed to curb the Islamic funda-
mentalists who had turned on Sadat (Heikal 1983:128-35), Pope
Shenouda was exiled from the patriarchate in Cairo. Amazingly, Sadat
banished Pope Shenouda III to a desert monastery, Deir Anba Bishoi!

Jehan Sadat remembers the decision of her late husband as a two-pronged clamp-down on sectarian extremism, both Muslim and Coptic (1987:437-38), but the matter is more complex than that. The Copts were never mobilized for political militancy and so could never mount anything like a threat to national security which warranted militaristic reaction. Nevertheless, the Islamic interpretations of Coptic communal advocacy and growing political self-awareness could be used to fuel a fundamentalist revolt against Western Christian influence in the Arab-Islamic nation. A crackdown on the Copts by Sadat, *as if* they were conspirators in national subversion, pre-empted Muslim extremists from playing the card of alleged Western infiltration of the government. Pope Shenouda's exile to the desert had the effect of placating a people who had been alarmed by their own propaganda.

Sadat inadvertently returned the patriarch to the place where his office was always energized. Even while silenced under house arrest, Pope Shenouda was a more forceful symbol in the desert than he had been as a free man in Cairo. The ancient hagiographical associations of persecution, martyrdom and desert exile were popularly reinforced. International outpouring of support for the Copts was worldwide; recognition they dared not seek for themselves was unwittingly granted them by an insecure president.

Pope Shenouda's exile lasted four years. One month into the pope's house arrest, Sadat was assassinated, which many saw as the finger of divine justice. When the patriarch returned to Cairo in 1985 by decree of President Hosni Mubarak, the city was paralyzed with jubilation (*New York Times*, 4 January 1985). The number of people who turned out to celebrate his return exceeded the city's Christian population. This highlighted the national role played by the patriarch, whose office is respected by many Moslems as the only link tying Egypt to its ancient pharaonic glory. The Moslems would not want a strong patriarch, but neither would they want to lose "the venerable See of Alexandria."

The divisions and problems which beset the Copts are still present and still serious, but without ever addressing any of them directly, the monks of Egypt have greatly increased the likelihood of Coptic survival. The monks have raised up a timeless symbolic standard which transcends temporal problems, and points to a divinely legitimated communal solidarity. Reinforced by the monastic sacrifice and re-

turned to their ethnic heritage by monastic leadership, the Copts are
not bowed under in that persecuted manner which precedes ethnic
dissolution. Their massive pilgrimages to the adiora are lively, song-
filled, and touched by an apocalyptic joy. Youth retreats and rallies
are ever more frequent, well attended, and religiously zealous. Church
reform is vital, even on the local parish level, and has spread from the
cities to the villages of the Delta and Upper Egypt. Ordinations to
the priesthood have dramatically increased, and vocations to the
monasteries are too numerous to house. New monasteries are continually being rebuilt on the ruins of ancient ones.

Stalin's rhetorical jest: "How many divisions has the Pope?" met
its rebuttal in the election of a Latin patriarch from the Eastern Bloc.
The Arabs are far more sensitive to the power of religious symbolism
than traditional Marxists. The question has been asked in Egypt more
than once in police interrogations, Islamic speeches and inter-religious
conversations: "Where are the weapons hidden in the monasteries?"
The question betrays the national sense that the Copts have some
secret device locked in the adiora. The failure of government searches
to find any weapons underscores the seriousness with which the issue
is taken, and the type of symbolic power the Copts possess.

The Copts have adopted a religious view of life which is focused
on the crucifixion of their Lord. They have been called "monophysites" by the Western Churches--a theological position which affirms
that the divinity and humanity of Christ were so intimately joined
that Christ had, as a consequence, but one unique nature. Hence, the
Cross of the human Jesus becomes the very Passion of God. The
humanity of God is, on the other hand, the very safety of the human
Christ. This paradox has given the Copts an inexhaustible meditation
on the meaning of their own suffering, its irony, its efficacy, and the
ultimate elusiveness of security.

Islam has no such parallel esteem for the mystery of suffering.
Allah's power is revealed more commonly in human success, social
advantage, pleasure, and order. Asceticism, celibacy, and solitude do
not appear as lifetime vocations in imitation of the Mohammed's
earthly suffering. If there must be suffering, it is redemptive only
insofar as it is explicitly strategic. The experience has no virtue in
itself. This condition has been called the fundamental difference

between Islam and Coptic or monastic Christianity (cf. Barclay 1982: 120-25). As such, the form of Christian life which most closely assumes the voluntary suffering and sacrificial mode will always be incomprehensible to Islamic understanding.

Moslems value martyrdom in a wholly different way than the Copts. For Islam, the militant ideal is to die fighting for one's faith. For the Copts, the ideal is to die while passively accepting persecution with grace. Hence, Christianity can have its martyrs in Egypt without eliciting widespread violent suppression. The ability of the Copts to live and die passively enables the martyrs to reinforce their values even as they rob their enemies of an opportunity to create a spiraling cycle of violent retribution.

Monasticism has been historically and spiritually linked to martyrdom in Egypt. Monks often ended up in the desert, historically, as a result of oppressive forces directed against the Coptic laity. Desert life is sometimes preferable to facing the pressures of prejudice. As such, it is itself a suffering induced, to some degree, because of religious persecution. In this way, the monks are also martyrs, but of a species only comprehensible to the Christians of Egypt. Their manner of sacrificial offering lies beyond the understanding of secular or Islamic experience.

The monasteries of Egypt provide the social and symbolic inspiration of martyrdom and sacrifice to the Copts. They also provide leadership to the Coptic Church and to the entire ethnic group, for Coptic Catholics, Protestants, and unbelievers alike are all part of their cultural following. Observers on the scene in Egypt only a generation before this study was undertaken did not anticipate the present monastic renaissance, nor did the conventional political and sociological wisdom perceive the role the adiora would serve in the future.

This historical overview makes no effort to obscure the ecclesiastical and monastic divisions which plague the Coptic Church. For example, when Pope Shenouda III was in exile, Abuna Matta el-Meskeen, the recipient from Sadat of one thousand feddan of reclaimed desert farmland (a government attempt to strengthen a divisive element within the Church) gave public approval to the banishment of his pope. Other church leaders, several of them bishops, quickly cooperated with the government to establish an interim ecclesiastical leadership. When Pope Shenouda returned to Cairo, the reversal of that operation found many of these officials ecclesiastically marginalized.

Such intrigues would normally cost a Church a decisive loss of credibility, but the inclusion of monastic personnel in the operation of Church government continually restores confidence. The real significance of monasticism to the Copts resides not in its political involvements, most of which are not coordinated or decisive, but in its symbolic operation. To some extent, this is even served by the popular perception of worldly organizational incompetence among the monastic leaders of the Church.

This chapter on Coptic monastic history closes with a reflection from the epilogue of Evelyn White's archaeological work on the Wadi Natroun:

> . . . lastly, we have seen the monasteries in their fall. That history is not ended yet. But the task of carrying on the record through the second half of the nineteenth century to the present day and of tracing the partial revival of the monasteries in modern times is one which cannot be attempted here. Much documentary material must be extant which can be studied only by an Arabic scholar and which is, perhaps, too confidential to be laid before strangers. Moreover, matters of ecclesiastical politics, controversies, even personalities are involved; and on these it would be impertinent for the Western student to pass judgment (Evelyn White 1973:436).

This historical survey is by no means intended to be an impertinent Western reading of the Coptic monastic heritage. Its interest is more anthropological, and hopes to challenge the often previous, facile interpretations of the Copts and their religious institutions.

Chapter VI

Deir Dwellers

Until now, the discussion has considered Coptic monasteries in a general way, across the entire spectrum. In order to better describe the interior life of a monastery, the focus now shifts to a single deir. However, this is not without problems. There are only a limited number of monasteries in Egypt which can be selected for analysis, but scrutiny of any particular deir might be deemed inappropriate by its inhabitants. The possibility of identifying actual personalities and current situations would be an unfair intrusion into the monastic community which hosted the fieldworker. For this reason, the deir to be presented herein is generalized from patterns of relationships, activities and behaviors common to most of the Coptic monasteries. The personalities portrayed are composites of impressions gleaned from the notes and recollections of the fieldwork.

Deir Anba Amoun (a fictional name for a monastery derived from an early monastic founder) is located in the Mount of Nitria, an elevated desert corridor running northwest to southeast along the western edge of the fertile delta in Lower Egypt. Anba Amoun was a desert father credited with giving rise to the so-called "Amonian system" of monasticism. This was a mixed version of Coptic asceticism which fostered both the solitary, ascetical life and the communal or cenobitic life. Traditionally, the monastery was not walled, but took the form of a *laura*, a collection of cells scattered around a church and a "tower of refuge" (a refuge from raiders) built roughly in the middle.

Deir Anba Amoun was destroyed in the seventh century by the Bedouins. However, its ruins were visited with some frequency by the Copts of the western Delta. The site was considered to be a place of blessing where the unmarried could better pray for a good spouse and the newlywed could pray for fertility. Monks from other monasteries occasionally celebrated the Liturgy amid the ruins on the feast days of its early saints.

In the nineteenth century, a widowed priest took up his residence in the ancient church and began to restore the building with the assistance of his former parishioners. Word of miracles began to spread about this priest, and the visits of pilgrims increased. Eventually, he was joined by a few unmarried men of marginal estate, and a quasi-monastic life was resumed on the Mount of Nitria. In 1932, the widowed priest died at an age said to be over one hundred. Shortly after this, a solitary monk of an indeterminate age, though not very old, unexpectedly arrived from a monastery in the Wadi Natroun where some of its monks had been monitoring the events that transpired at the ancient site. Without the complete support of his monastic superiors, Abuna Jonah settled in at the church to restore formal monasticism to Deir Anba Amoun.

Abuna Jonah welcomed the return of the traditional waqf of Deir Anba Amoun from his cousin, a delta bishop, as the legitimization of his role as a monastic refounder. He hired numerous youthful *fellaheen* (peasant field laborers) to work a portion of the land, paying them a fraction of the produce they grew. He sold the rest of it in the city of Damanhur and then proceeded to rebuild the monastery from the profits. By 1950, the building was sufficiently restored to house twenty-five monks although, in fact, it contained only eight, six of whom were collected from other monasteries. Abuna Jonah died that year and the fortunes of the monastery began to wane.

During the period of the legal deconstruction of the waqf in the early years of Nasser's rule, Deir Anba Amoun lost the greater part of its delta estate. The monks were forced to live on pilgrim donations, and the physical plant deteriorated. By 1965 the deir was nearly depopulated. However, in that year, the Coptic patriarch took note of the decline of this once-famous monastery and appointed a longtime associate of his as *uskof-hegoumenos* (bishop-abbot) of the deir. The patriarch visited the deir on three occasions and reconsecrated its altars, cells, and gardens. The relics of several of its ancient founders were recovered during the construction process while the bones of two saints were discovered during the digging of new wells. Moreover, the bones of one of the founding saints were returned from the reliquary of a Catholic monastery in Jerusalem, which had kept them since the time of the Crusades. Thus, with the increased prestige of the deir and the mounting pressures on the local Christian population, the monastery was soon filled with pilgrims, and the number of vocations dramatically increased as well.

Today, Deir Anba Amoun is a thriving monastic center of ninety monks. With modern pumping techniques, they draw fossil water from far below the desert surface, and now cultivate 350 feddan. Patriarchal grants and private donations supplement the economy of the deir as do the donated estates of many of the candidates who enter. An analysis of the operations of this deir will provide useful insights into most of the Coptic monasteries of Egypt, making them more comprehensible.

It is a commonly held impression that all the inhabitants of a monastery are monks. Proceeding from this position, treatises about monasticism often become somewhat idealized in their description of monastic routines and perspectives. No doubt, this image is what the monasteries intend to create. After all, monks are supposed to be viewed as set apart from mundane affairs. A description of their sources of revenue and their manner of interrelating to the complexities of civil law, public finance, and ecclesiastical politics are aspects of their lives which might detract from the angelic aspect they are meant to exhibit. And so, perhaps, the ideal representation of monasticism is not concerned with the relationship of the monks with their lay employees who contribute so much to the essential well-being of the monastery.

Anthropologists are certainly interested in the ideal picture which social institutions attempt to project and which are often embedded in the foundations of a group. But they are also interested in the social and material base of that society. Hence, it is not enough to state that the inhabitants of Coptic monasteries are monks. Perhaps it is only the monks who embody the spiritual ideal of monasticism but, in reality, Coptic monasteries have a lay population which often far exceeds the number of monks who live there, and these inhabitants are a vital part of the social, religious, and economic institution of every deir. This is true, moreover, of nearly all monasteries everywhere throughout all periods of history. The inhabitants of the Coptic deir, then, are comprised of two broad classes: the monks and their employees.

Today, most of the employees (*mozafeen*) of Deir Anba Amoun come from Upper Egypt, usually via the Wadi Natroun. They are hired from the unemployed faithful by arrangements with the Coptic parishes of that region. Since so many men desire employment in the Wadi Natroun beyond the number who can be hired, the excess applicants are sent to Deir Anba Amoun or Deir Mari Mina in Mariutte near Alexandria. All of the employees are male, both because of the nature of the work, and also because this is deemed appropriate for laborers in constant proximity to the monks. The majority range in age from thirteen to thirty, although a few are special-case workers of a much greater age which include three lifelong bachelors and a widower. At present, the number of mozafeen at Deir Anba Amoun equals the number of monks, although this number fluctuates according to the varying needs of the deir, as well as the seasonal availability of the labor supply.

An employee of the deir may work there anywhere from a single season to several years. The youngest mozafeen tend to be more seasonal, however, being most numerous in the spring and summer. Many of them are accompanied by their older brothers, uncles, or cousins. None of the workers are married, nor are any engaged. The mozafeen are to be celibate, if not virginal, for so long as they work under the monks. This is not only because their wages are too meager to support a wife and a family, but it is also part of the purity by association which each employee is expected to possess while working with the monks.

Mozafeen usually remain at Deir Anba Amoun with little incentive to leave for the duration of their stay. All their needs are provided for in the monastery as part of their wages. A shop in the mozafeen quarters of the deir sells personal goods such as stamps, pens, paper, soap, tissues, sweets and the like. Their wages vary, depending on the level of work performed by each employee. It is difficult to accurately represent the wage levels of the mozafeen because of the inflation of the Egyptian pound, as well as the way Egyptians gauge the relative value of money in their Third World economy. In 1987, two Egyptian pounds were roughly equal to one American dollar. A beginning civil service employee in Cairo might have made between forty and fifty pounds a month at that time. Since that sum is not considered sufficient for a married couple, it either required a second job, or both spouses working for basic survival.

In Deir Anba Amoun, the highest-paid employees are the older, stronger men who are often found working the longest hours in construction jobs or in other strenuous tasks. Such a man might make two pounds per day, plus room and board, which is considered a good salary since most of it can be saved. Younger men of average build generally make one and one-half pounds per day, while boys make one pound per day. In addition, there are a few apprentices who come to the deir to learn certain skills from the monks trained in former professions, usually in the areas of machine maintenance, bookkeeping, engineering, hydraulics, electricity, or even crafts. The apprentice is not paid, but is only supplied with his bed and board. The majority of the paid workers save their money to take home with them whenever they leave the deir, or they send it back with visiting relatives to help with their family's expenses. Actually, these men have often been sent to the deir for this purpose.

Another motive for working at the deir is to make possible job contacts through the recommendation of the monks who might be pleased with the quality of the labor produced. Monks are sometimes solicited by Coptic businessmen to release qualified mozafeen to their employment. Owners of such companies are often benefactors of the deir. A monk may retain professional contacts from his former secular life, and can then be alert to job placements for particularly good employees. Moreover, a worker may find that gaining the patronage of a monk is a consolation in the burdensome task of arranging his future in economically uncertain times.

The jobs performed by the mozafeen are numerous, although the majority of those who are hired are fellaheen who tend the farm of the monastery. However, planting and harvesting are only a small part of their work, as the maintenance of the farm's irrigation system takes most of their time. Many of them may regularly be seen dredging, leveling, repairing, or extending the narrow canals. There are also numerous construction projects in process at the newly expanding deir; for example, the building of solitary cells, a library, a second retreat house and a garage. Consequently, construction workers form the second largest labor group. Six older boys work in the bakery; five work in the craft shop and in the print shop. Of the three kitchens in the deir, the largest one which serves the monks employs three mozafeen assistants. The mozafeen kitchen has two men in charge; the guest kitchen has only two young boys under monastic supervision. There are numerous other tasks the mozafeen perform, some of which are ad hoc. Finally, some of the mozafeen are the personal assistants of a few of the more prominent monks; two older monks each have a lifelong servant.

The mozafeen take corrections from the monks without resistance. None desire to anger a monk for fear of dismissal. A worker may lose his job if he is considered too lazy, accident-prone, complaining, rebellious, or irreligious. There is no recourse for the decision to release an employee from his job, and the possibility increases when the seasonal labor declines, or when greater numbers of candidates apply for work.

Although many monks at Deir Anba Amoun supervise some of the mozafeen each day, Abuna Rafael el Amoun is generally responsible for all the workers. He hires the mozafeen and dismisses them, although he often does so in consultation with other monks. Abuna Rafael pays the weekly wages of the mozafeen, determining the precise rate and hours himself. He assigns each employee to his job or his labor group as the mozafeen line up for their orders at 7:00 a.m. each morning. The overseer constantly receives requests from monks seeking laborers for their projects. Hence, his relationship with the monks may be a determining factor in the number of workers assigned to them and the length of time in which their projects are completed.

Typically, the overseer rotates workers from one assignment to another with some frequency, thus acquainting the mozafeen with a wide range of jobs. This practice also prevents any of the mozafeen from becoming an expert at any particular task or, more importantly, from becoming possessive of a job. A responsible monk, an "*abuna robeyta*," is always placed in charge of a work area, and it would not do for one of his workers to have a greater competency or sense of ownership than he. The policy of frequent rotation creates considerable tension among the mozafeen who quietly complain that they are needlessly made to feel incompetent.

Mozafeen almost never work unsupervised since there is tacit agreement among the monks that they are lazy and need constant prodding. Moreover, the monks insist that the quality of the work suffers in the absence of a supervisor. Hence, at every work site, except in the mozafeen kitchen, a monk is on hand to give directions. Acting as a foreman, he often holds a long stick with which he can point to direct a new course of labor, or which he can use to encourage better work, greater attention, or less distraction.

The mozafeen, most of whom are from Upper Egypt, are typically simple, even primitive, agrarian people in the view of many inhabitants of Lower Egypt. Deir Anba Amoun is situated on the edge of Lower Egypt, and most of its monks are from delta towns and cities. The geographic division of the two groups reinforces the social convention of unequal relations between the monks and the mozafeen. The nature of the relationship of employer to employee already generates inequality, but that division is given further definition by the prevalent interregional sentiments. However, the situation is somewhat different in the monasteries in Upper Egypt where both monks and the mozafeen derive from the same region and speak with the same accent.

The mozafeen are generally religiously observant. They all assemble together in the body of the main church of Deir Anba Amoun for the Kodes every Sunday and on major feast days. Ten or more may also participate in the Kodes on weekdays; some even assist the monks as lower-order deacons during the Liturgy. A few priests prefer the assistance of the same liturgically competent employees every day. The mozafeen are invited to attend a catechetical class on Saturday evenings. There a monk, not normally assigned to supervise the workers, teaches them basic church doctrine and answers their questions. These queries often involve the nature of heaven, the character of angels, the purpose of fasting, the moral and spiritual effects of adolescent sin, reported visions of the Virgin Mary and the second coming of Christ.

Mozafeen spend much of their spare time playing games. At Deir Anba Amoun, they draw checkerboard designs in the sand and play an ancient version of checkers with two colors of stones. Some wrestle on the dusty road within the mozafeen quarters, or swim in the concrete irrigation cisterns at the far ends of the deir. In addition to their recreation, some of the older boys teach the younger ones to read Arabic letters and words, to sing popular songs, and also advise them on how to better handle their problems at work.

Mozafeen hold hands with one another as they walk, in typical Near Eastern style. Internal relations among the mozafeen are left to the employees themselves to control. Since most come from interrelated parishes and villages in Upper Egypt, there is already an implicit hierarchy among them based on their kinship, physical size, age, and occupational prestige. One of the leaders of the mozafeen at Deir Anba Amoun, a charismatic youth in his twenties, is the elder cousin of a great number of younger relatives who are also employed at the deir. Older men among the mozafeen are usually not leaders, although their age is respected. They leave the younger men to form their own informal social organizations, claiming that they are not fathers to them. Fighting among the mozafeen, even if it occurs in plain view, is not curbed by the monks. This is a matter for the workers to monitor and resolve themselves.

The following items were found in the room of a *moazuf* (worker) at Deir Anba Amoun: seven mattresses (some stacked, and some laid out on the floor to be used as couches during the day); a wooden picnic table; a hot plate and a water pot for making tea; a plastic-capped bowl for tea grains, a smaller cardboard box of mint leaves; a stack of flash cards with Arabic letters; a battery-powered transistor radio with an ear plug, and seven boxes of various sizes for personal effects. There are numerous paper wall icons of St. Mary, St. George, St. Therese of Lisieux, St. Antony, St. Amoun, Pope Kyrillos, Pope Shenouda, and others. The room, which measures six by seven meters, is similar to the fifteen other rooms in that building. It is windowless, with only a few vent-like openings near the ceiling. Cement floors stretch from wall to limestone wall. At the edge of the quarters, along the exterior wall of the deir, an outside latrine is constructed on a natural slope in such a way that its overflow falls down the hillside outside the habitation.

The mozafeen wear the traditional peasant galabeya, the beltless caftan garment of the fellaheen. As over half of them are well under eighteen years of age, many do not yet shave. But no mozafeen may be bearded. They explain: "In the monastery, a beard is the sign of a monk. In the world, it is the sign of a Moslem."

As Mary Douglas notes, each society will give its own charged interpretation to the physical aspects of the human body, including facial hair (cf. 1978:121). Among the Copts, a full beard indicates a return to a natural state, which, if not accompanied by the grace of a special holy status, would be a negative and dangerous condition, a return to "fallen nature," without even the "grace" of the civilized habit of grooming. But for the monk, the body is a site of divine worship so that natural aspects, such as a beard, are the signs of a restored original nature and holiness which others should not appropriate to themselves lightly.

The mozafeen are in constant contact with monks all day and, as a result, are not expected to make the same ceremonial gestures of deference, such as kissing the monks' hands, touching their fingers to the ground near the monks' feet, and then kissing the monks' fingers, as pilgrims are wont to do. However, once they leave the employment of the deir, that behavior is expected to be resumed. While at the deir, the mozafeen simply avert their eyes, or touch their right hand to their heart in silent greeting to the monks. That gesture is the same one the monks use to greet one another without disturbing their silence.

At Deir Anba Amoun, the mozafeen have lately begun to be addressed by the title *akh* (brother). In former times, the title was reserved only to monks not yet ordained to the priesthood, although today all monks are called *"abuna."* The monk-candidates who are in the period of probation before priestly consecration are still called "akh." However, no one ever mistakes the status of the "novice monk" with an employee by the use of that title. More likely, the title of "akh" is used for the mozafeen to remind them of the quasi-religious state of their employment, and also as a polite means for the monks to evade having to remember the workers' names when addressing them. The title used to address mozafeen may also serve as a means of humbling the novice monk.

Monks may walk through the mozafeen quarters, but they never enter the limestone houses which serve as their sleeping quarters. These buildings were constructed on the far side of Deir Anba Amoun, away from the common entry gate.

Public access to the deir is generally limited to the front of the monastery, where the churches are clustered amid courtyards and gardens. The deir is so arranged that the enclosed churches, cells and cloistered monastic sections border on the desert on three sides. The fields, retreat houses, garages and employees' quarters adjoin the walled section on only one side and fan out from the back of the monastic quarters. The entry gate is so angled from the desert that the larger part of the deir is obscured by the enclosed monastic section. A high internal wall separates the work areas and mozafeen living quarters from the visitors' area. Since it is of the same height and texture as the external front wall, it adds to the impression that what is seen initially is the entire complex. Hence it is possible, even likely, that pilgrims can visit the monastery without even being aware of the fact that the greater part of it remains beyond their courtyard where the guest master monk has brought them tea and has spoken to them of God. Deir Anba Amoun is not unique in this layout; it de-emphasizes the material operation of the monastery--a concept which fits perfectly into the intermediate position the deir holds between heaven and earth.

Peter Brown suggests that the body of a monk is, in itself, a spiritual landmark which designates a point of connection between humanity and the holy which is, at the same time, a special class of body that is separated from the secular body of the temporal social

order (cf. Brown 1988:243,257). By extension, the dwelling place of
the monks has the same significance. The deir attempts to diminish
public exposure of its material base and to emphasize its spiritual
properties. No effort is made to deny a material base, of course, but
it is regarded more as an incidental matter, or as providing the means
of enabling the monks to express their spiritual qualities. For instance, the monks involved with farming remind the pilgrims that
God created a garden in Eden, or that Christ was taken to be a gar-
dener after the Resurrection. The monks involved with building
projects point out that God blessed the temple of Solomon and visited his people in places built by human hands.

Pilgrims who visit the deir today are a vital part of the social
mechanism of monastic life. They reflect back to the monks a sense
of monastic transcendence for that is what, among other things, they
came to see in the desert. They are not a part of the internal society
of the monastery, so their contribution in that regard is necessarily
limited.

The mozafeen, however, are a vital part of the monastic life. Although they do not socialize with the monks according to the casual
meaning of the word, their conventional distance and deference
constitute part of the social matrix of the deir. Their distance represents the opposition of secularity; their deference and respect represent
the laity who attempt to commute between the secular and the holy
by their emulation of the desert monks.

Erving Goffman discusses the value of "team performance" in the
creation of a social persona. Any individual who wishes to credibly
represent a recognizable role must perform the gestures and recreate
the image of the ideal type which the role reflects. One must look his
part, but there is no better way to convincingly portray that part than
to have others formally demonstrate belief in it. These people would
be his "team" (1959:77-78). They are the supporting cast of social roles,
just as nurses are to doctors--not so much by their practical assistance
as by their deference to, intimidation by, and respect for physicians.
The mozafeen can also be viewed in this light. Their deference to,
fear of, and reverence for the monk serves to further establish and
confirm the dramatic persona of the monk.

A Moment in the Deir

If a visitor were to walk through Deir Anba Amoun at eight o'clock in the morning on a Saturday in late November, the following activities might be observed:

In the courtyard before the church, two boys are raking the sand floor of a walkway to remove the debris of yesterday's pilgrims. Another youth is pounding the raked sand with a flat board to compress it so it cannot be too easily wind-carried. Abuna Bessa, the guest master of Deir Anba Amoun, is the supervisor of the boys, but just now he is in the guest kitchen on the ground floor, directing its cleaning. Akh Wallid is walking to the kitchen and will assist Abuna Bessa today, as the crowds will probably be large just before the holy season of Advent when the monastery is usually closed to guests. The kitchen only serves tea and bread cakes; the bread is a conventional form of blessing. The pilgrims bring their own picnic foods. Further on, by the shed at the side of the church, two boys are carrying cement bags. They are part of a construction detail working at the retreat house outside the wall.

In the church, the sound of finger cymbals and the faster beat of quarter-tone chant, sounds which are heard at Communion time, indicate that the Kodes is ahead of its normal daily speed. Abuna Arsenius, the librarian, is presiding over the Liturgy today; his rate of chant is one of the fastest in the deir. Serving him at the altar are several youths, one of them, a bit older, is actually the apprentice of Abuna Arsenius in the library. Three thirteen-year-olds are sleeping on the floor in the back section of the church. They are part of a work detail which includes the deacon servers of the Kodes. They will shortly be awakened for Communion.

The grape arbors beyond the church are presently dormant. Sitting alone at their center is Abuna Marcus Muttawahad (our Father Marcus, the hermit), who was once a solitary for nearly ten years in the desert of the Wadi Rayan. He was one of the graduate students who sought religious perfection at the bidding of Abuna Mina in the 1950s. When Abuna Mina became Pope Kyrillos VI, Abuna Marcus was among those ordered back to the monastery in an effort to reduce the risk of their establishing potentially divisive, charismatic, and independent monastic institutions. Abuna Marcus is sitting on a barrel with a cat on his lap alongside a thick volume of church literature.

A large construction site can be seen outside the monastic quarters of the deir, behind the wall which separates the desert reclamation zone from the cloister. Ten young men are building a garage and a vehicle shop where farm machines and cars can be maintained; ten other men are on scaffolds erecting a new water tower. Each group is supervised by monks in their mid-thirties who have engineering degrees from Ein Shams University in Cairo. The monks are carrying long wooden sticks which they use to direct the workers' movements. A flatbed truck is driven through the side gate, laden with limestone. Many of the workers from both sites come to fetch stone from the truck, forming lines to convey the stones with less footwork. Their *galalib* (long, beltless garments) are girded above their knees to avoid tripping. They are wearing rubber thongs on their feet, or are barefoot.

At the water tower, men are sawing and hammering and mixing cement. The various floors are connected by ramps in order to facilitate the carrying of heavy stones. Cement, ready to be poured, is carried by cable and cranked from floor to floor. All in all, this low-tech, labor-intensive operation best suits the needs and resources of the monastery.

Little is growing in the fields which stretch out for dozens of acres beyond the construction site. Still, a few boys are clearing sand deposits from the canals which water the orange grove. Across the fields in the bakery, six boys are working under Abuna Tadros, an unlettered monk, baking bread. The ovens are massive and the boys are quite active, pouring water on the flour, churning dough, and shaping cakes. This activity guarantees the provision of fresh bread for the pilgrims on Sunday.

The barn is located at the far end of the fields. A number of boys are distributing feed to the chickens and rabbits. Some are cleaning cages. Abuna Maximus is on the roof seated at a table in the morning shade of his cell. His laundry hangs around the edge of the roof in the early sun. His cell is built into the side of the barn, and nearby are the recently built, free-standing cells of a few other monks.

Two older mozafeen are guarding the main and side gates of the deir. One of them, a lifelong bachelor, has been working at the deir since he came there in his early teens. He can deal with most of the guests until 10:00 a.m., when the guest master's assistant, Akh Wallid, will take charge. There is no telephone connection from the monastery to the outside world; the gate is the bottleneck through which all transportation and communication must pass. Older mozafeen and monks take charge of it day and night.

The other workers are divided between the retreat house and the wood shop. A wall is being built at the retreat house to enclose the site. In the wood shop, a monk teaches his apprentice how to use a jigsaw to make wooden silhouettes of the saints, the cross, and other religious symbols. Several mozafeen are sanding freshly cut crosses and varnishing them. At present, there is no one in the print shop next door. Ink fumes waft out from the stacks of literature, mostly copies of Pope Shenouda III's latest sermons, which are mounded inside.

Custodial, repair, and construction work dominate the deir at this time. In another season, it would be planting or harvesting. These tasks are supervised by a different group of monks. The monks are seldom as visible as the workers. Most are indoors alone and, with notable exceptions, are not in the public eye of either the workers or the visitors throughout the year.

The Monks

The great majority of the monks of Deir Anba Amoun are between the ages of twenty-seven and forty-five, which seems to be true of most Coptic monasteries in the present restoration period. The average candidate who presents himself to the deir is between twenty-five and thirty-five years of age. All of the present candidates are college-educated, which reflects both a greater interest in monasticism among the professional classes, and the disinterest of monasteries in receiving uneducated men. Both conditions represent significant departures from the past.

Nowadays, unless an applicant comes to the monastery with a strong recommendation from a bishop, he must not only be college-educated, but should also have experienced previous gainful employment. The conscious intention of the kommos of the monasteries is to upgrade the caliber of monastic personnel. Monks who have successfully sacrificed the very life styles which their society holds out as its primary benefits have, to that degree, transcended the symbolic bondage of their culture and have become participants in a greater symbolic order. Education, leading to profession and marriage, has been the chief social benefit promoted since the Egyptian Revolution. The willing sacrifice of that status by those who have already attained it, is interpreted as no small challenge to the priorities of the secular society.

This practice stands in marked contrast to the caliber of the majority of monastic candidates in past centuries. In previous ages, they were often widowed, old, lame, or otherwise unfortunate. Only an individual who hoped to rise to an episcopal seat, or the occasional true devotee of Coptic Faith, would enter a deir while still young and productive. This seems to have been the case since the plague of the fifteenth century. The monastery retained its sacrificial aspect due to its own pervasive folklore among the Copts. They remembered monasticism for what it was in its earlier, more vigorous centuries. Hence, its recent revitalization is not seen as a break with its dimmer history so much as a rebirth of monasticism's long-hidden, inner essence which had been concealed in the Church and in the deir for centuries.

In Their Own Words

A social analysis of the Coptic monastery runs the risk of being unduly abstract unless some of its members are permitted to speak in their own words about their motivations for entering the deir and remaining therein. The statements below were gleaned from personal interviews held with the monks during several visits over the course of a decade. They serve to flesh out the cultural landscape of the inhabitants of the desert monastery. Details which would identify the monk or his monastery have been omitted.

The personal motives of candidates who enter the monastery are quite diverse nowadays. A number of those awaiting full monastic consecration in Deir Anba Amoun expressed their dissatisfaction with their former careers. One stated: "Everybody said how lucky I was to be a dentist, but I did not feel lucky." He felt that God was making him restless until he chose the proper vocation. Another said: "In the world, I was anxious all the time. Here, I am at peace because God wants me here." Two had been frequent pilgrims to Deir Anba Amoun and determined that after so many happy visits, they belonged in the monastery. One said:

> I first came to the deir because I liked to picnic with my friends. Later, I grew to enjoy the presence of so many uninhibited Christians in one place. It gave me a sense of belonging to be with all of them at the deir. Finally, the monks themselves made me feel like I was welcome here, even though I had been a great sinner. My parents had big plans for me, but I told them God was calling me.

Another candidate was present at an apparition of the Virgin Mary in a church in Shoubra, Cairo, where she was seen by the crowds in the 1970s and 1980s. He stated: "When I saw the Virgin, I knew that God had a special plan for me. She did not say anything to me, but I felt that Mary wanted me to offer my life to God."

One candidate was in the monastery as a result of the healing of his mother.

> My mother was dying of cancer. My father is a doctor, and he couldn't do anything. I came to the deir and cried on the relics of Anba Amoun. I promised him that I would enter the monastery if my mother got better. The kommos heard me crying and told me to go home for now because my prayer had been heard. Within a week, my mother was in complete remission, and is perfectly well today. So now I am here, and I am very happy.

Another candidate at Deir Anba Amoun came to the monastery because his spiritual director, a priest in his home parish in Alexandria, encouraged him to do so.

> My (spiritual) father knew everything about me. God gave him a deep knowledge of my soul, and I could depend on him for good advice. When I told him that I had taken a job as a hotel engineer, he told me that God wanted more from me.

One candidate for the monastic life at Deir Anba Amoun has an apocalyptic rationale for his vocation:

> One day soon, the fundamentalists will take over Egypt. Then they will burn down our churches, and the soldiers will not come to protect us, but to arrest us. They are already planning to destroy the Copts. They want our property and our money in order to give life to a new Islamic state. We are like the Jews in Europe. No one but God can save us. Only God can save us if we worship him better and are not so materialistic. Or maybe they will force the Christians out of the cities into the desert. Then the monasteries will be places where the Copts can wait for God. That is why I am here.

Another candidate for the monastic life was summoned to the monastery by the patriarch. He was a graduate student in computer science in Canada, from a prominent delta family, and was recalled to Egypt for the monastic life. This last vocation is a special case. He is not expected to be a monk for long, before he is given an ecclesiastical post in Cairo which leads to the episcopacy.

The blind cantor (*arif*) of a deir in Upper Egypt shared the following story. He entered the monastery as a teenager, and is now regarded as an elder monk there.

> I remember seeing. My father took me to the Church of St. Girgus in our village, and I saw the blind deacon. He sang like an angel. Everyone admired him and said that God gave him to the Church when He took away his eyesight. I was very young, but I used to imitate his voice at home. When my aunts came to our house, I sang to them the songs of the Kodes. I didn't understand any of it, but they made a great fuss over me. My father never said anything. Maybe he knew.
>
> When I was in the first year of school, my eyes became infected. In only a few months I could not run with my friends anymore. Nobody thought that this was a disease which could be cured. We did not think like this. My father once shouted at my mother and her sisters, "Why did you encourage him to sing?" But I realized that God wanted me to "know how to see" the mysteries. After this, I was always in the church.

Paradoxically, the word "arif" means "one who sees," but the word "see" here has the same connotation as the English words "to know."

> When I was just fifteen, the priest of St. Girgus told the bishop of Beni Suef about me. He said I was the best cantor in the diocese! The bishop, who is my mother's cousin, sent me a message through the priest that he wished the monastery associated with the diocese would have a good cantor. I felt that God had called me. He arranged everything. My father permitted it. What could I do for him? I was seventeen when I came here. I know this place so well that I dream about it and see it in my dreams. Every monk here I taught to sing. Even the new cantor I taught. He can see, but people tell me that he cannot sing as well as I do.

A senior monk from an upper Egyptian monastery which hosts a fair-sized *mulid* (festival) for its patron saint each year shared this:

> Every year that we have the festival, we are visited by the saint. On the wall of the monastery, he makes his silhouette in the evening light, or in the night we hear him chant from the desert. Last year, two sisters saw him during the baptism of their niece. Many have felt their angels around them. Always there are miracles. Too many miracles!
>
> The crowd is always very large. Everyone has needs. Everyone wants a miracle. You may be sure that many Moslems are also with us. We do not care if they come. Why not? Let them come.
>
> We have to know that they are always nearby. We can never forget. Even at the festival, we must remember that God has made us to be martyrs. But they have to know that if they want the blessing of the patron saint, they need us for the festival. Our saint never goes to their festivals. If they say they see him at their festival, where are the miracles?

Another reflection comes from an aged kommos of a monastery in the Wadi Natroun:

> The condition of the monastery is very different now than when I came here. Only a few men were coming then. It was hard

for them. The road through the desert was unpaved and there were no access roads from the desert highway to the monastery. We had no electricity because the Aswan High Dam was not yet even planned. We drew the water up ourselves from the well, so we did not have a lot to use except for minimal necessities. I told many of the young men to reconsider joining. You could see that they were afraid when they got here to make a retreat.

The old monks in those days were a different kind of men. They were simple. Some really could hardly read, but they were good monks. Even then, without cars and roads, pilgrims came to be blessed. Those monks could pray. They just placed their hand-cross on their heads, and the people were blessed so much. We did not have brochures and cassettes to give them. We just had faith. People learned what they needed to know from the childlike wisdom of the old monks. The pilgrims did not ask so many questions. They only wanted blessings.

The changes started when the monks got involved in the university, when one or two went into the city and spoke to the students, and when the churches began sending them here for more retreats. At the same time, the university was becoming less welcoming to the Christians. We welcomed them when they did not. But that is what happened when the changes started. That is not the cause of the changes. Some monks were sent by God who became great saints in the solitude of the desert. Even before they died, they were like angels more than men. These monks prayed. God answered their prayers and more men came to the monasteries. When they saw these saints, they were not afraid anymore. Many of them joined.

Finally, one of the middle-aged guest masters of a monastery in the Eastern Desert made the following observations:

When the pilgrims come, they are always amazed. God is so close to them here. All of them are surprised at how God is speaking to them. So many young people are brought here by their friends or by the Church just for a visit, just for curiosity. Maybe they have given up their faith or they do not care about it anymore. They only want to dance or to spend money on sports and drinking, you know. But once they are here, you can see them change.

At first they are shy. They stand far away and look. Then they ask a few questions. They are surprised to hear answers which satisfy them. They did not expect a monk to be able to speak to them on their level. But we also went to the university. Pretty soon they feel they can be friendly. They tell us about their exam fears, or about their family's fight, or always about the problem of finding a good job. Only God can help them, and we tell them, "Why not pray with us? Why not ask St. Mary to pray for you? Why not enjoy God's mercy? He knows our weaknesses."

And they come back to the Church. They are crying and laughing at the same time. They feel that we love them. They want to stay after that. This is the beginning. They have far to go, but the beginning should be sweet. When they come back to visit the monastery, we tell them that the life of faith is hard, but it is easy if you have the holy love of Jesus Christ. They believe us, and by then they are ready to accept this. So they keep coming back because they cannot get this encouragement as much in the city.

Such commentaries as these offer a glimpse into the desert monk and his views. Their words are direct and disarming.

Beneath these individual motives for entering the monastery lies a social current. In nearly every case, the choice of the monastic life proceeded from the individual's subordination to what was perceived as a transcendent reality. The monks are deeply engaged in the symbolic work which the Coptic community assigns to them; they are players within the sphere outlined for them by the cultural values ascribed to the monastic state.

Chapter VII

Forming the Monastic Persona

The three levels of the monastic life are easily recognized at Deir Anba Amoun by the wearing of color-coded garments. The first is the pre-candidacy period, when a young man presents himself for consideration, but has not yet been accepted by the kommos as a potential vocation. He keeps his own name and wears a blue galabeya suitable for manual labor. For so long as he remains in this status, he is little different from the other laborers inasmuch as he is not a part of the monks' community social group.

The pre-candidate lives in a special wing of the monastic guest house and eats in the laborers' mess hall in the mozafeen quarters. However, he is permitted to join the monks in their common prayers and liturgies. The pre-candidates are often uncomfortable with this status. Most of them have not worn a galabeya since childhood, and consider the blue version to be more proper to uneducated fellaheen. Moreover, the length of their pre-candidacy is undetermined. Of the five men in pre-candidacy in Deir Anba Amoun, one has been there over a year, one for six months, and the other three for just two months or less. The kommos is free to adjust the duration of the time as he wills. The candidate who was summoned by the patriarch to Deir Anba Amoun from Canada was a pre-candidate for less than a week.

At Deir Anba Amoun, the pre-candidate is accepted without ceremony. A monk is delegated by the kommos to direct him, and to report to the kommos about his suitability. The characteristics required of a pre-candidate include diligence, respect, calmness, and cheerfulness. Orthodox spirituality is presumed. If the pre-candidate meets the requirements, he is eventually admitted into monastic candidacy, the second level, during a feast day celebration of a monastic saint. The brief ceremony is appended to the Kodes. Should the monastery be celebrating the consecration of a candidate to full monkhood, the promotion of the pre-candidate may follow that ceremony.

The promotion itself is a simple affair. A white galabeya is placed over the blue one (which will later be shed), and a white knit cap is placed over the head of the applicant. A blessing for perseverance is read over him. The new candidate kisses the ground at the feet of the kommos, and then kisses his hand and hand-cross. He still retains his baptismal name, but he is now addressed as "akh." The color of the galabeya, white, is a recognized liturgical color, and the head covering is a sign of religious dedication. The akh feels well on the way to becoming a monk. He now lives in a special wing of the common cells building, just behind the back wall of the original deir. He eats in the monastic refectory at a table next to the kommos. Abuna Bishoi, the administrative assistant of the kommos, becomes the spiritual and practical director of the candidate. He sits at the table of the kommos and discusses the progress of the candidate with him after the daily evening meal.

The candidate is free to leave the monastery at any time, and the kommos can reject him on short notice. Should this happen, the departure is quiet and unannounced but, in fact, few candidates actually leave the deir. The essential act of vocational discernment at Deir Anba Amoun is the pre-candidacy period, when discouragements to the monastic life are made subtly so as to allow the would-be monk to depart graciously on his own.

As with pre-candidacy, no one but the kommos determines the

duration of the monastic probation period. On average, it lasts anywhere from one to three years, with certain exceptions shortened to
six months or less. When the time for monastic consecration is
announced, it is usually with no more than a day's notice.

The akh is told by the kommos to prepare for consecration, and
is given a secret new name, not to be made public until the next day's
celebration. Meanwhile, the akh sends out word of the upcoming
event to his family through the pilgrims. If they are close enough,
they will come for the consecration. The candidate spends the night
before his consecration in the church of Anba Amoun. He is to
reflect on the significance of his new name, and on the life and
holiness of his heavenly patron. Each of the monks will come to the
church during the night to give him a word of advice or insight.

The candidate must not sleep during this night. The ceremony of
the next day is entered into more properly with the tension of
sleeplessness and the preparation of many hours of prayer. Moreover,
the upcoming ceremony must not be tainted by any bodily impurity.
Hence, the possibility of nocturnal pollution is evaded. Finally, the
candidate notes that Jesus was sleepless in prayer the night before his
Passion while his disciples slept in the Garden of Gethsemane.

Passion and death are the themes of the consecration ceremony.
The candidate is ushered to the reliquary of Anba Amoun, and told
to lie down on the floor. The wool covering of the saint's coffin-like
reliquary is removed and placed over the prostrate candidate. He
remains motionless in a state of intense heat, excitement, weariness,
and near airlessness for over one and one-half hours. Above him and
his funerary pall, the monastic community chants the funeral prayers
for the dead. That is to say, these are the same prayers and chants of
the Coptic funeral, invoking the saints to assist their brother who has
died. The essential part of the consecration is thus accomplished, not
by vows that are professed, but by the willingness of the candidate to
lie down in ritual death.

When the pall is removed from the new monk, the abbot announ-
ces his new name and vests him in the black galabeya of Coptic
monasticism. Additionally, the kommos gives a the leather *hezan*
(belt) for around the waist, and a distinctive black cotton cap (*kalaswa*)
which is said to resemble the cowl of St. Antony. The leather belt is

interpreted as a reminder of the denial of bodily satisfactions. One monk frankly says: "The belt reminds us to deny our stomachs. It also deprives our lower bodies of excessive hormones which conflict with chastity."

In the past, before the medical view of the suppressive use of the belt became common, it was worn on the outside. Now this acknowledged use of the belt induces many monks to wear it beneath their outer clothing rather than over it. However, since the symbolism of the belt may lose its public value when worn on the inside, the monks speak of "the hidden belt," even if they are not wearing it at the moment due to the heat or some other problem. The verbal reference to this hidden symbol may exercise even more evocative power precisely because concealment generates mystery and, therefore, power, in religious garments.

The monk's kalaswa has six crosses embroidered in black on each side, representing the twelve apostles, for the monk is said to lead an apostolic life for the Church. A clearer symbol for the ecclesiastical involvement of the monks, who otherwise avoid social entanglements, could not be imagined. In the Coptic Church, an apostle is equated to a bishop, and since no one can become a bishop except a monk, the apostolic significance of the crosses denotes the exclusive monastic claim on the episcopacy.

Strings are attached to the cap so it can be tied under the chin. It extends down the back below the shoulder blades somewhat like an apron. The monks claim that this design purposely resembles a bib for young children to indicate the monk's distance from the world. A further symbol of that distance is the cut along the top of the cap which is cross-stitched in a contrasting color. Following the hagiography of St. Antony, a monk is said to be pulled between heaven and the world, between angels and devils. The world's pull against relinquishing the monk is so strong, that violence is done to him in the process. He is torn. Only God can heal the wound, which is signified by the cross-stitching. Such symbolic woundedness enhances the sacrificial aspect of the monastic persona.

Finally, an additional cross is embroidered atop the cross-stitching as a symbol of divine authority over the monk. He is under no worldly authority. In short, the headpiece of the Coptic monk is a statement of paradox. It proclaims that the monk is a citizen of another world and, yet, he is the proper director of the Church in this world. The sagittal tear implies that the monk has been profoundly damaged by his renunciation of the world and, by virtue of having integrated that wound, is now equipped to challenge that world, no longer subject to its intimidations. It cannot coerce him by allurements to the flesh, or by holding any hostages to fortune (i.e., wife, children, job, estate), for he repudiated these enticements before they could be played against him. Symbolically, the monk is potentially dangerous and revolutionary, just as his hagiography indicates. For the Copts, even the unrealized and unattainable potential of that danger is, of itself, a source of ethnic solidarity.

A newly consecrated monk at Deir Anba Amoun is a likely candidate for ordination to the priesthood. Fewer than ten percent of the monks who entered Deir Anba Amoun in the last decade declined to seek the priesthood. The percentage of priests in Egypt's monasteries is highly variable but, in general, the adiora are undergoing a strong process of clericalization. This is another sign of the greater role being played by the monks in the Coptic community.

Monks seek ordination for a number of reasons. For some, it is the natural expression of the monastic spirit: "My sacrifice of wife and family, of job and comforts, is a sharing in the Cross of Christ. To celebrate the Sacrifice of the Kodes as a priest is just a deeper sharing in the Cross." In Lower Egypt, the Coptic Church has lately ordained only educated men as priests to serve in parish ministries, in contrast to earlier times when priests could be completely unlettered. Since most of the monks of Deir Anba Amoun are now college-educated, the modern convention urges that their ordination occurs after they have been formally consecrated as monks.

A priest is a more integrated member of the ecclesiastical institution than is a brother. He possesses the rites of the Church, exercises most of its sacramental mysteries, and dispenses its saving graces. Pilgrims who come to Deir Anba Amoun seek blessings, absolution, exorcism, anointing, and Communion. These rites can only be offered by priests. Brothers in the deir sometimes avoid the pilgrims simply because they are so frequently requested to provide the sacraments they cannot administer. Since they wear the same garb as the priests and have the same title, brothers are placed in an awkward social position. One said: "All I feel is pressure to be ordained. The monastery has taken the look of a house of priests, so that those of us who are not priests must not disturb this image by our appearance or title."

At present, a few more Coptic brothers are declining to seek ordination than in the immediate past. These monks often express their lack of willingness to be utilized for the parochial ministry of the Church. "I came to the deir to seek God in solitude. If I am a priest, people have a right to lay hold of me just as if I were a father with children. The kommos could ask me to leave the desert to work in a city church or to be a missionary to the Coptic immigrant churches." A number of monks from Deir Anba Amoun are presently serving the Church outside the deir. One is in a Coptic parish in Germany, another in Australia. Several work in the patriarchal offices in Cairo, so the brother's remarks are based on fact. One such monk admits feeling frustrated because he will never have any role to play in the administration of his House: "Because I am not a priest, and because I am not an engineer, I have nothing to say. Sometimes I feel that I am just an employee here." Nevertheless, he does not dream of departing.

The guest master of Deir Anba Amoun is an engineer, but not a priest. Presently in his forties, Abuna Bessa refuses ordination because he says he is "unworthy" to serve on the altar. Since he is constantly in the public eye, assisting pilgrims, guests, and notable visitors, it actually serves Abuna Bessa not to be detained by priestly ministration among the crowds which press into the deir. Moreover, his oft-expressed humility, which inhibits him from ordination, enhances his monastic reputation and increases his chances of being invited to an even higher ministry in the Church. "He takes the lowest place in the banquet," murmured one peer of Abuna Bessa. The implication, based on an allusion to the Gospel text, is that Abuna Bessa is postured to be invited to move to the head of the table.

Monks are ordained to the priesthood at the direction of the kommos. In Deir Anba Amoun, the kommos is a bishop and is able to ordain his own monks. In the past, the patriarch sometimes came to the deir for ordination. During such visits, he could also survey the condition of the monastery and monitor prospective vocations. However, since his desert exile and release in 1985, Pope Shenouda has been able to visit the deir less frequently.

After ordination, a monk in Deir Anba Amoun is prepared to assume responsible monastic positions. Certain kinds of prestigious occupations are considered desirable by many monks. To take charge of the library, for example, is to hold a very respected position in the deir. The modern esteem for education has made the library, once a neglected corner of the deir, a site of renewed activity and interest. The library of the monastery contains nearly 3,500 volumes of printed materials, including encyclopedias and bound journals. The bulk of the material is religious, mostly Western in origin, and largely about the first desert monks and the patristic period of the early Church. Since the recent ideological work of the Coptic Church is the recovery of its heritage and apologetics, that is, the defense of its doctrines, the monk in charge of the monastic library is automatically recognized as the chief agent of this effort.

The eleven monk-engineers at Deir Anba Amoun enjoy great status, partly as a result of the special place Egyptians in general reserve for this occupation. The enormous building projects of the Church and the adiora have made them especially important at this time. Engineers from the monastery are sometimes invited to oversee the renovations of churches in the Delta and are consulted in the building projects of prominent and generous Copts in the construction business. A parish priest in Cairo said: "An engineer is believed capable of doing any work. A monk-engineer is thought capable of being a bishop." The commonplace metaphors of "building the church" or "edifying the Coptic community" reinforce the sacred sense of engineering skills.

Likewise, the physicians in Deir Anba Amoun who administer to their fellow monks and the mozafeen are highly regarded. They are also called out of the deir at times to assist the needs of the Coptic clergy in the Delta. The priest-physician is occasionally invited to rural villages to address the Copts about proper hygiene and health practices, while pilgrims to the deir often seek either the physicians or pharmacists for assistance. There is a dentist chair, a pharmaceutical store, and instruments for simple surgical procedures in the monastery.

Seven physicians and dentists and five pharmacists reside as monks at Deir Anba Amoun. Christ's role as healer is frequently alluded to in their regard.

A large number of monks graduated from business colleges before they entered the monastery. A business degree, in itself, does not have so much prestige as a medical or engineering degree. A degree in law, social science, or the humanities has even less. Young men who wish to enter the monastery with degrees in these fields, but without exceptional ecclesiastical recommendations or family connections, have more to prove in order to be accepted as a candidate. They are expected to have acquired successful careers before they seek admission.

The kommos of the deir explains the reasoning of the selection process:

> What does it prove when a poor man comes to the deir and lives better than he did in the world? Who will be edified by his choice? Nobody but himself and his mother. We had men like this in the early monasteries of Egypt, and the Church was weak because it had too few examples of asceticism. A man must surrender something of value if anyone is to believe he has offered up his own life.

This line of reasoning presumably applies even to those candidates who, without having acquired credible evidence of sacrifice, are accepted because of ecclesiastical and family connections. If they had sufficient connections to enter the deir without educational or professional qualifications, then those connections in themselves qualify as testimony of an ascribed status which a man is willing to apply to monastic formation, rather than to secular gain.

Nowadays, university education is available to all qualified young Egyptians. Copts from poor family backgrounds may, by studiousness, position themselves to become acceptable for monastic admission. However, truly poor families may not be able to allow their sons to attend school since they need them to seek gainful employment for economic survival.

The monks who are not degreed are more likely to be found among the groups of men who entered the deir in the 1960s. Many of these unlettered monks had no particular ecclesiastical recommendation to enter. In those days, before Deir Anba Amoun was filled, entry was considerably easier than it is now. None of the unlettered monks from that period are priests. Two of them rotate the supervision of the main gate at night; another is the personal servant of the kommos. Two from this group are virtual recluses and live in neighboring cells at the northeast edge of the mozafeen quarters. Another three are not living at Deir Anba Amoun, but are serving local bishops in their homes as servants. These bishops are benefactors of the deir, and urge qualified vocations to seek entrance at this monastery.

The oldest monks are more difficult to classify. Many of them did not initially enter Deir Anba Amoun, but were transferred here later. Transferring monks is a delicate subject in the monastery, second only to their defection to the secular world. Coptic canon law discourages monks from leaving their monastery to join another deir and precludes them from leaving monastic life altogether. Those who have transferred have done so for multiple reasons. Some are from Deir Abu Maqar and have left that monastery to join others because of its estrangement from the patriarchal office, or because the kommos of that deir emphasizes what many feel to be excessive labor for the monks. "At Deir Abu Maqar, we had to work side by side with the mozafeen all day," one complained. Laboring in the same class as fellaheen, without any chance of ecclesiastical promotion, is not what drew these monks to the deir. Moreover, excessive work, which is usually considered to be more than four hours a day, is deemed incompatible with the life of monastic prayer and solitude.

At Deir Anba Amoun, some of the elder monks transferred from monasteries which were subjected to the renewal of Pope Shenouda in recent years. This mandate entailed changes of custom and authority and was met with considerable resistance by many older monks throughout Egypt. Hence, a number of them were transferred from their reformed houses due to political alienation. They have little social position in the deir and are more often found to be away from the monastery visiting friends and family in the cities, or helping out in local parishes by performing baptisms and weddings.

The Spiritual Father

The most important relationship of any monk is with his spiritual father, who is his advisor in all matters, both religious and mundane. A monk entrusts his soul to his spiritual father and obeys his directives entirely. The eremitical ideal of solitude is based upon this privileged relationship, as all the desert fathers of old first began their vocation by finding a competent spiritual director who led them on the road of solitary perfection. Today a monk is known by the distinguished lineage of the past generations of his spiritual father, and a spiritual father is known by the number and quality of his "sons."

The word for a spiritual father, "hegoumenos," is shortened to "kommos" in daily use. At Deir Anba Amoun, as in many Coptic adiora, there is but one kommos, who corresponds to the Western monastic position of "abbot." The kommos in charge of a deir is sometimes called *raeese-deir*, or the "president" of the monastery, in order to distinguish him from another spiritual father, if another one resides in that deir. He can also be designated *kommos-raeese*. In Deir Anba Amoun only one monk, the kommos who administers the affairs of the whole community, is the spiritual guide of each member of that community. To join Deir Anba Amoun is to be adopted by a common father.

Not all monasteries have only one hegoumenos. Some adiora have three or four such fathers who are subordinate to a kommos-raeese. This is especially the case when a kommos grows old or becomes ill and is no longer able to direct a great number of monastic souls. Additional or potential spiritual fathers can be rivals for the future control of a deir. Who and how many monks adopt rival fathers as their directors, and how the spiritual fathers relate to the bishops and patriarch are factors which may determine which of them eventually assumes full control of the deir. This rivalry, however, if it becomes operative, must be played out in restrained stylized forms, for the participants must be compatible enough to co-exist in the same deir for the remainder of their life. If the rivalries are too deep and too divisive, some monks may have to relocate when a kommos-raeese is finally chosen.

Even when there is but one kommos in a deir, other monks may position themselves to be future spiritual fathers. Should something happen to the kommos, it would be too late for an interested monk to suggest himself as hegoumenos just at that moment. He must be prepared ahead of time for that eventuality.

He can do this in several ways. First, he must attain the status of an abuna robeyta, a "father controller," who has a recognized area of responsibility in the deir to which all defer. Such positions would include having charge of the employees, or the library, or the farm, or the pumps, or the clinic, or the supplies, or the retreat house. Such monks may informally preside over groups of other monks. These ad hoc associations may appear as no more than casual recreations around a pot of mint tea, for instance, but they form well-known groups which have significant social implications in the deir.

Since the abuna robeyta is being considered here in an informal social role as the center of a non-canonical social segment of the deir, the term "robeyta" will be used to designate the role, even though the title is also used as another term for the abbot. Since no formal or canonical term exists for this role, the word "robeyta" will be used when the context is clear that the abbot is not intended.

The informal groups of monks meet in the domain of the abuna robeyta, i.e., in the clinic, the library, the retreat house, or the cell of the "father controller." The father robeyta takes a central position within the group, often at a desk. He initiates the topic of discussion and responds to each comment. He is not contradicted, and he elicits questions from the group for which, it is assumed, he will have the answers. He will meet with each member of the group individually at other times, taking a paternal interest in his affairs. In all of this, the abuna robeyta is a small-scale model of the kommos who acts similarly when presiding socially. Hence, the abuna robeyta is tacitly preparing to become the kommos if called upon to do so. However, not all abuna robeytas are motivated to become a kommos. The sheer size of a deir and the external ecclesiastical concerns of the kommos may make it impossible for him to tend to each of his monks personally. In that case, an abuna robeyta may simply be responding to a social need of his monastery. The monastery, itself, may also be positioning him in response to the inaccessibility of the kommos-raeese.

The formal structure of authority in the deir is a simple one. The kommos is the head; every monk is equally subject to him and, there

fore, stands in equal relationship to every other monk in the deir.
This model is the ideal, however, and does not take into account the
inequalities which inherently exist in the social diversity of the men
who enter the monastery, such as in education, professional experience, family background or ecclesiastical connections. Moreover, this
model, formed from the eremitical ideal of ancient Coptic monasticism, does not provide the hierarchical positions required in the
more integrated cenobitical monasteries which have evolved in Egypt.
The robeyta monks fill this vacuum in the hierarchy of classical
monastic authority.

A monk may also be a more likely candidate to become an abuna
robeyta, or even a kommos, if he is already a spiritual father of many
pilgrims. When a monk is so sought after by pilgrims for advice or
blessings that he must make efforts to evade them in order to recover
monastic quietude, he becomes, *de facto*, a candidate for the role of
hegoumenos whether it is his goal or not. The monk who draws spiritual children also draws monastic income and candidates. He embodies the symbolic function of the deir in Coptic society.

In Deir Anba Amoun, several monks have acquired the honorary
distinction of "spiritual father" because of their skills and success with
pilgrim ministry. They are not recognized as a hegoumenos in the
deir, however, for that internal distinction is still the preserve of the
kommos-raeese. A monk may be viewed as a spiritual father outside
the deir, or even by the mozafeen, but may not be considered as such
by the monks within the monastery. All the monks honored as spiritual fathers by the laity are robeyta monks; most of them actually
request such informal titular recognition, ostensibly to give legitimacy
to their public ministries. All of them earned professional degrees
before entering the monastery, and most of them are from prominent
Coptic families. Social hierarchy in the deir often, though not always,
mirrors social hierarchy in the world. The social capital of the one
translates, in rough proportions, into the spiritual capital of the other
through the value-inverting process of ascetic sacrifice.

The nature of the relationship between the monk and the
kommos is ambivalent. The kommos is a real, although analogous,
"father." The term is not to be dismissed too hastily as a mere title.
He has the full responsibility of the monk in his care and speaks to

his "son" with full authority. Beyond the deep and complex bonds of paternal and filial loyalties, little exists by way of a contractual relationship between the two monks. Fatherhood is not just an incidental metaphor for the kommos. The Middle Eastern and Mediterranean role of "father" deeply, though not exhaustively, defines the spiritual fatherhood of monks.

The monk respects and fears his kommos. This respect borders on veneration, for the father is portrayed and perceived as a vicar of God's fatherhood. A monk expects his spiritual father to speak to him on behalf of God, to express the divine point of view, and dispense divine mercy. A kommos, by definition, has deep, grace-filled insights into his son and, by a few words, can probe his heart and penetrate his soul.

The monk is expected to bare his soul without reservation to his spiritual father, exposing every thought, private distraction, secret sin, personal shame, and unguarded imagining. Most of the dialogue between the spiritual father and a monk may consist primarily of ascetical matters: how many daily prostrations the monk performs; how many hours of sleep he forgoes for prayer; how silent he is; how much he meditates on the ancient fathers and their sayings; how well he keeps the fasts; how he deals with temptations; how often he walks in the desert by night in contemplation; how well he keeps detached from guests, pilgrims, and employees while exemplifying holiness to them. According to Coptic piety, the act of baring the soul in such a holy setting grants the monk an opportunity for an otherwise unattainable purity and holiness.

By transcending his sinful past and his fleshly inclinations, the monk eludes the material bondage of the secular society and the Islamic state, or at least it is so regarded by the Copts. The spiritual father grants the monk this fundamental aspect of his vocation, and the unrelieved honesty demanded by and offered to the kommos is an essential element of monastic sacrifice. For yielding up the intimate contents of one's memory and emotions is an act both painful and purgative, violating the soul, even while upbuilding the spirit. The benefit of this sacrifice is the belief of the Coptic community that the bondage of the world (read here "the Islamic state"), the flesh, and the devil can be surmounted. Offering such a sacrifice to the kommos in no way diminishes the oblation which the monk offers of himself to God. Indeed, God is the guarantor of the spiritual father's ministry.

The kommos decides when the candidate will be consecrated as a monk, when the monk is to be ordained, what position he will hold in the deir and whether or not he may ascend toward a higher degree of monastic perfection with the recognition which that entails. A monk may therefore fear the kommos who can withhold promotion, detain him from consecration or ordination, or even expel him from the deir. The disapproval of a kommos disorients the monk and causes great grief. God is felt to be thereby inaccessible; his consolation is unreachable.

Should the kommos indicate disinterest in the monk, the very ground of the monk's world is felt to be shaken. The monk broods on the implications of his spiritual father's words and silences, his gestures, absences, and lack of interest. "Who has he been speaking to now? What is he thinking of me? When will he seek me out? How would he interpret my seeking him out?" Although the monk is no child, and although he consciously contextualizes these concerns, the structure of his relationship with the kommos is such that he can hardly avoid the consuming preoccupation of these questions. There is too much in the hands of the kommos for him to be regarded casually. A monk will do everything in his power to regain the interest and approval of his father. A brief visitation with such despair will serve to generate additional energy to comply with the demands of the kommos. Eagerness to perform the prescribed ascetical works will give evidence of his compliant will.

The kommos has the responsibility of transforming his sons into monks, recognizable to themselves and to their world. Attaining monkhood is a process which occurs in the dynamics of the dialogue between a spiritual father and his son. In all of this, the real fatherhood of the kommos is clearly evident. He "begets" monks, inasmuch as his sons are formed into monks by listening to his words attentively. He views his monks with special insight and interest as does any faithful father with his natural children. He governs his monks and sets their future. This power grants ready meaning to almost any of his actions, just as a natural father's are fraught with meaning to his son.

At Deir Anba Amoun, the kommos-raeese is a bishop whose name is Anba Amoun, so named after the patron saint of the monastery. Anba Amoun has the care of ninety monks plus the lands and estate of his deir and the ecclesiastical concerns of the local Coptic Church. He is away from the deir for weeks at a time, and his absence causes considerable anxiety among his sons.

At Deir Anba Amoun, the robeyta monks have become more outspoken, and their groups have become more defined than they had once been. A process of adjusting to the absence of a unifying kommos is at work, as separate groups of monks begin to emerge. Those who remain loyal to the kommos will bring the matter to his attention when he returns to the deir, and he will attempt to re-establish his paternal hold. This pattern may be repeated indefinitely.

Another group of monks, however, or perhaps a coalition of robeyta monks or their followers, may eventually take their concern about an absentee (or otherwise problematic) kommos to the patriarch, the "spiritual father" of the Coptic Church. If the patriarch is still well-disposed to the kommos he installed years earlier, he will likely recast the objections of the monks in the form of filial love and respect for him, and promise that the kommos will respond well to their solicitude. The patriarch may then speak to the kommos and encourage him to take greater care of his monks and not to punish the robeyta monks who criticized him. But the vicissitudes of the Church may be such that the kommos no longer enjoys the favor of the patriarch as before. In such a case, the patriarch may hear the robeyta monks more sympathetically. He may, in fact, undermine the kommos by appointing other spiritual fathers in the deir, leaving Anba Amoun the kommos-raeese of a divided house.

Chapter VIII

Behavioral Embodiments of Value

In the secular world of Egypt, a man who hopes to become a leader on any social level must evidence certain social skills. He must demonstrate confidence in himself and his abilities, engage others freely and easily in conversation, be decisive in his dealings, prove his credibility and be articulate and persuasive in expressing his point of view. Although the Egyptian style of communicating these traits may differ from that of Western leaders, resembling instead a Mediterranean, male-oriented formality, these qualities are not altogether foreign to Western models of social promotion (Gilmore 1990:16). Yet the Coptic monk, who attains a high status in his ethnic society, projects a decidedly different kind of persona for credibility and social acceptance.

Erving Goffman perceived that any general role in society proceeds from an ideal human type who perfectly embodies that role. He calls efforts at establishing credibility in a role "performance." A person, in order to project a believable selfhood, must embody certain consistent patterns of behavior which are measured against the ideal. To the degree that a person approximates that ideal, he attains social weight and influence (Goffman 1959:252). A person may be "taken in" by the role performed and may come to believe in it as though it were the essential self (1959:17). Considerable effort will be required to protect this image, which is intuitively perceived as fragile and vulnerable to damage by the appearance of cross signals (1959:141). For Goffman, there is no essential self, merely the dramatic effect of the performance that is inter-subjectively believed (1959:253). Suffice it to say that a coherent social perspective of a group depends upon the consistent self-presentation of its members.

For the Copts, this same insight also holds true of monastic figures. The credible performance, or self-presentation of the monks, reflects a specialized social perspective and reinforces the unique culture of the Copts. The monks have a different style of expressing openness toward social status. Because they have ostensibly rejected the prevailing models of the secular world and have based their persona upon the sacrificial model of religious existence, the monks must not promote themselves for leadership in the deir in any direct way which would be immediately intelligible to the secular world. They must, in fact, avoid leadership and ambition in dramatic ways if they intend to pursue ecclesiastical and spiritual status. As Simon Tugwell states:

> What is, at first sight, surprising is that many of them [the monks] acquired a position of considerable authority and power. The explanation is probably that, by their total renunciation of ordinary human structures, they came to represent a completely different kind of power, which can then be used to challenge the political and economic power which is normally operative in our society (Tugwell 1985:15).

The social history of the Coptic monasteries depicts the essential revolutionary spirit of the early monks. They rejected the oppression of the Copts under imperial rule, and opted out of its stranglehold over Egypt by taking to the desert and living a countercultural life. The credibility of their indictment of the Empire rested upon the idealism of their life styles in counterdistinction to the mercenary ambition of the country's leaders. To that end, they repudiated the secular lust for power and, instead, adopted the powerful symbol of self-denial and powerlessness.

The monks enlisted the Gospel to support this strategy by recalling Christ's words: *"For everyone who exalts himself shall be humbled, while he who humbles himself shall be exalted"* (Luke 18:14). They freed themselves from the economic restraints of the secular world by renouncing marriage and families which would give them greater responsibility for acquiring income and property, and would set them on the track of striving, earning, and social climbing. Instead, they formed counterfamilial structures based on spiritual fatherhood, rather than the carnal paternity which typifies the basis of the secular, social organization.

Such reversal of the secular order and the inversion of its values became essential components of desert monasticism and defined it for centuries, even when other sociological facts indicated the need of significant adaptation of monasticism to its social milieu. The institution of monasticism seems, therefore, perfectly suited to historical analysis. In its counterpoint to the world's secular order, monasticism provides for the ethnographer a village-level inversion of the symbols of the complex, dominant state.

Another reason for preferring the desert wilderness in establishing monasteries is that the desert is not only physically barren, but also has no social markers or boundaries. By definition, it is without internal borders, property titles, pathways, human associations, and historical references. The desert is an undifferentiated whole. As such, the arid wilderness is a blank screen onto which an inversion of the secular social order may be projected. Occupied lands present too many distortions coming from the ascendent cultural structures for this to occur. The Western Church also prefers more sequestered regions when establishing its monasteries. When that is not possible, special care is taken to consecrate sufficient "cloistered" zones within and around the monastery to create *terra incognita*, a zone of mystery, at least in the estimation of the surrounding believers.

Because monasteries transcend the coercive structures of the secular order, they are expected to provide a special context for the critical appraisal of the "outside world." Asad has noted that the monastic penitential practices of medieval Europe, for example, provided the culture of that time with the catalyst to scrutinize moral life with great deliberation. Not only were the customs and behavior of Christians studied, but all manner of their religious competitors was examined and codified. The behavior of heretics, Moslems, Jews and pagans was presented to provide moral context for converts and sinners who came to repent. Asad concludes that the West's well-known curiosity for understanding and describing the "Other" is rooted in this monastic practice. Ascetic disciplines require a systematic type of knowledge.

> In other words, forms of interest in the production of knowledge are intrinsic to various structures of power, and they differ not according to the essential character of Islam or Christianity, but according to historically changing systems of discipline (Asad 1996:5).

Western monasticism is, then, a "system of discipline" which has the power to orient the culture which produces it toward a certain kind of mentality. Analogously, Coptic monasticism also shapes the Christian cultures of Egypt. Its unique origins and long history profoundly strengthen this role.

Coptic monasticism presents a microcosmic inversion of the pluralistic values of the state on the stage of a desert community. The monastery, then, is a key to understanding that pluralistic state. How its monks attain leadership roles may be a case in point.

The ritual for the installation of a Coptic patriarch contains, in a revealing way, precisely what it attempts to conceal. As mentioned earlier, the patriarch-elect, a monk from the desert, is brought to the installation ceremony literally bound in chains (Burmester 1960:55). Coptic history and hagiography abound with stories about contented hermits being forced out of their solitude by a Church which needed their holiness and wisdom. So apparently unwilling were these hermits to submit to ecclesiastical status that they had to be fettered in iron in order to be brought to the site of their consecration. The ritual suggests that this occurred so frequently that the chaining of the patriarch-elect eventually became customary. It also suggests that the patriarch-elect realized that, by living in the desert, he was already in the spiritual heartland, the symbolic capital of his ethnic Church, and consequently did not want to be "exiled" to the merely functional center of the Church.

Curiously, no one has suggested that the symbolic function of these fetters outstrips in importance its once practical utility. No one really believes that the Office of Patriarch in the Coptic Church has been consistently occupied by a series of unwilling popes. In point of fact, the sacrament of Holy Priesthood and the consecration to the episcopacy can only be conferred upon a willing recipient. Such canons are held universally in apostolic Churches. Moreover, should an unwilling monk somehow be consecrated as patriarch, once installed, he would be the ultimate authority in his Church and, therefore, free to express his unwillingness without further contradiction. He could return at once to the desert! Finally, should he be forced, somehow, to remain in office, he would make life difficult for those who forced him from desert retirement. Consideration of these consequences would inhibit the ecclesiastical apparatus from ever choosing such a monk to begin with.

The hagiography of the unwilling hermit seized by a Spirit-directed electoral body and the rubric of fettering a monk-to-be-patriarch are extremely successful symbols in the Coptic Church, with analogues in other Churches as well. They are symbols of power which are shunned, for power unsought and a position evaded are the hallmarks of credibility for monastic leadership. A monk cannot ostensibly be an ambitious man, for this appearance would undermine the meaning of his own vocation. Should he become a leader, he does so, as it were, unwillingly. Of course, he does not really assume leadership unwillingly, but he accepts the leadership role with a proper attention and respect to the inversion of secular ambition to which he has pledged his life, that is, with humility. Moreover, the charisma of the power he holds would be dissipated were he to grasp that power too deliberately. The delicacy of the monk's position in relationship to power is safely guarded in the hagiography and rubrics of the Coptic Church.

Thus, a patriarch-elect, himself, need not wish to evade his new office, nor need his predecessors have wished to do so. He needs only to cooperate with the custom of *appearing* not to want the position during the proper ceremony. He thereby preserves a ritual innocence toward ambition, and the Church demonstrates a value of crucial importance in its internal life. The observance of this particular ritual serves as an example of monastic leadership roles in general.

Desert Poetics

In the desert today, some monks circulate stories about the manner of their ordination to the priesthood. Each one relates how the patriarch or another bishop called him to serve as a deacon assistant in the liturgy and that, in place of a simple blessing during the celebration, the bishop imposed his hands on the head of the unsuspecting monk, making him a priest. This story is more often told about other priest-monks than claimed about oneself, but both cases exist in some numbers. The story is similar to the ritual of the patriarch-elect in chains. In both cases, imputed unwillingness to pursue ecclesiastical promotion serves as the guarantor of a monk's purity of intention. The private intentionality of a monk in legitimating his authority is of greater importance than for secular leaders who pursue power more directly. Zeal and ambition are common in secular leaders, but a monk is expected to have renounced personal ambition. Its reappearance in him would not only negate his claim of disinterested service, but would also undermine his basic identity as a monk.

The projection of an appropriate personal image which corresponds to one's role is more than a private concern. Culture itself supplies the proportions of a persona to which individuals attempt to conform (cf. Goffman 1959). Coptic culture is no exception in regard to the role of the monk. Hagiography supplies much of that proportion and provides the rules for inverting the secular social order in individual monastic lives. But even without hagiography, the inherent logic of secular-value-inversion would direct the monks to embody the lofty ideals proper to their religious vocation.

Following Goffman, Herzfeld has described the process of projecting a personal image onto social roles. He calls that process "poetics," which at once recognizes the set structure of certain roles and the individual's ability to embody them. Hence, there are certain stylized behavior patterns which supply actors with a full repertoire of activities proper to their personae and incorporate them into an historical movement, giving them the power to embody a tradition and recapitulate an ideal (Herzfeld 1985:10).

Coptic monasticism has its own poetics in this sense. The Coptic monk has a repertoire of behaviors which allows him to embody hagiographical ideals and to dramatically invert the secular values of his day. He invests himself by specialized speech, garments, food and gestures with the power of his ancient desert heroes from a bygone age of spiritual giants.

There will always be a certain question of credibility in the appropriation of such heroic roles and the projection of such lofty ideals onto actual men. People will remember the earlier, secular lives of the monks and will recall their former human frailties or temporal ambitions. They will also notice the present shortcomings of a monk which do not conform to the ideals he projects. The distance a monk takes from the world is critical in this regard. Distance is not just a geographical matter. The monk must not be a familiar of the world, just as the desert is not familiar to the world. He must be distant in the sense of being detached from casual human commerce so that the contradictions between his life and role will not be too apparent. Herzfeld notes that an actor of poetics must take care to suppress any sense of incongruity which is inevitably created by projecting roles of "grandiose implications" (1985:10).

Nothing could be more "grandiose" than for a human being to claim to live the life of an angel. Yet the monks of Egypt claim just such a life! The secular and Islamic detractors of this role are numerous and powerful; hence, the Coptic affirmation of it is serious and intense. Consequently, the Coptic monk does not typically employ humor in his analysis of the monastic life. When humor is evidenced, it is marginal to the essential aspects of his daily routine and activities. What is truly heroic does not need to be, indeed, ought not to be, diminished by irreverent or mundane associations. Distance and humorlessness, then, typify the behavior of the monks in relationship to the laity and to the world.

What of the poetics of the monks in relationship to one another? How do they present themselves to each other in terms of leadership and respect? How do they disregard the incongruities which they perceive in one another at close range?

As already noted, a monk recommends himself for authority and position by deliberately making counterindications of these interests. These gestures have evolved into patterns of behavior which can be recognized, although they are not necessarily consciously employed or explicitly understood. Such behavior is, nevertheless, symbolically communicative within the social matrix of the deir and the Coptic Church.

Self-deprecation is one such behavior practiced in many forms in the deir. For the monk to present himself properly for notice and esteem, he must verbally negate himself in whatever area he is tending to pursue. "Books are too burdensome for me to bother myself with. They belong to brilliant people who can appreciate them more than I can." Such are the expressed sentiments of a monk candidate in Deir Anba Amoun who has an advanced degree in library science.

Monks frequently express deprecatory remarks not only about their competencies, but also about their holiness. "I am really just a beginner in matters of the spirit," is an oft-stated sentiment. "I am a weak man who needs the monastic life because of my weakness with temptation," said one monk living a celibate life for over twenty years. "Theological talk is beyond me. I cannot understand deep matters of religion," is another common declaration. But the quickest way to gauge the real meaning of such sentiments is to agree with them when they are expressed. The reaction to such agreement is often consternation and silence. The intent of the behavior, therefore, was not agreement, but contradiction, or at least tacit disbelief.

Alter-adulation is another method of self-promotion in the deir. Monks frequently extol the talents and holiness of each other, especially when the other is present: "Abuna Sylvanus is a visionary. Anba Amoun, the saint, has appeared to him and instructed him."

"No, no, Abuna Meshack, you are the visionary. You are pure of heart and God's holy light shines on you."

"Abuna Sylvanus, you are too humble. You must not hide your light under a basket."

The conversation can go on at length and can be modified for pilgrims in attention or for fellow monks, where it is somewhat more subtle. The dynamic of the dialogue is more powerful than self-deprecation by itself. It permits the statements to be explicitly contra-dicted, and thus engages the monks in mutual endorsements. Yet at no time does the monk explicitly boast; he retains a formal humility.

Self-abasing gestures are also an important stylized form of role-defining behavior for the monks. They customarily greet each other by a stylized kissing of each other's hands, i.e., by sliding their palms over those of a confrere in an abbreviated motion of grasping his hand, and then taking their own hands to their lips with a kiss. This represents a symbolic kiss of the other's hands which they would have been holding. By this gesture, two monks can kiss each other's hands simultaneously without awkwardness. But, frequently, monks will attempt to kiss the other's hands actually, not just figuratively. One will attempt to grasp the other's hand while he is unsuspecting, and quickly press it to his lips before his confrere can resist. The impli-cation is: "You are holier, for I take my blessing from your hand. We are not equals, for I have honored you first, and I am therefore subordinate to you."

Of course, the other monk cannot allow this to occur too often. If he does, it will be apparent that he is in danger of permitting per-sonal aggrandizement and, by that very appearance, he will lose credi-bility. He would not be embodying the poetics of monastic humility, but evidencing the prestige-seeking behavior of the secular world. Therefore, he tries to grasp the hands of the approaching confrere, even as the monk tries to grasp his. Often, then, the monks can be seen in a tug of war over who will be humbled before the other. The intention of expressing abasement is even clearer when the ritual is extended. A monk will try to touch the feet of another monk and then take his own hands to his lips in a symbolic kiss of the feet he has just touched. Or he will touch the ground on the place where the other has walked and kiss his hand as if to say, "I kiss the ground on which you walk."

The social meaning is well conveyed: real monks are humble, and humility is the only possible meaning of such gestures. The paradox is that over-expressing humility exalts oneself, to one's own detriment. The struggle is unresolvable and unending. Significantly, monks who engage each other in such public acts are more often members of the same informal intra-monastic group, rather than monks from less familiarly associated ones. Reinforcement of the group seems to result from their mutual reinforcement of each other.

Self-deprecation, alter-adulation and self-abasement are dramatizations of communicative behavior which is intentionally evocative. They define much of the social sphere of the deir and its internal divisions in sheer opposition to the self-promoting behavior in the secular world. In the secular society of Egypt, as in so much of the world, a man tends to directly promote his strengths, denigrate the weaknesses of his rivals, and posture himself to the fullest advantage in his business dealings.

The credibility of the monastic community rests on its opposition to secular values and symbols. One might object that any contradictions to secularity in the deir are only strategic appearances. But this is not the case. The monks do not simply "enact" their behavior. The project of any primate society entails the interpositioning of each of its members according to prevailing behavior patterns of competition and hierarchical formation (cf. Bramblett 1994:75-85). Social coherency requires this strategy, even if the individuals in a specialized human society have renounced it as their primary mode of operation. The deir exhibits the irreducible social directives of humanity, even if it ostensibly repudiates one particular cultural configuration of those directives. The monks' repudiation of self-promoting social positioning does, in fact, condition their own countercultural expression of it. That the monks have not transcended humanity altogether is hardly a matter of duplicity or guile. Rather, their behavior is an expression, although a tortured one, of essential social forms.

Still, for the symbolic work of the deir to be accomplished in Coptic society, it is often necessary for the rather limited transcendence of secular strategies to be dramatized as the full transcendence of a fallen human condition. Hence, exaggerated claims about the lives of the monks, their fasts, their silences and their mysticism are frequently made by one monk about another, or by the laity. Exaggerations, however, are inlaid on existing lines of reality, and often call attention to important areas of counterculture which might otherwise be missed.

The behavior of the monks among each other, their distance from the world, and their relentlessly serious concern about who they are and how they appear constitute much of the poetics of their deir. Poetics, as the word connotes, implies drama. A monk is a dramatic, heroic persona, even if his own character is actually rather ordinary. The claims of a religious order are better served by heroes than by doctrines. The Copts, who depend upon their religion for ethnic survival, will discern or impute heroic ideals in their monks because to do so invests their religion with greater symbolic power and social efficacy (Herzfeld 1985:xiv). The monk must provide the dramatic persona onto which a religious counterculture can be safely projected. If he embodies these ideals well, so much the better; a living saint may be perceived to add new vitality to the Copts' voluminous hagiography. If he does not, the public presentation of monastic poetics still preserves the ideals which grant the Copts ethnic viability.

Finally, there are a number of monks within the deir who do not exhibit the self-promoting social behavior described above. They are self-effacing, rather than self-deprecating. The latter tends toward anonymity, while the former is directed toward self-advertisement. Their desert walks are not calculated to be noticed by conspicuous departures or returns. They do not belong, or belong exclusively, to one robeyta monk's group. They are not in the line of monks who greet the kommos on his return, or welcome the patriarch on his visit. They do not seek a desert cell or cave, although they are reclusive enough within their cell.

These monks are to the monastery what the monastery attempts to be for the world. They appear detached, transcending the temporal stage whereon they walk. They grant a legitimacy to the deir; they manifest not its margins, but its silent heart. If other monks do not quite embody the special qualities of monastic transcendence, they can be comforted that the whole monastery is not so undermined. But those who do embody these ideals grant the whole community sufficient reason to continue its cultural course. These monks derive no visible benefit for their service which, if it were publicly noted, would be an undesired indictment of the rest of the community. Thus, their monastic lives are, in reality, something of the sacrificial act that all monks' lives are projected to be. They generate a degree of credibility to the deir among the monks themselves, which redeems the whole monastic project from explicit showmanship. The integrity of Coptic culture would be called into question if the monks were exposed as uniformly, self-consciously ambitious; that is, the integrity of the minority subculture, which endures oppression and persecution as a form of sacrifice after the example of the monks, would also be endangered. In a sense, the rare and nearly invisible monk, so difficult to analyze because he is not a player in the complex field of the daily dynamics of the monastery is, by the same token, a willing oblation offered for the sanctification of his religious order and the salvation of his people.

The Monastic Regimen

Nothing might appear to be a more straightforward matter than the daily routine and diet of the monks. Westerners expect that monks, above all people, have achieved a regularity in their schedules and a uniformity in their practice. This may have once been the case in most Western monasteries and is still true in some, but those of Egypt are quite different. Regularity and uniformity do not obtain there.

Coptic monks follow a course of daily life which is unstructured, that is, they practice a form of monasticism found more typically in the Eastern churches which permits a great range of individual variation. Part of the reason that this model is prominent in Egypt is that the most important social relationship in the monastery is between each monk and his spiritual father, as already noted. Thus, the ideal of the eremitical life is somewhat maintained by this arrangement.

There are no community meetings or common recreations, no shared retreats or general conferences at Deir Anba Amoun. A formal community exists in the monastery as an accidental consequence of the number of individual monks clustered around the same spiritual father. The aggregate community is important in some respects, for it provides a base upon which the monk can more successfully live out his private vocation, and it serves as a collective dramatization of monastic sacrifice which might be more obscure if projected only by individuals. And, of course, the collectivity of a monastic institution is more capable of ecclesiastical interplay than that of isolated ascetics.

Still, the Coptic monk retains the primary sense of his own individuality. There is little which cannot be negotiated by the consecrated monk with his spiritual father. The progress of his personal growth is very much a process of privatization of religious practice. The hours of prayer performed standing upright in the church among fellow monastic candidates are soon translated into private devotions in his cell, once a monk receives the full monastic habit. The daily Kodes and Communion give way to occasional liturgical celebrations, for instance, when it is the "turn" of the monk-priest to officiate. Austere common meals yield to simple meals prepared in one's own cell. With so much private practice of the monastic life, advertised schedules of daily religious activities in the deir are somewhat misleading.

In spite of the enormous extent of individual practice and the impossibility of knowing the range of privatized devotions, the monks of Deir Anba Amoun readily supply the pilgrims with a "horarium," that is, an hourly schedule of the monastery. This has more value as a symbol of monastic asceticism than as a prediction of where the monks may be at any given time. Nevertheless, it provides information regarding the whereabouts and activities of the monastic candidates, as well as those monks who may occasionally participate in community activities. The schedule of the Coptic monastery of Anba Amoun presented below is a description of its official routine which describes the ascetical ideal held by all monks:

3:00 a.m. to 6:00 a.m.	Morning Psalmody and Incense in common.
6:00 a.m. to 9:00 a.m.	Kodes in common.
9:00 a.m. to 1:00 a.m.	Work projects, followed by rest.
2:00 a.m.	First meal in common.
3:00 p.m. to 5:00 p.m.	Spiritual reading; meditation.
5:30 p.m. to 6:00 p.m.	Evening Prayer in common, followed by rest.
7:00 p.m. to 8:00 p.m.	Evening meal in common.
8:00 p.m. to Midnight	Desert walks, social discourse, common spiritual study, rest.
Midnight to 3:00 a.m.	Private monastic prayers; prostrations, followed by rest.

Some commentary on this regimen may be helpful. The spiritual exercises which last from 3:00 a.m. to 9:00 a.m. are performed with the monks on their feet almost the whole time. These six hours of standing are the great ascetical work of most monks for, as candidates, they performed this feat daily. The monks stand in two antiphonal scholas during the endless psalmody and incensing. The droning chant, the aching legs and back, the heavy acrid smoke and the dim light are conducive to a kind of minor hypnosis, which the monks regard as an inducement to pray more than a bystander might.

Although everyone is awakened by the relentless ringing of the bell at 3:00 a.m. (the call to prayer) the morning exercises are the most poorly attended common events in the deir. The candidates and the monks who are newly consecrated, but have not yet been ordained to the priesthood, are well represented. The blind cantor is escorted to the church by one of the monastic candidates. At 6:00 a.m. the priest in charge of the monk-recruits arrives and notes those in attendance. He is acknowledged in a deferential ritual greeting by all who preceded him. He then begins the hour-long prayers of praise which initiate every Liturgy. While he does so, a few priests arrive and are vested. Just as one taper may light several candles, several Masses may be celebrated from the same opening prayers of this group. A priest who arrives at 6:30 a.m. may join the prayers at this stage, and then go off to another altar within the sanctuary to begin a separate Kodes.

Various lay employees of the monastery also arrive at this point and, with the monks who have come earlier, are assigned as liturgical assistants to the officiating priests. By the chanting of the Gospel around 7:30 a.m. (the last possible moment a concelebrating priest or monk-communicant may arrive), the number of monks attending the morning exercises may have reached twenty-five. After this point, all the monks disappear behind a curtain in the wall of the sanctuary and participate in the core of the Liturgy as a distinct body, separated from the laity in attendance, i.e., the pilgrims, retreatants and mozafeen. Unseen by the others, they may be seated on the sanctuary floor, or making prostrations during the more sacred moments of the ritual. The monks explain that they have a reserved space in the Liturgy closer to the altar because their life of sacrifice unites them more closely with the sacrifice of the altar. In the Coptic view, what happens in the sanctuary is of heaven, and the monks who serve there commute from earth to heaven.

The first meal at 2:00 p.m. in Deir Anba Amoun is communal and is well attended. It consists mainly of rice and falafel beans called "*fule*." Secondary dishes may include oranges, tomatoes, lettuce, leeks, lentils, olives and carrots. Barley-bread cakes are served at every meal.

The monks are seated in a U-shaped configuration of connecting tables with the kommos at the center. At his left is the youngest (i.e., the newest) monk in the deir, and at his right is the oldest--mirroring the supposed seating arrangement of Christ at the Last Supper where John, the youngest apostle, and Peter, the senior, sat on either side of Jesus. The monastic community fans out in proper order from these anchored positions, with the consecration date of each monk establishing his place at the table. During the meal, a monk reads from the ancient desert literature to the silent, eating assembly.

Not all monks attend the meal. Some may be fasting or eating alone. Most monks have some provisions stored in their rooms, with hot plates on which to prepare the food. The evening meal is more likely to be eaten in this way, as this communal meal has less structure. There are no readings and no secondary dishes.

As fasting foods, the items above contain no animal products in their preparation or serving. Fast days in the Coptic calendar account for over two hundred days of the year in which no animal products are to be eaten. The average Copt might only fast on the more important days, for instance, in Lent, or in August before the feast of St. Mary's ascent to heaven, but the monk is supposed to observe all the fast days. Monks are generally believed by the Copts to be vegetarian, and many are. Nevertheless, on Sundays and major feasts, hard boiled eggs, milk, butter, cheese, fish, chicken, and lamb may appear on the communal table.

The kinds of food a monk may store in his cell vary according to his tastes. All the foods mentioned above, as well as fruit preserves, jellies, juices and candies may be found there. Small personal refrigerators are not uncommon in Deir Anba Amoun, although they are not found in most other monasteries. The acquisition of hot plates, small refrigerators and other appliances is a matter for each monk to negotiate, first with his spiritual father, and then with whatever resources

he can negotiate through his visitors. The deir usually does not provide these "extras," but may permit them in a monastic cell. The cell
of a monk is never a place where guests are entertained and fed, or
visitors are hosted, with the possible exception of prospective monastic recruits.

The modern cells of the monks at Deir Anba Amoun are fairly
standardized, most having been built around the same time. The
greater part of the cell is a circular affair, with a bed and a desk
beneath a high-domed roof, five meters in diameter. The bed is little
more than an elevated wooden mat. Each monk is free to choose fur-
nishings and decorations for his room. Typically, there are icons,
lamps, extra chairs, small tables and shelves, but little in the way of
modern appliances. All the floors are carpeted with throw rugs.
Beside this larger room, the cell has an added smaller rectangular
"prayer room," two by four meters and less than two meters in
height. The site allows the monk to pray without the distraction of
his personal effects and bed in view. He may store the Bible with
some other spiritual books in the "inner cell," where he ideally spends
his time, unless he is walking alone in the desert.

The external facade of the cell is made from limestone blocks
which are used everywhere in the monastic buildings. There are no
eye-level windows. For light and ventilation, the cells have narrow
vertical slits in the area where the vaulted roof connects to the wall.
The inner wall is plastered. In addition to the numerous individual
units, a building of common cells has also been built. Its cells have
the same space, and function as the others; it houses forty monks. All
monks, whether in single units or in a common building, share
common sanitation and lavatory facilities, although some monasteries
have provided them in each cell.

There are seven structural parts to the daily prayer routine of the
monks. These parts are called the *Agbeya* (Liturgical Hours), much as
in Western monasteries. For the Copts, each hour commemorates a
critical event in Christ's saving work; most, therefore, are associated
with the Cross. The praying of the Agbeya incorporates each day of
the monk's life into the timeless mystery of Christ's Passion, further
uniting the monks to his sacrificial role.

The Agbeya explicitly presents the monk in the role which he portrays by his "poetic" behavior, as discussed above. The monk is perceived by the Copts as one who continually offers up the prayers of the Agbeya, and he is thereby invested with the fullness of its associated meanings. The performance of these daily prayers somewhat resembles the traditional image afforded to Western clergy, who have been pictured in the constant recitation of their breviary. The monastic regimen does not proscribe seven separate interludes of prayer. The Coptic monk, like his Western counterparts, combines these seven separate "Hours" into more inclusive prayer times in the morning and in the evening.

The Evening Prayer of Deir Anba Amoun includes substantial clusters of psalms, petitions, readings, and collects. Nevertheless, the whole prayer lasts less than half an hour, even though the number of psalms alone would ordinarily take several hours to recite or chant. After the monks assemble in response to the invitation of the bell, they stand in rows in the main body of the central church. The psalms are distributed, one per monk, so they can pray all of them simultaneously. This collective recitation of the psalms expedites the prayer quickly. The monks explain this practice by stating that if one prays a psalm in faith, all monks enjoy its benefit. Such a phenomenon is a reflection of the mystical economy of the Body of Christ. Attendance at the evening prayer may increase to half or more of the monks of the deir.

Around midnight, each monk is to wake from sleep to begin an hour of private prayer in the inner room of his cell. During this time, he spends the excessive energy of his body in a series of one hundred fifty prostrations or more which are designed to sanctify the night, a time which is believed to be dangerous to the purity of a monk's body and imagination. These profound bows, called *metanoia*, which bring his body flat upon the floor, are said to sublimate passion into prayer, or at least, to exhaust bodily restlessness. The privacy of these prostrations and the delicacy of their significance make them impossible to satisfactorily monitor. The manner in which each monk performs this ritual is conditioned by the advice of his spiritual father, but the difference between the ideal of the private ascetic act and its performance by each monk (e.g., the number, duration, and degree of prostrations) cannot be observed.

The Coptic laity are encouraged to pray the Agbeya whenever possible for their state in life, and pilgrims often join in the monastic prayer in the deir. There is, however, a special "eighth hour" of prayer which is reserved for the monks alone. This prayer, called "*sitar*" (the veil), is prayed in conjunction with the monks' common evening prayer, after the sequence of the regular "Hours." The word for veil, "sitar," is used because it recalls the modesty of Mary, the mother of Jesus, who is pictured in the Near-Eastern imagination as veiled. A monk "veils" himself in prayer as he anticipates sleep, for sleep is a potential threat to modesty and purity.

The Gospel read during the sitar, that of St. John (6:15-23), concerns the desire of the crowds to make Jesus king. Jesus must flee from them into the wilderness to evade their plans. Interestingly, the sitar "veils" the monks most explicitly from the temptation of ambition. Lust, sloth, and gluttony are less proximate to their religious role and are less likely to surface than the desire to gain social and symbolic advantage.

Chapter IX

Coptic Culture and Monasticism

One contemporary monk's version of a popular Coptic religious lesson was recounted to me in a monastery of the Wadi Natroun:

> In Egypt, religion is a simple matter understood by all the Copts from childhood. In fact, religion is as simple as the alphabet. [The word "alphabet" has some currency in Egypt due to centuries of Greek, French, and British influence.] "Alpha" is the sign of the eagle, the symbol of the Spirit of the highest heaven. It stands for God and all the members of God's court, the angels, and the saints. "Beta" is the sign of a house, the place of human habitation. It stands for the realm of the earthly and familiar. "Alpha and Beta" have been combined through the Incarnation of God, Jesus Christ, and the Christian can speak about religion in one such simple term. The eagle has perched at the window of our house. God and all his hosts have come among us. Everywhere we see signs of their visit, and we are not surprised. In the West, the eagle has flown far above, more like a black dot in the sky than a bird in the house. So far away is the dot, many cannot even see it. But for us, there is little else to see. Religion is so simple, like the alphabet.

The old monk's story, whatever its origin, illustrates the essential character of Coptic culture. Life is felt to be permeated with religious significance. Angels accompany people, especially children, in all of their comings and goings. Patron saints watch over their devotees and obtain special favors for them in times of stress. *El Adra* (the Virgin Mary) visits her dedicated family and is visible above churches in the movements of strange lights at night. *Meri Girgus* (St. George) is seen in shadows which play upon church and monastery walls. Crosses appear miraculously on skin, clothing, walls, trees, leaves, stones and sand. Blessings linger upon household objects, places and people. God governs the weather, the Nile and the forces of nature. He holds a real but inexplicable authority over states and leaders, and may speak directly to the hearts of holy monks through the lips of spiritual fathers. Women, as well, may hear God through "spiritual mothers," i.e., cloistered nuns. Common social and economic elements such as oil, salt, bread, wine, wax, wool, paint, wood, and water can be sanctified and impart divine touches and significance.

The transcendent God is close. Holiness is immanent everywhere, pervading homes, relationships and objects. Some areas embody more holiness than others. The sanctuary with its altar has more than a sock drawer containing a holy card, but holiness, the insinuation of divine persons and forces, is hard to evade. Herein lies a grave problem.

While God is spiritually proximate, an enormous moral distance remains between human and heavenly persons. God is infinitely good, totally other, perfectly pure, all light and truth. Humanity is, even without reference to God, obviously flawed and incomplete. Juxtaposed to the goodness of the Almighty, sinful humanity is failed and fallen, shadowed, shameful and worthy of contempt. In the Coptic view, humanity deserves to be punished; people deserve to be afflicted for their impurity when it is asserted in the face of such a proximate deity. The world is a dangerous place, according to a spiritual worldview as simple as the alphabet.

Peter Berger holds that religion is the enterprise by which a sacred cosmos is established from the basic social data in a culture (1967:25). For the Copts, the sacred cosmos is so coincidental with their secular world that real discomfort often results. Copts often avoid building their homes too close to churches because their ordinary domestic faults are all the more disturbing in proximity to the site of the daily Kodes. A father may feel inhibited in expressing anger at his children if the cross of the local parish church is plainly visible outside the window of the family's flat. A mother may feel guilty for under-paying a domestic servant when she hears the droning chant of the monks wafting into her home. Children coming of age may feel restricted from adolescent indulgences because their house is over-charged with holiness; even the fragrance of incense occasionally invades their rooms from the religious services next door. The press of the divine presence can be costly.

Secularity, in fact, does not exist for the Copt as it does for the Western Christian. Secularity is but the systematic behavior of a moral avoidance of holiness. A sense of shame repressed, and sin de-nied, are better descriptions of the Coptic experience of secularity, for these feelings give testimony to the impossibility of forever evading the spiritual realities which fill the Coptic world. Behavior without positive or negative reference to religion, however desirable for some, is virtually unattainable for the Copts.

Some Copts may seemingly lead secular life styles from the Wes-tern point of view, but even their lives are full of religious meaning, for all Copts are inhabitants of their ethnic society and must act out their lives as players in that arena. Even if some consciously reject this environment, it is the one in which they were baptized and enculturated, the one which is shared among all Copts as the medium of symbolic discourse and exchange of meaning. It is the only viable alternative to that of the Arab or Islamic world. Copts, just by being Copts, negotiate their life-ways to greater or lesser degrees within the cultural and religious details of their ethnic society.

The Copts associate their ethnic survival with their religion. To repudiate Coptic orthodoxy not only weakens their Church, but un-dermines the cohesion and viability of their beleaguered community. Therefore, irreligious life styles are laden with guilt, but even guilt is a payment to the spiritual consensus. The possibility of guilt-free, secular Copts would be the real danger.

One monk from a monastery near the Red Sea tells the story of his nephew, Emir. Emir was a popular and gifted graduate student in

engineering who had repudiated the beliefs of the Coptic religion. He
met a female student to whom he was attracted, and they began to
date. She was from a Muslim family, but she too was a non-believer.
They both thought that they could elude the entanglements of mixed
religions by their Western-styled secularity. So long as their relationship was regarded as casual, no great difficulty arose, but when they
proposed the idea of marriage, however, both of their families objected
vehemently. Suddenly they met opposition at every turn.

Marriages in Egypt must be contracted religiously, but no minister
of religion, neither Christian nor Muslim, will preside over a mixed
religious service. Unmarried couples cannot rent apartments, and sexual relations between the unmarried are illegal. Moreover, the Near
Eastern convention that a woman join the religion of her husband put
Emir in a dangerous position. He was liable to be accused of attempting to force a Muslim woman into apostasy which is a crime in the
Arab Islamic Republic meriting stiff punishment. Emir and his fian-
cée were devastated by the obstacles that affected their relationship.

Their lives were so disordered by the stress of their conflicted
engagement that they had to leave graduate school. Eventually, Emir's
intended spouse was sent by her family to relatives in Upper Egypt,
and he was bereft of her companionship. In his grief, he was abandoned by his graduate colleagues, but was surrounded by new friends
from the Church.

Emir's uncle arranged for him to make a retreat in a desert
monastery where, in fact, he encountered angels during one night of
sleeplessness. Emir was overwhelmed with a sense of shame for his
former disregard of faith and his neglect of prayer. He realized that
he had been in flight from God all along. God caught up with him
in his life's reversals, and angels came to retrieve him. Emir is now
driving a taxi in Alexandria and serving as a deacon in the Church,
even teaching Sunday School classes to secondary school students.
The resolution of the flight from God into a guilt-ridden return to the
Church is a testimony to the viability of the Coptic Faith. Even situations which at first do not seem applicable to this process may eventually yield similar results.

Not only the secular Copts, but also those who adopt variant
versions of Christianity experience a sense of guilt. They know that

Egypt's monolithic Islam preys upon the divisions within Christianity. They know that they have weakened the fabric of Coptic resistance to the Islamization of their people. Hence, they choose to be considered as "Coptic Catholic," or "Coptic Evangelical," or "Coptic Protestant." These variant religions recognize the social discomfort of their new flocks and adapt themselves to conspicuous displays of their Coptic character. They print pictures of Pope Shenouda on their literature; they plan regular pilgrimages to the monasteries for their youth, and maintain high profile public relations with the Coptic hierarchy. The Coptic Catholic liturgy, moreover, is practically indistinguishable from that of the Coptic Orthodox Kodes, and bears almost no resemblance to its Western equivalent. Many Copts who attend other Christian denominations for regular Sunday worship are, nevertheless, baptized, married and buried from the Coptic Orthodox Church. Coptic Orthodoxy, with its rites and its belief in the immanence of holiness, holds its own.

Evidence of the tension of the intrusion of holiness into mundane life is everywhere apparent in the Coptic religion. Since Copts in general, and the monks in particular, perceive holiness in terms of moral purity and divine perfection, the evidence of human acknowledgement of its proximity is always an acknowledgement of human imperfection and impurity. Following the alpha-beta analogy, the only way to "house" these conflicting sentiments is to adopt a position of thoroughgoing contrition. Coptic prayer and ritual are filled with such expressions.

The Orientation of Prayer

The entire corpus of Coptic ritual could be presented to demonstrate its contrite and supplicatory nature. However, the immensity of Coptic ritual discourages its insertion into a work of this nature.

The common prayers of the monasteries have become the devotional life of the popular Church. Except for the sitar, the "prayer of the veil," much of the monastic prayer is also potentially the prayer of the laity. The monks, however, intone these prayers more regularly, intensely, and with greater attention to structure. This similarity between monastic and lay prayers marks the Coptic Church as thoroughly monastic in character. The penitential prayers of the Copts are not merely expressions of ritual impurity to be avoided by religious leaders engaged in liturgical rites. They also reveal the more basic moral discomfort of the Copts in their own world and society. They experience relief in the proper enactment of the prescribed prayers and liturgies, especially those which implore divine mercy. For the Copts, the re-enactments of traditional worship is a matter of great gravity; failure to do so would serve to aggravate human discomfort with divine proximity.

The application of the word "religion," derived from the Latin word *re-ligere*, meaning "to execute painstakingly and by repeated efforts" (De Waal Malefijt 1968:20), may be found in the Coptic ritual. Throughout the liturgy, references are made to the unworthiness of the assembly to implore God's mercy and blessing. On numerous occasions, supplications are made to revered saints and ancestors to join their prayers to that of the assembly. The Copts believe that God will not dismiss or grow angry at feeble prayers which have become the agenda of those he favors.

The ability of the Copts to shift the burden of their moral discomfort with the proximity of God and His Holiness onto the shoulders of accomplished spirituals of the past greatly enhances their ready reliance on professional religious of the present (Doorn-Harder 1995: 183). This ability marks a profound and essential shift from the theological to the social realm. The Copts maintain a posture of spiritual tension with God which corresponds to the interrelations of segments within their own society. Their spiritual vision and its embodiment in prayer forms, center them around a class of religious experts and spiritual symbols.

The title *labesa saleeb*[1] ("cross-bearer"), given to their monks by the Copts, has several references in the liturgy. The vicarious atonement of Christ's Cross is a well-known theme of sacrifice in Christianity. The sense of Coptic ritual is that the ascetic sacrifices of the monks are redemptive for the Copts in general. Asceticism may be theologically efficacious only because it is linked to Christ's Cross, but the monks' sacrifices also contribute effectively to overcoming the social discomfort experienced by lay Copts living in a world overwhelmed by the holy while governed by the infidel.

The moral distress of the Copts is a force which binds them to a heritage of saintly ancestors and heavenly intercessors, as well as to desert ascetics (Doorn-Harder 1995:155). This distress promotes conservatism with regard to ritual activities, and enhances the role of ritual specialists who know how to properly enact the liturgies so that they diminish the tension of a mundane society visited by divine agencies. The moral distress of the Copts is a sense of impurity common to many religions, but it is extended here to the general social sphere of ethics and personal integrity.

The overlapping of the categories of moral rectitude and ritual purity is visible at many points in Coptic worship; for instance, it is found in the prayer calling for the absolution of the mother of a child to be baptized:

> O Lord, God Almighty, the Creator of the ages, He who ordered his servant Moses in the Law, and taught him the laws of purification to be observed by all confined women, to remain some few days without being permitted to touch hallowed things or even to come near to the holy places . . . we ask and entreat Thee, for this Thy handmaiden, she who has observed Thy law and kept Thy Commandments, and desires to enter into Thy Sanctuary, longing to partake of Thy Life-giving Mysteries. . . . Bless Thy handmaiden, purify her, absolve her from every defilement and impurity. Let her be pure in her soul, body, and spirit. Let her be set free from every blamableness, and from all her old works. Forgive all her iniquities. Let her be worthy of the fellowship of Thy Holy Mysteries without falling into condemnation (Gregorius 1975:22).

The text presents a striking spectrum of sentiments. The woman to be blessed is deemed to be observant of God's law and commands by virtue of her maternity. She is introduced as a person subjected to ritual impurity by reason of her exposure to blood in the delivery process, but then she is absolved of blame for sinful works and "iniquities" and prayed for because of her moral failures.

Women hold positions in paradoxical relationships, much as do the Copts. The Copts are marginal inhabitants of a land where they are deeply indigenous. They are economically and educationally advantaged, but politically handicapped and socially endangered. They are citizens of Egypt, but unable to support the popular Arab-Islamic form of patriotism. They are Christians in the apostolic tradition, but unable to assert a solidarity with similar Western Churches.

Women in Egypt, and also cross-culturally, provide the basis of human bodily genesis, personality formation and cultural transmission, yet find themselves unable to attain meaningful roles in political, economic, and intellectual activities. They are regarded as relationally gifted, but they are often organizationally isolated. They are committed to the stability and progress of their society, but are regularly deprived of the means of securing such ends. They share many basic, common needs and aspirations from nation to nation, but are generally unable to draw upon the strength of their own consensus. Subcultures and minority peoples, like the Copts, often endure a status which is "feminized" vis-a-vis the dominant culture.

Living under such pressure obliterates all sensible distinctions between moral fault, ritual impurity, inherited prejudice, the natural opposition to subcultures, bad luck and poor strategy. The Coptic religion intuits just this state of affairs in its self-understanding. The only means of relief is in the midst of the ritual supplications of the Church, the only institution which embodies the paradoxes of Coptic society as well as the women within it. The symbolic reinforcing of this institution is the one societal act allowed the Copts. The desert monks loom large in this effort.

The Validation of Worship

In spite of the formality of their devotional activity, the Copts regard their own prayers and the religious exercises of the monks, that is, their supplications, rituals and sacrifices, as profound interrelational acts among the believers themselves. More explicitly, the relationship is between the transcendent and the earthly order which is subordinated to the Christian God. The Copts regard their worship as deeply interactive and the worship of others as mechanistic. This criticism is not unusual for Christians, nor even for religious leaders.

Hebrew prophets indicted ancient Israel for hollow ritualistic display, while Israel criticized the religious shallowness of the nations round about them. Jesus chastised the Pharisees for excessive formalism, and Paul challenged the Jews for empty legalism. Protestants repudiate alleged Catholic "paganism," while Catholics reject biblical fundamentalism. Moslems reject Christian sacramentalism as quasi-magical while the Copts consider Moslems as intimidating absolutists. The tendency to define the character of one religion in reference to the supposed decadence of another is pervasive. Anthropologists may be no less guilty of this behavior than others, sometimes ascribing "religion" to state-level societies, and "magic" to tribal groups (Douglas 1978:22).

Coptic worship and sacrifice are not perceived as generic religious exercises, but are intimately enmeshed in Coptic culture. Their worship bears the stamp of a highly stylized religious perspective and is conditioned by the omnipresent specter of the Cross in Coptic life and belief. This does not preclude the probability that Coptic cult activity has great implied religious significance, but these symbolic functions are subordinate to its primary orientation to the Cross, and are often interrelated with it.

For the Copts, as for other Christians, although with varying emphasis and degree, the moral tension between God's perfection and human limitations and moral fault came to a head in the human Incarnation of God. The advent of Christ, of course, has many joyful aspects, but it forever traumatized humanity with the presence of a God who looks directly across into human faces, rather than simply down at them from far above. One may hear an echo of the terror of God's proximity in the Coptic view, for it encompasses and overwhelms even Christ's perfect humanity in its wake. Even if the humanity of Christ, perhaps by its moral purity, could endure being conjoined with divinity, how could sinful humanity endure God's complete immanence?

The Copts have faced national absorption and ethnic suppression since well before the Christian era. Forces of history, economics and politics have burdened and threatened them with great intensity and consistency. The religious mind would not have to meditate too long to feel the pressure of God in this struggle. The alienation of the

Copts in Egypt through the ages is the social theme most frequently commented upon by outside observers. Alienation and anxiety are precisely what Coptic Christianity expresses in terms of God's overwhelming proximity.

A structural interpretation of Coptic survival might see the genius of their religion in the substitution of a negative value of ethnic submergence by a hostile majority with the positive value of being overwhelmed by a perfect, all-powerful God. The translation of the social despair generated by the former into the spiritual anguish of the latter permits momentary release and a new opportunity for ethnic reinforcement in the monastic presence. The Copts, as well as the Moslems, are left to wonder how the social pressures which could have disintegrated them have failed to do so. The intended message is that God has saved his people because of those who came to him in supplication, especially the desert ascetics.

God's saving work of his suppliant people is expressed almost exclusively in terms of the Christian Cross. The affront of human sin to God's perfection is deemed so serious that violence must result. Ordinarily, this violence might be expected to take the form of retribution, or even apocalyptic wrath. Human suffering, persecution, sickness, accident, disaster, or death would result.

The Copts, therefore, have a ready response to any suffering, injustice or adversity. "We deserve it, and much worse besides," a Coptic housewife and pilgrim laments. "Even the smallest sin of ours is an absolute offense!" She understands that the juxtaposition of infinite perfection with flawed humanity makes every human sin, no matter how slight, appear with infinite gravity before God. In justice, God could thereby visit such a one with immeasurable punishment. How much more so, then, the "great sinners" described in Coptic worship? The fact that Coptic suffering is relatively measured rather than apocalyptic, is evidence of divine forbearance and mercy. If this analysis seems somewhat harsh to Westerners, it must be kept in mind that, for many traditional peoples, suffering injustices and adversities without a metaphysical purpose, however undefined, is generally even more dehumanizing to endure.

For the Copts, a zone of practical, or at least symbolic safety has been created for that part of humanity which is faithful, for Christ reversed the directional flow of violence which divine immanence evoked. Christ absorbed the violence into himself on the Cross, becoming a sacrifice for his people. Penance, petition, asceticism, sacrifice and supplication place the Copts in that zone of sacrificial safety. The degree to which the Copts experience external harm is the degree to which they must examine themselves for straying into unsafe areas of retribution.

Coptic Liturgy

The Liturgy of Coptic worship, the Kodes, like the Catholic Mass, is regarded as the re-presentation of the sacrifice of Christ on the Cross. As in most ritual settings (though not in many Protestant churches), the prayer and gestures of the presider and the worship of the assembly transcend secular time sequences, and place the community back in the timeless area of divine epiphanies (Grimes 1982:44-45). The divine epiphany re-presented in the Kodes is the Passion and Cross of Christ. The Communion of the Kodes carries the Copts through a divinely endorsed ritual medium into the mystery of Christ's sacrifice, into the zone of safety wherein the violence marked out for humanity was absorbed by the God-man. Like their European Orthodox and Catholic counterparts, the Copts revere the bread and wine of their ritual sacrifice as the actual body and blood of Christ in his timeless sacrifice.

The Kodes is more than a communal meditation on a salutary event which confirms Coptic social values. The ritual is a generative event of Coptic culture, for it translates disintegrating and chaotic tensions into a meaningful and ennobling, although stressful, social challenge. This broader function of ritual which makes it more compatible with present social concerns, has a broad philosophical rationale. Victor Turner sees that, in simple terms, a society is not a static reality which can merely be "preserved" by the reinforcement of certain ideals, some of which are ritually endorsed. Rather, society is a process unfinished which proceeds from the affirmation of certain values and the enactments of certain rituals (Turner 1974:24).

Peter Berger may also have been driving at this more dynamic view of religion and religious rites when he states that religion is:

> . . . the establishment, through human activity, of an all-embracing sacred order, that is, of a sacred cosmos that will be capable of maintaining itself in the ever-present face of chaos. Every human society, however legitimated, must maintain its solidarity in the face of chaos. . . . The world of sacred order, by virtue of being an ongoing human production, is ongoingly confronted with the disordering forces of human existence in time. The precariousness of every such world is revealed each time men forget or doubt the reality defining affirmations, each time they dream reality-denying dreams of "madness," and most importantly, each time they consciously encounter death. Every human society is, in the last resort, men banded together in the face of death. The power of religion depends, in the last resort, upon the credibility of the banners it puts in the hands of men as they stand before death, or more accurately, as they walk, inevitably, toward it (Berger 1967:51-52).

The death-dealing, disordering forces which confront the Copts collectively are, and have long been, far more threatening than the challenges faced by most societies. Special adaptive behavior and institutions have been required of the Copts in response to their stressful social setting. Monasticism is a special aspect of that response.

A basic point emerges that ritual is a force which resolves the complicated problems embedded in the burden of Coptic social life. The Coptic Kodes is a sacrificial rite in Egypt which bloodlessly re-presents Christ's bloody sacrifice on the Cross. The substitution of this bloodless rite for a bloody death both conceals and reveals another subtle substitution operative in the Coptic religion. Great unresolvable problems which could easily lead to social disintegration find resolution in their rituals. The problems in both cases remain, but by rerouting the social problems into a divine matrix--a substitution which carries at least proportional anxiety--the Copts can momentarily diffuse the resultant tensions by faithfully and properly entreating God. The highest form of the latter act is the Kodes whose ritual fulcrum is the Cross.

The Kodes, however, is hardly the only lever operating on the fulcrum of the cruciform. The Copts perform other sacrificial functions based upon the same Christological dynamic such as the intensity and duration of their fasts. They consider themselves purified by entering Christ's paschal desolation by self-denial. They disdain the "fasting" habits of Egypt's Moslems who, in Ramadan, actually increase their ingestion of food several-fold, though it is all eaten after sundown. The Cross makes the Copts capable, they quietly assert, of "*real* sacrifice." The absence of the Cross, they maintain, impoverishes Islamic attempts at sacrifice, making the great daytime Muslim "fast" a nocturnal feast.

Along with fasting, many married Copts practice sexual abstinence during the fasting days and seasons. These fasts include an Advent of more than forty days, a Lent of over fifty days (including Holy Week), a several-weeks fast for the feasts of Saints Peter and Paul, and a long August fast for St. Mary. Additionally, the Copts fast every Wednesday and Friday (except in the few weeks following Easter) and have many other fast days as well.

Islamic family size in Egypt is generally larger than that of the Christians, owing to the Muslim practice of polygamy and divorce, while Christian family stability, urban preference, and professional occupation are most often cited as reasons for the relatively smaller family size of the Copts (Chitham 1986:78). The Copts, however, often claim that their sacrificial abstinence from sexual relations is a contributory cause. Nothing prevents social and religious traditions from mutually reinforcing each other, even as temporal and ideological forces may work in parallel fashion (Rappaport 1971:68-69).

The amount of sexual abstinence required of the Copt, it should be noted, is fairly extensive. Christ, who is believed by the Copts to have been a lifelong celibate, is held to have been completely deprived of human solace in his Crucifixion. This state of desolation is symbolically relived by the Copts when they abstain from sexual activity as well as food on fast days.

The Coptic Liturgy itself has an added sacrificial aspect well-known to the assembly, that is, the duration of the Kodes. The ritual commonly lasts over three hours; most of it is prayed standing. Thick incense smoke and the interminable droning of quarter-tone chant permeate the Kodes during the entire service. The discomfort of standing, inhaling smoke, and being subjected to the incomprehensible Coptic chant is often increased by liturgical "extras" on feast days, which can extend the Liturgy an hour or more beyond its normal length.

Moreover, the Copts must fast the entire day prior to attending the Kodes, so they often lack sufficient strength to worship well. Coptic baptisms, weddings and funerals, as well as major feasts, all entail very long rituals. In all of this, the Copt may only comment that Christ endured many hours of suffering, and his people must be willing to do the same in union with him. The "Week of Suffering," which corresponds to Holy Week in the West, is intended to be a moment-by-moment journey with Christ en route to his Cross. The Copts may spend eight, ten, twelve, or more hours a day in church during this period. Their monks certainly do.

Monastic Prayer and Sacrifice

Perhaps the most significant cultural and sociological example of sacrifice for the Copts is monasticism. The manner in which a monk and a monastery interacts with Coptic society and the manner in which the ideal of monasticism operates in Coptic culture reveal a mode of sacrifice which requires special consideration. Not merely does a monk live a sacrificial life as his vocation, but for the Copts, the monk literally *is* a sacrifice. His asceticism, isolation and prayer designate him as one who is separated from society as an offering to God, an offering permitted and even endorsed by the society he appears to repudiate, precisely because he becomes an offering for its salvation. A monk diffuses the explosive violence implicit in the immanence of God in human society and vents the communal frustration of his ethnic Church by his silent, yet eloquent, rejection of the structures of the non-Coptic economy and society.

The relationship of sacrifice to the economic systems of a society is not new to anthropologists, especially when economy is understood in its larger social context, and not merely as a formal system of markets.

Raymond Firth makes an important equation between the apparent material loss in sacrifice and its clear social and symbolic gain.

> Situations continually tend to arise, then, in which some sacrifice of economic benefits is judged necessary to maintain or raise one's social status, or to help give reality to social ideals which one thinks are important (Firth 1961:153).

Although he does not consider asceticism or monasticism in this context, the equation can be extended to this type of sacrifice as well. The monk raises his social position and gives reality to social ideals by his ascetical behavior. This extension of the analysis of ritual sacrifice to sacrificial life styles appears to be productive, if not novel. Monasticism may, indeed, be the maximization of the sacrificial principles outlined by Firth.

In one sense, nothing is novel in the view of monasticism as an agency of (usually) bloodless human sacrifice. Sympathetic religionists have so often praised the institution for its sacrificial aspect that the description has become standard devotional use. The French medievalist, Georges Duby, makes the following commentary on Western monasticism which applies equally well to its Coptic counterpart:

> A society that attributed so much value to set formulas and gestures and lived in constant apprehension of the unseen world, needed rites to still its ghostly fears and to make its peace with the supernatural powers; it called for sacraments and, therefore, priests. Still more necessary seemed the duty to "pray without ceasing." These prayers took the form of liturgical chants rising in clouds of incense towards the throne of God, sounding His praises and entreating His mercy. Hence the need for monks.
>
> Their primary function was to pray for the community as a whole. For at that time, the individual did not count; he was a mere unit in a group, all personal initiatives were merged completely into the activities and collective obligations of the community. Just as the vengeance of a family was a joint enterprise in which all its members took part and reprisals were directed not only against the offender but also against all his kinsmen, so the whole body of believers felt responsible, in God's eyes, for the acts of each of its members; tainted by the crime that one of them committed, purified by the holiness of others. For most

> men saw themselves as too paltry or too ignorant to attain
> salvation by unaided efforts.   Rather, they hoped to win
> redemption by a sacrifice performed by others. . . . The agents
> of this communal redemption were the monks (Duby 1967:131).

Duby's assessment of medieval collectivism over the individual and
this connection with the blood feud lacks refinement, but variations
of such communities are hardly restricted to medieval Europe. Even
today, they are common to Coptic society and to much of Egypt.
Blood feuds are an integral part of the kinship system in Upper Egypt
even in modern times. But the placement of monasticism in a setting
of the dread of the divine proximity is insightful, and it offers a real
understanding of its sacrificial spirit. Further, the burden which the
divine immanence represents is a paradoxical symbol for all of the
vicissitudes which beset the Copts from beyond the boundaries of
their social whole. Hence, the sacrifice which the monks embody
grants the Copts a certain sense of having communally overcome their
alienation with God and his world.

There is a formidable body of casual, Western, post-Reformational
opinion which holds that a monk is a supreme individualist, interested
in no more than the salvation of his own soul or the perfection of his
own life (Workman 1913:23). This view would seem to be a popular
modern notion, and perhaps even more properly ascribed to the
Orthodox Churches of the East which do not exhibit the same kind
of cenobitic ideal or institutional centralism as the Western Church.
But such a notion is at odds with the sacrificial role of monasticism.

As Hubert and Mauss described it, the nature of sacrifice is to first
separate that which is to be offered and the one who offers it from
their mundane associations (cf. 1964:19-20,29). The individualism so
apparent in monasticism, therefore, serves as a testament to the radical
separation from mundane social contacts which any sacrificial life
must exhibit. After the monk separates himself from the world, it is
of considerably less social interest whether he joins a community of
monks in their collective self-offering, or remains an island of self-
immolation.

Michael Foucault accepted the premise that monastic asceticism
was genuinely sacrificial, and distinguished traditional Christian reli-

gion from that of other sacrificial religions (1988:35). Of course, Christian sacrifice is always predicated in terms of the Christian "Paschal Mysteries." Hence, ascetical sacrifices are atoning, by extension, as acts conjoined to the redemptive suffering of Christ.

Now, an anthropological analysis of a religion and its institutions, while it must be informed by that religion's views of itself, must not simply interpret that view as the essence of the religion. Monks may well be serving critical functions sociologically and spiritually, but society does not usually extol their efforts by analytical prose. In Egypt, the monk's role is ritually highlighted but, in other places, he may serve a vital, but silent, place-holding role in a non-sacramental system. Nevertheless, he will always be conspicuous by his prominence, or his anonymity, for the place he holds is beyond the claim of others charged with symbolic credibility. His life is endlessly fascinating. Hence, even if a monk were deluded into thinking that his was a solitary life without social implication or consequence, he would still be caught up in serving a sociological function whose dimensions are beyond his understanding.

Stark has attempted to describe the role of the monk along these lines. To that end, he translates Wurmseer (1924:108-109) as follows:

> Any conception of the monk . . . which sees in him merely a man devoted to personal sanctification, is too narrow; indeed, it fails to appreciate the deepest significance of monasticism and could hardly yield as much as a bare justification of its existence. . . . Now, religious man has always tried to please and pacify Almighty God by sacrifice: such were the firstlings of Abel's flock which were found acceptable on high. But even lambs are only possessions, only things, something which man can surrender without too much pain to himself. Yet he has something better to offer up than that: his own *self*, and that too he owes and should give entirely to God. For ordinary man this is difficult, if not impossible, for he is absorbed in the struggle of survival and cannot totally devote himself to penance and prayer. But it is different with the human race as a whole. The human race as a whole has the possibility of laying before God a much more appropriate symbol of its devotion by surrendering the secular services of some of its members, especially their participation in the procreation of offspring and in the production of

commodities, and by therefore separating them off from the rest and dedicating them exclusively to the immediate service of God. . . . We find in the end that the God-given mission of monasticism is the fulfillment of the sacrificial duty of humanity as a whole. *The meaning of monkhood is to be humanity's sacrificial offering*, a sacrifice in the name of humanity and for the sake of humanity, with all the purposes which sacrifice in its widest connotation subserves . . . above all, expiation (Stark 1970: 224-25).

Stark's translation of Wurmseer's insights are helpful to the present discussion on several levels, but, first, a certain premise must be understood. The human race as a whole may well be intended as a spiritual beneficiary of monastic oblation, but, sociologically speaking, the only people who can be affected by the benefits of a monastic vocation are the ones who belong to the culture from which the monks derive. In those smaller human subsets of societies which share a common cultural view, the monk may occupy a place which grants him a functional impact, even on those in that society which remain practically indifferent or even morally hostile to monasticism.

Democratic investigations into the nature of religion often fail to discover its primary operations precisely because most individual practioners may not be able to explicitly express their religious views or entirely explain their religious actions. The theoretical expressions of a religion reside in the interrelations of religiously acting peoples and, somewhat more fully, often only in the minds of religious specialists who operate on the intersections of these interrelations.

Wurmseer's insight into the universal spiritual function of monasticism seems better understood as its sociological function *within* particular societies. Each society with monastic institutions would tend to impart to these institutions the properties in their nature which reflect the formation process of that society's history and present conditions. Coptic monasteries are formed, not out of the response to a universal monastic ideal, but in relation to the particular features of Coptic experience. Hence, when Wurmseer notes that the "struggle to survive" in the secular world is antithetic to the democratic exercise of sacrifice and is, therefore, antecedent to the self- sacrifice of the religious specialist, he offers a clue as to how the Copts' struggle for survival for almost two thousand years is a precursor and conditioning factor in the genesis and maintenance of Coptic monas-ticism and monastic sacrifice. The chapter on Coptic monastic history corroborates this view.

Even before the advent of Christianity, the Copts had already become a people long associated with living in ethnic servitude and suffering. It seems quite natural that they should eventually generate a class of people to shoulder the moral burden of their ethnic alienation. By the symbolic potency of the sacrifice of that class, the ethnic burden would be spiritually transformed from an external social threat to transcendent social affirmation. If the Copts must suffer at the hands of their occupiers, their sacrifice is turned by the monks, and by the sacrificial dynamic which the monks embody, into an engagement with the terrible and immanent God. The ground of that engagement is suffering; its axis is the Cross.

Wurmseer noted the inferiority of animal sacrifice. The sacrifice of lambs is, after all, not very painful for the people who offer it. Inferred is the idea that sacrifice requires pain in order to be efficacious (Stark 1970:224). In this inference, we come close to the assertion by Girard that sacrifice must be thought of precisely in terms of the fascination which its necessary violation always evokes (1977:2).

Human sacrifice is more painful and its violence more riveting, more capable of centralizing itself, in the religious mind. While monasticism often lacks great overt violence in its human sacrifice, Wurmseer regards the deprivation of sex as a violation of a monk's natural humanity. More than this, monastic asceticism has celebrated accounts of monks who "went too far" in their self-mortification. No Church has collected more illustrations of this phenomenon than that of the Copts. So-called "excessive" acts of asceticism are the proper lore of monasticism, sociologically speaking. Unnatural fasts, sleeplessness, self-flagellation, exposure and self-mutilation are only some of the more graphic activities with which hagiographically rounds out the sacrificial image of abstemious monks--at least in Egypt, and perhaps in an earlier Western epoch as well.

The discussion above has so far treated the role of the monk as a sacrificial offering only on a theoretical level. Abundant ethnographic data verifies this designation as certain linguistic evidence will show.

The most frequently used term to denote a monk in colloquial

Egyptian Arabic is "raheb," which has the literal meaning of "one who dreads." It is tempting to interpret this word in terms of the Christian-Islamic virtue of the "fear of God," and to see the monk as one who stands in awe of God's power or goodness. But while such a fear of God is esteemed in Egypt, "raheb" has a different connotation. The nature of the dread implied by "raheb" is that which anticipates violence. It is a consuming expectation. One who dreads in this fashion feels overwhelmed by danger. Yet, the danger of God's all-too-close proximity is precisely the feature of Coptic religion which has been suggested to be the ground for the existence of monks. The monk bears the brunt of the danger of God's immanence. He faces God first in the desert as a kind of moral lightening rod. His life is sacrificed to this danger so that the rest of the community will find God's indignation deflected.

Sometimes the greatest dangers said to face a monk in the desert are not from God, but from the devil. Hagiographical accounts of desert monasticism are filled with references to monastic combat with evil (cf. Mohler 1971). Modern commentators tend to regard these battles solely in terms of the individual monk's projections of sexual or psychic restlessness (Mohler 1971:20). Frequently, these encounters with evil are quite violent to person and property. It is also possible to suggest a sociological function of monastic encounters with violent demons.

Girard notes that violence is an inherently ambivalent reality for humans, especially on the social level (cf. 1977:52,58). Violence left unfocused can disintegrate a community. However, when focused on a sacrificial victim, it can discharge a community's dangerous levels of tensions and actually consolidate its internal bonds. Monastic sacrifice in Egypt accomplishes this on two paradoxical levels, by absorbing the danger of divine immanence and by battling with demonic powers. Both acts are the expression, or social construction, of the monks' primary functions: (1) to symbolically transcend and, therefore, to diminish the threat of external pressures upon the Copts; and (2), to avail the Copts of the benign aspect of divine immanence by addressing God in his moral absolute perfection. Both tasks, each at seeming odds with the other, are paradoxically conjoined into the sacrificial act of monasticism. Rituals and symbols, in their many levels of meaning, can do what single concepts and words cannot.

On the sociological level, the demonic powers with which the monk does combat derive much of their threat from Coptic ethnic insecurity and anxiety about outside persecution. Such collective insecurity readily translates into personal crises and domestic tension. The student suspects she has been awarded a lower grade than she deserves because she is a Christian; the government clerk is passed over for promotion because he is a Copt; the housewife whose television show is interrupted regularly for Islamic prayer is reminded that Egypt is an Arab-Islamic country; the wife who has just argued with her husband about family matters hears him threaten to become a Moslem in order to divorce her. Broad collective alienation shows a threatening face to individual Copts who encounter personal demons. Monks who flee to the desert transcend powers which cannot be broken in the Delta. Their ascetical lives further serve to prevent this power from spiritually breaking the Copts. Hence, they do combat.

External social institutions, foreign values and religions, political movements and economic trends have been unkind to the Copts since the inception of Christianity into the region. The genesis of monasticism cannot be understood in a sociological framework without reference to this ethnic concern. In fact, the Copts are largely unable to effect a reversal of their plight. Incredibly, after a thousand years and more, a Coptic sense of helplessness has not effected the dissolution of the group. Monasticism may be partly credited with this feat. The monk has done battle with the demons of ethnic helplessness, even if he could not exorcise their external material progenitors. Pope Shenouda states:

When saints are fought, their power is revealed and they conquer; but sinners are defeated. . . . However, God may allow sometimes that saints be defeated--temporarily--for their own benefit. . . .

Indeed, how frightful are the words of Revelation about the beast: ". . . and it was given unto him to make war with the saints and to overcome them. . . ." (13:7). And how frightful is what follows: . . . *and power was given him over all kindreds and tongues and nations, and all that dwell upon the earth shall worship him* (Revelation 13:7,8).

However, lest some would despair, it is stated that those
worshippers are those whose names are not written in the book
of life since the establishment of the world . . . that is, the sons
of perdition . . . though they are undoubtedly abundant, a matter
which shows the severity of the wars of the devil and his power.
. . . We are comforted in this respect by the statement that the
beast and the devil were cast into the lake of fire and brimstone
(Shenouda III 1989:18-19).

Pope Shenouda perceives that "wars" by "worshippers" of the beast
may thwart the Church, and that the devil may temporarily subdue
the devout monk, but God has the final word wherein justice will be
satisfied. Pope Shenouda thereby equates communal stress under a
hostile majority to the personal struggles of the diligent monk.

Of course, the Copts do not explain their religious views in the
categories supplied by Emile Durkheim nor any other social scientist.
For them, the demons are real spiritual foes who seek the ruination
of souls and the disruption of the life of the Church. Without reference to the metaphysics of the question, however, demons and the
external secular forces around the Copts have many overlapping traits.
Both phenomena are hostile to the welfare of the Copts and are
invasive of the Coptic community, attempting to break down its
family life, values, church life, peace and prosperity. Both forces are
exceedingly powerful and dangerous, and can destroy anyone who
attempts to engage them apart from the community. Each cooperates
with the other so closely that it is often hard for the Copt to tell
where one leaves off and the other begins.

Moreover, language practices among the Copts frequently portray
the enemies of the group as "demonic," "led by devils," "came from
hell" and "controlled by Satan." Concrete social realities appear to be
subsumed under spiritual categories when certain levels of helplessness
are reached. Random acts of unfocused rage are more than symbolic
in their value to the terrorist. They are sacrifices which dispel the
demons spawned by helplessness under external pressures. The terrorist must be endangered by his acts, and must be prepared to be
joined to the sacrifice at any moment. Likewise, the demons fought
by the monks are not unrelated to the ones which oppress their
fellows. Their asceticism, and the love of it, has a sacrificial intent.

As previously noted, the linguistic designation of a monk in Egypt is "labesa saleeb," which means "cross bearer." The term clearly associates the monastic life with the Passion and death of Christ, the quintessential sacrifice of Christianity. The rigors of monastic life are steps along the route of Christ's Cross, taken for the salvation of those who put faith in the cross-bearer. The sacrifice of the monk, like that of Christ, need not be explained in all of its operations in order to be effective. Indeed, few Christians can actually tell precisely how the Cross has merit for believers. The mechanism of sacrificial benefit is often elusive, or even unspeakable, but it appears to operate just as well, if not better, unvoiced. As Beidelman points out, few anthropologists would debate that sacrifice lies at the very heart of religion, even if they are remarkably lacking in an understanding of how it functions (1987:548). The anthropologists are not alone, as even religion specialists cannot often explain the efficacy of religious works. Apparently, the tendency to offer sacrifice is so deeply embedded in cultural formation and social relations that it does not rely upon conscious assent to be effective.

The New Adam

The linking of the monk's sacrifice to that of Christ accomplishes something toward which ritual sacrifice tends; it ties a modern sacrificial act to a primary and timeless religious event. The Cross of Christ is the source of the Christian community, transforming all those who come under it into a new spiritual solidarity. The cross of the monk's life also serves to echo this community-building function.

The Copts continually sense a source of new blessing on their community from the ascetic practices of the monks. The ability to make a community anew is illustrated by another linguistic convention of the Copts. A monk is said to be *Adama Kadeed*, "a new Adam." The term likens the monk to Adam, the first human in Eden, before the creation of Eve. The classical term *monachos*, from which the word "monk" derives, is also used among the Copts. This term specifically connotes the state of "aloneness" typified by celibacy. For Adam, God acknowledged that "it is not good for man to be

alone," i.e., monachos. But now, in Christ, and through the blessing
of a divinely endorsed sacrificial life, a man could do well to be
monachos (alone) in the desert. A new era of society is introduced
which engenders new life--not from marital fruit--but from the fruit of
sacrificial celibacy. For this reason, the Coptic monk often refers to
the barren desert environs around his monastery as "a paradise, a new
Eden," from which a new creation springs forth.

The monk's refusal to cut his hair or beard or, in many cases,
even to bathe, is a similar assertion of the Adam-like stature he embodies. As Adam in paradise was considered to live such a perfectly
ordered life prior to the Fall that he never needed to groom or wash
himself, so the "Adama Kadeed" assumes this attitude in the "Eden"
of the desert. The curious onlooker wonders about the practical
particulars of such personal habits. Any visitor to the deir can clearly
see that the monk's simulation of the pristine condition of humanity
in paradise fosters a wildness of appearance, but fails miserably on a
basic hygienic level.

Under his black wool cap, which is never removed outdoors or in
public (no matter how severe the sun or heat may be), is the stringy,
unwashed hair which is never cut. It grows down the monk's neck
and is tucked beneath his black tunic where it grows during his entire
monastic life, ever downward to his waist. Its length is generally
mitigated only by the rate of its periodic falling out, according to the
vicissitudes of health, diet, physical pressure and age. The same is true
of his beard, but it tends to coil up into itself and mat somewhat,
especially given the heat, perspiration, and residue of food and drink
which find their way into its texture. Visually and olfactorily, this
creates an impression of great rusticity.

Although Copts, especially pilgrims to the monasteries, are very
reluctant to voice their impressions about this aspect of the appearance
of their monks, it undoubtedly figures into their sense of their charisma and symbolic role. While the laity cannot imagine living in
such a state, the monk once again demonstrates his transcendence of
the temporal world.

The monk also creates the impression that he resides in an alternative world where his physical irregularities are transformed into
spiritual benefit. Such a world is not accessible to the senses of the

uninitiated, but the plausibility of its existence is enormously increased by the ease by which the monk maintains his rustic persona. This process of transformation of negative reality into positive symbols is entirely consistent with the sacrificial role of the monk as described above.

In the monastery of Anba Samwil, the kommos assigned to an elderly monk the task of escorting this ethnographer several miles across the desert, up a treacherous mountain to the prayer cave of the ancient founder. The kommos directed us to make the journey on foot as a requirement of my status as "a pilgrim." The month was July, and a terrible heat wave held the region in temperatures over 130°F. While I nearly died (literally) from heat exhaustion, sun prostration and dehydration, all along the trek the elder monk was chanting in a barely audible voice: "Thank you, thank you, Holy Founder, St. Samwil. You came into this paradise and grew a garden in the sweet sunshine. Thank you, thank you, holy God. You let me stroll in this pleasant park wherein is all delight."

Now the monk was old, bent, and gaunt. The landscape was sweltering, blistering, and barren. The comfort level of other pilgrims at the monastery was also nil; indeed, the excessive heat resulted in real medical problems. Yet the prayer-chant of the old monk indicates the assimilation of an altogether different perspective of the world. He had within himself the means of a perceptual transformation of reality. When the heat is actually high enough, such an alternative perspective becomes more persuasive than when desert conditions are more normative. Moreover, it should be recalled that since, in one manner or another, the Copts live with the "heat" of their minority status continuously, the cultural value of the role of the monks is all the more appreciated.[2]

Chapter X

Transcendence of Time and Space

As the sacrificial victim of his society, the Coptic monk is separated from mundane associations in order to better mediate the moral chasm between an all-too-immanent, but perfect God, and an all-too-corrupt, but aspiring people. In this middle distance between God and the ethnic folk, the monk is immolated through asceticism and, at the same time, he overcomes the evil forces which threaten the welfare of his Church-community. All this occurs on a sacred plane, which is to say that on one level it is hidden, and on another it is on a stage. It is hidden because the monk's life is private, remote, unattached and silent; it is on a stage because it is in the desert that this takes place.

The monk's isolation from worldly entanglements in Egypt is both geographic and temporal, that is, it spans both time and space. On the temporal level, the Coptic monastery follows an entirely different calendar from that of the secular society of Egypt or, for that matter, the Islamic and Western worlds. Thousands of years before Christ, pharaonic Egyptians had calculated a solar calendar of 365 days, constructed of twelve thirty-day months, and one so-called "small month" of five days. These calculations were based upon the relationship of solar and stellar activity (sidereal calculations) and the seasonal variations in Egypt (Matta el-Meskeen 1988:3-4). The seasonal variations involved in crafting the ancient pharaonic calendar were the flood cycles of the Nile and the agrarian life of the fellaheen. The calendar was divided into three, rather than four seasons.

The Coptic Church inherited this calendar and employs it for her liturgical year. The major feasts of Christmas, the Epiphany, and any number of saints' festivals are fixed on the ancient Nilotic calendar, and then translated onto calendars of more ordinary, popular usage. The monks, however, live entirely within the ancient calendar by which they reckon their days throughout the year.

As noted above, the Coptic calendar does not consider the "Christian Era," beginning with the supposed date of Christ's birth, as the beginning of the present dispensation of time. The concept of "B.C." or "A.D." is not grounded in the Coptic system of temporal measurement. Rather, the Copts reckon their time to begin with the year memorialized by their greatest historical martyrdom. Under the Roman Emperor Diocletian in the Latin calendar year A.D. 284, the Copts were brutally suppressed by imperial legions for their ethnic aspirations which were contrary to Roman colonial governance. Since the Copts conjoined their new-found Christian religion to their ethnic resurgence, they interpret this military suppression as religious persecution. The outpouring of blood ushered in a new consciousness of ethnic victimhood, and inaugurated the calendar which is specifically Coptic: "A.M." (*Anno Martyrium*, the Year of the Martyrs). Since Coptic monasticism is perceived to be the linear extension of martyrdom, the life of the Coptic monk is regarded as synchronized to the dispensation of sacred time in Egypt.

In the monastery of St. Amoun, the kommos leads a candlelight procession of monks out of the gates of the deir every year, just before dawn on a mid-September night, according to the Western calendar. The monks proceed in the hypnotic quarter-tone chant of Coptic psalmody until they reach a place where the desert opens wide and low to the east. Minutes before the sun appears, a lone bright star rises above it, the *stit*, in the Coptic tongue. The star is Sirius of the constellation Canis Majoris, and it appears in this pre-dawn display but once a year. The Copts call the star "flood-bringer," because proximate to its rising in this conjunction, until recently, the Nile began its yearly rise until it flooded the valley and delta lands with its life-giving water and rich alluvial mud.

As stit appears, the monks intone the *owshia*, the special liturgical prayer which distinguishes each of the three Coptic seasons. A new Coptic year has begun. The rising sun is incensed and the monks return joyfully to the monastery, having sanctified time for themselves and for their realm.

This para-liturgical rite is illuminating. Undoubtedly, some form of it antedates Christianity in Egypt when a pharaoh or his priest might have actually invoked the star and the subsequent flood. The incense and chant; the awareness of astronomical signs and their associations with Nilotic movement; the intercession for the cattle in particular--all derive from an earlier epoch long before the Aswan High Dam stilled the Nilotic waters. Early pharaonic Egypt might well have been more similar to the Nuer cattle culture of present Sudan than to the agrarian society of ancient Mesopotamia. Indeed, the oldest Egyptian mythological figures are more animal-like than human, and cows were figured therein with remarkable prominence (cf. McKinnon 1995; cf. Evans-Prichard 1940).

The calendar of the ancient Egyptians begins each year with ritual recognition in the Coptic Church and, in particular, in the monasteries. On the one hand, this special demarcation of sacred time separates the monk from secular time; he is always out of sync with the notations of days and months which are everywhere else employed. Even the average Copt only knows the transcribed dates of the Church's feasts; it is thought too difficult for him to keep track of two concurrent calendars. On the other hand, the Coptic calendar used by the monks is arcane, not because it is radically foreign to the Copts, but because it is so deeply buried in the depths of their heritage. This calendar separates the monk in time from his society, but it also embeds him in the timeless rhythm of its culture. Moreover, the desert locale of the monk's intercession seems spatially far removed from the agrarian realities of river-valley and delta life. But the content and formality of monastic prayer is often Nilotic in orientation and timing. This, too, reinforces the sense that the monk is somehow closer to the heart of the people precisely because he has fled to their margins.

Near the end of October, forty days after the New Year has begun, the flood waters ordinarily begin to subside.[1] The prayers of the Church turn to concerns about vegetation. Likewise, from the third week of January to mid-June, alternative prayers are chanted for the coming of seasonable winds, not so strong as to damage crops, but constant enough to assist pollenization and fruitfulness.

The seasons of the liturgical year situate even the most remote desert monk in the sacred timeliness of his people. He is reminded of the rhythm of their lives, even when the desert would otherwise obscure the seasons. His prayers are always turned to their needs, "the poor, the widow, the orphan, the stranger, the visitor, and for us all" (Abdel-Massih, Melika & Michail 1982:54). Indeed, the monastic vocation cannot simply become a private life of personal sanctification; it is essential to the processes of communal healing and redemption.

The months of the Coptic calendar which underlie the three seasons of the Egyptian year are as follows:

1.	*Tut*	September 11 (New Year's) to October 10.
2.	*Babah*	October 11 to November 9.
3.	*Hatur*	November 10 to December 9.
4.	*Kihak*	December 10 to January 8. (Includes the Advent season and Christmas.)
5.	*Tubah*	January 9 to February 7.
6.	*Amshir*	February 8 to March 9. (Lent always begins in this month.)
7.	*Barmahat*	March 10 to April 8. (Easter falls in this month.)
8.	*Barmudah*	April 9 to May 8.
9.	*Bashons*	May 9 to June 7.
10.	*Baunah*	June 8 to July 7.
11.	*Abib*	July 8 to August 6.
12.	*Masri*	August 7 to September 5. (Month of the Marian Feast.)
13.	*Nasi*[2]	September 6 to September 10.

According to the traditional calculations of a feast day, some of the Coptic holidays are immoveable, that is, fixed on specific days each year; and some are moveable, variable within a given latitude of days. The same holds true of Western Christianity where Christmas is fixed on December 25, but Easter falls on various dates in March or April from year to year. Moveable feasts are set according to lunar calendric signs, whereas immoveable feasts are set by the more invariable signs of the solar calendar.

The Coptic monks observe all the seven Major Feasts and all the seven Minor Feasts of the Coptic year as follows:

The Major Feasts

1. The Annunciation, Barmahat 29.
2. The Nativity, Kihak 8.
3. The Epiphany, Tubah 11.
4. Palm Sunday, one week before Easter.
5. Easter, moveable.
6. Ascension, forty days after Easter.
7. Pentecost, fifty days after Easter.

The Minor Feasts

1. Circumcision, Tubah 6.
2. Miracle of Cana, Tubah 13.
3. Candlemas, Amshir 8.
4. Maundy or Holy Thursday (Last Supper), Thursday before Easter.
5. St. Thomas Sunday, the Sunday following Easter.
6. Flight of the Holy Family into Egypt, Bashans 24.
7. Transfiguration, Masri 13.

Noteworthy is the fact that virtually all the feasts, major and minor, are Christological. The Annunciation, for instance, while it highlights the role of the Virgin Mary, is really the feast of Christ's conception in her womb at the visitation of the archangel. Likewise, the purpose of St. Thomas Sunday, one week after Easter, is to highlight Christ's divinity, as Thomas exclaims before the Resurrected Jesus, *"My Lord and my God!"* (John 20:28) Candlemas is the feast of the baby Jesus being brought into the temple for dedication to God as the first-born, whereupon the aged prophet Simeon exclaims: *"My eyes have seen your salvation . . . a saving light to the Gentiles"* (Luke 2:30-32). All candles used in Coptic worship are blessed on this day when the "Light" is revealed. The Epiphany is the feast of the star which draws the Magi to worship Christ. The other feasts listed above have more obvious connections to Christ, even to the post-Christian Western reader.

Additionally, seven feasts dedicated to the *"Theotokos,"* the "God-bearer" or Mother of God, are observed. These include a special annunciation of her birth which parallels the annunciation of her Son's; her nativity; her death; her assumption into heaven; and a special new feast which commemorates her recent apparitions over a Coptic church in Cairo in the 1960s. Mary's perpetual virginity is especially emphasized in all these feasts as a special means of her total dedication to God. She is thereby regarded as a favorite model of monastic holiness by the monks who celebrate her feasts.

Times Sanctified by Fasting

In conjunction with the feasts already mentioned, a number of fasts are part of the monastic regime which serves to sanctify the monks' passage through time in the monastery. Once again it should be noted that the rigorous schedule of fasts is recommended from the pulpit to all Copts, but it should be obvious that few lay Copts would actually be able or willing to sustain the whole routine. Instead, the sense of the laity that a minimal spiritual life is beyond them only increases their participation in the liturgical contrition of their Church. It fosters in them a greater respect for, and reliance on, the monks who are presumed to follow, and even well exceed, the minimal fasts as part of their intercessory mission.

First of all, in every time of fasting there is also implied a shorter time of abstinence. This means that fasting, properly speaking, simply changes and delimits the kinds of food which are eaten, whereas abstinence requires the cessation of all food or drink. For instance, on a given Friday fast, the monk fasts from all animal products all day, and abstains from all food and drink from sunset of Thursday until

3:00 p.m. on Friday, the time of the Crucifixion. Few lay Copts attempt the traditional rule of abstinence, for it applies, among many other times, to every Wednesday and Friday of the year, save during the Easter season. Manual workers, fellaheen, commuters, machine operators and busy parents all complain that such protracted abstinence weakens them, diminishes job effectiveness, and even endangers their health. "This rule was made by monks, for monks, but they keep telling us to obey it too!" one Copt complained to his parish priest. "Do what you can do," the pastor rejoined. Many take it for granted that only the relatively non-physical livelihood of the monks could sustain such abstinence.

Second, the nature of the Coptic fast is somewhat more severe than the traditional Western Catholic fast. In addition to meats, all animals products are also avoided, including fats, milk, cheese, and eggs.

Explanations for this practice are varied and overlapping. A Sunday School teacher in Tanta explained to his adolescent students that meats and other related products stimulate hormonal secretions that increase aggression and lust. (The Copts, like their Muslim counterparts in Egypt, talk of hormone levels and moral behavior often and with a great sense of surety.) A more general explanation is simply that animal products taste better and, therefore, their avoidance is a more authentic asceticism.

In the monastery of Anba Amoun, the aged anchorite explains the matter a bit more graphically: "Animals reproduce in heat and mount each other in lust. The meat we would eat is the product of their sexual urge. Now, fish reproduce outside their bodies; the meat of fish, therefore, is allowable on some fast days." The anchorite's explanation is undoubtedly widely dispersed in Coptic theological circles. Not only are various classes of animals distinguished by it, but the problematic nature of the sexual impulse is located in terms of an exercise of ritual avoidance. Coptic married couples are instructed to forego their conjugal rights during all fast days and seasons. Anecdotal evidence suggests that their low birth rates somewhat correspond with these injunctions.

The fasts that are rigorously observed in the monasteries of Egypt are as follows:

1. Every Wednesday of the year, except during the fifty days of the Easter season, because on this day (Wednesday) Judas betrayed Jesus.

2. Every Friday of the year, expect in the Easter season, because Christ died on a Friday.

3. The forty days of Lent. Lent exceeds forty days in length, but the Copts do not consider Sunday a true Lenten day inasmuch as Christ rose on a Sunday. While the monks fast during Lent, not all abstain from food in general until 3:00 p.m. on Saturday and Sunday.

4. Holy Week. The seven days prior to Easter are the most rigorous Coptic fast days. Most monks eat only bread and salt during this week, inclusive of Saturday. Such a diet does dramatically alter a sense of time, especially since the greater majority of this time is spent in liturgical exercises--standing!

5. Advent. This season is forty-three days in length, beginning on the 16th of Hatur and lasting till the 29th day of Kihak (January 7). Fish is eaten in Advent.

6. The Apostles' Fast. The duration of this fast is difficult to determine inasmuch as its beginning is calculated by a moveable feast day, Pentecost. It ends on the 5th of Abib (July 12), the Feast of Saints Peter and Paul. In general, this fast is more than a month in length.

7. Nineveh's Feast. Three days in length, this fast is a preparation for Lent, starting two weeks before. It commemorates the biblical story of Jonah who called pagan Nineveh to repent.

8. St. Mary's Fast. Fifteen days in length, this fast ends on the 16th of Masri, the Feast of the Virgin's Assumption into heaven (August 22).

9. The day before the Epiphany, the 10th of Tubah. This fast is a preparation for the blessing and the festive meal to come.

When major feasts occasionally fall on fast days (e.g., Christmas on a Wednesday), the requirement of fasting is lifted. Yet the number of fast and abstinence days may still exceed two hundred each year! Beyond this, most Coptic monks are given to various shades of vegetarianism all year long. And, of course, conjoined to the whole question of fasting is the fact of monastic lifelong celibacy. Monastic asceticism and sacrifice are oriented in time to a progression of religious mysteries, the liturgical cycle of worship. This cycle lifts the monk well out of the secular sense of time which is experienced outside the desert.

The Space of Sacrifice

Hubert and Mauss observe that sacrifice:

> . . . cannot take place at any time or anywhere. . . . The place of the ceremony must itself be sacred; outside a holy place, immolation is mere murder (1964:25).

The Coptic monk's lifelong celibacy makes him a proper candidate for sacrifice, and the Coptic calendar provides modulation and punctuations to his offering throughout the year. The monk's life of asceticism, celibacy and continuous prayer would be regarded as lunacy by the Copts if it occurred outside the desert and independently of the sacred cycle of the liturgical calendar. The body of the monk is at once the locus of the sacrifice and the agent who enacts the offering. The benefits of the sacrifice are received by that agent and through him, by the community. As already noted, Hubert and Mauss call the beneficiary of the sacrifice "the sacrifier" who:

> . . . is sometimes a collectivity--a family, a clan, a tribe, a nation, a secret society. When it is a collectivity, it may be that the group fulfills collectively the function of the sacrifier, that is, it attends the sacrifice as a body; but sometimes it delegates one of its members who acts in its stead and place (1964:10).

The desert monk is such a delegate. The desert is the place where he is set aside, and benefits for his work are bestowed on all his people.

Hubert and Mauss's classic study of sacrifice concerned chiefly Hindi and Greco-Roman cult activity, but their observations were intended to have universal application. About the sacrifier they say:

> These [priests] will progressively strip him of the temporal being that he possessed, in order to cause him to be reborn in an entirely new form. All that touches upon the gods must be divine. . . . To this end a special hut is built for him, tightly enclosed, for . . . the world of the gods is separated from that of men. He is shaved and his nails are cut, but according to the fashion of the gods--that is to say, in the opposite order to that which is usually followed among men (1964:20).

A number of other requirements of the sacrifier bear relevance to this comparison:

> He dons a brand-new linen garment, thereby indicating . . . a new existence. His head is veiled. . . . He must have no contact with men of impure caste, nor with women; . . . he must not be touched. He consumes only . . . the food of fasting . . . until his body becomes translucent. Then, *having, as it were, sacrificed his former body*, . . . he is fit to sacrifice (1964:20-21). [Italics mine.]

The associations of these treatments with the temporal and spatial characteristics of the monk in the desert are profound and numerous. The monk is "stripped of the temporal being that he possessed" by his loss of secular employment, renunciation of home and family, refusal of mate and children and his desert exile.

"All that touches upon him" is divine, as the temporal realm of the monastery is sacred calendar time. All the architecture of the monastery is suffused with religious use and sacred ornamentation and is immersed into the desert. "A special hut is built for him," inasmuch as his cell is deemed an inviolable sanctuary of meditation and solitude, and he aspires to retreat to distant caves for solitary prayer and retirement. He wears his hair and beard "according to the fashion of the gods," if not quite supernatural, then, at least according to the supposed purity of the preternatural Adam, which is "opposite to that order which is usually followed among men." By his habit "he dons a new linen garment," and "his head is veiled." By his virtue and isolation he avoids "impure" men (most especially the Moslems), as well as by his chastity he has diminished "contact with women." And of course, he consumes only "the food of fasting." Understandingly, no one else in the Coptic Church, except the monk, will accomplish the observance of *all* the fasts and abstinence, *all* year long.

Hubert and Mauss come surprisingly close to the thesis of this text when they state, almost parenthetically, that the sacrifier "having, as it were, sacrificed his own body . . . he is fit to sacrifice" (1964:21). Now, they mean that he is fit to offer up to the priest the object of sacrifice in order to enjoy its spiritual benefits. But a play on words is easy to infer: "he is fit to sacrifice" can easily mean that he is, himself, disposed to be sacrificed. This interpretation is perhaps gratuitous, except that the phrase is introduced with the notion that the body of the sacrifier has already been given to sacrifice by its thorough separation from the secular world.

Accordingly, the Copts possess a religion absolutely bound to and centered on the Cross of Christ. The symbol of human sacrifice as the place of reconciliation with God and redemption from all evil is axial to their worldview. Can they separate the sacrifier from the sacrifice in the work of their monks? Hubert and Mauss could hardly separate the two categories when analyzing more primitive sacrificial cults.

Finally, these French social science pioneers in the field of sacrifice make an additional contribution to this study. Concerning the sacrifier, which is here the monk, and also the people whom he blesses by his self-offering, they state that:

> . . . purity is required. The advent of the divinity is terrible for those that are impure; when Yahweh was about to appear on Sinai, the people had to wash their garments and remain chaste. . . . The sacrifier must fast, . . . put on clean garments, or even special ones. [There is] the "wearing of the veil," the sign of separation and consequently of consecration. . . . The "warding off of evil spirits" . . . [introduces] him step by step into the sacred world (Hubert & Mauss 1964:22).

As was explored at length above, the need for sacrifice is not in this case to make a distant deity draw near, but to make expiation to an all-too-near deity for the impurity with which he is affronted by his advent. Hubert and Mauss's grasp of this kind of sacrificial need renders their research especially useful to this work. Beyond their analysis of the sacrifier, they make analogous claims of the "sacrificer" and the victim (cf. 1964:22-45). In the act of sacrifice they maintain that:

> ... the victim, who already represents the gods [let us say here, the monk who represents Christ Crucified], comes to represent the sacrifier also. Indeed, it is not enough to say that it represents him; it is merged in him. The two personalities are fused together (Hubert & Mauss 1964:32).

For the purposes of this discussion, the monk is "fused" with the Coptic community which is thereby reconciled and redeemed by his extension of the Crucifixion in his monastic asceticism and prayer.

The body of the monk is transformed into a place of mergence. Forces converge in him which oppress the Copts: the hostility of the Islamic majority; the secularism of the West; the temptations of materialism and guilt for carnality versus the all-seeing eye of God. As sacrifier, he embodies the Coptic community. As victim, he embodies Christ Crucified. As sacrificer, he embodies the Church in all aspects of the sacrifice which are positive, and the non-Coptic oppressors in all aspects of the sacrifice which are negative. Tensions and conflicts which span a cosmos from God to the devil, from the heart of a community to the margins, are discharged in the "violence" of monastic asceticism.

A time and a place exist in the Coptic world for sacrifice. The time is liturgical, the place is the body of the monk in the desert. The desert is also the medium of sacrificial offering. Cassian of Marseilles recounts the following:

> The abbot Abraham . . . was silent for a long while, and then with a heavy sigh, at last he spoke. . . .
> "We could have built our cells in the valley of the Nile, and had water at our door, nor been driven to bring it to our mouths from three miles off. . . . We are not ignorant that in our land there are fair and secret places, where there be fruit

trees in plenty and the graciousness of gardens, and the richness of the land would give us our daily bread with very little bodily toil. . . . But we have despised all these and with them all the luxurious pleasure of the world: we have joy in this desolation, and to all delight do we prefer the dread vastness of this solitude, nor do we weigh the riches of your glebe against these bitter sands. . . . It is a little thing that a monk should have made a single renunciation, that is, in the first days of his calling to have trampled on things present, unless he persist in renouncing them daily. Up to the very end of his life the word of the Prophet must be in our mouths: '*And the day of man Thou knowest I have not desired.*' Whence the saying of the Lord in the Gospel, '*If any man will come after me, let him deny himself, and take up his cross daily, and follow me*' (Waddell 1936:224-25).

Cassian's account of Abbot Abraham recorded more than 1,500 years ago could have been spoken today by any number of contemporary desert fathers. The Copts throughout their history have avoided the systematic religious philosophizing of Western Christendom. Nevertheless, in their hagiographical accounts, maxims, catechetical instructions and anecdotes, much of the view offered above can be cited.

To Pelagius, the Western Pope in A.D. 555, came the task of translating Greek texts of the ancient desert into the vernacular of the West. The text, *Verba Seniorum*, or the *Sayings of the Elders*, supplies exemplary materials for this discussion. Regarding the burden of divine immanence, the brief vignettes below describe the Copts, and especially the monks, as being driven to constant, tearful repentance and sharp compunction:

Syncletica of holy memory said, "Sore is the toil and struggle of the unrighteous when they turn to God, and afterwards is joy ineffable. For even as with those who would kindle a fire, they first are beset with smoke, and from the pain of smoke they weep, and so they come at what they desired. Even so it is written,'Our God is a consuming fire': and needs must we kindle the divine fire in us with travail and with tears" (Waddell 1936:95).

The abbot Mathois said, "The nearer a man approaches to God
the greater sinner he sees himself to be. For the prophet Isaiah
saw God, and said that he was unclean and undone" (Waddell
1936:163).

Paschasius the Deacon has preserved certain sayings of the desert. In
one short verse he relates a sense of the power of monastic sacrifice to
transform the negative forces which converge in him to positive ones
of benefit to himself and the Church community. Moreover, by doing so, the monk overcomes evil:

> The abbot Macarius said, "If, to a monk, scorn hath become as
> praise, and poverty as riches, and hunger as feasting, he shall
> never die. For it is not possible that a man who doth rightly
> believe and doth loyally worship God, should fall into uncleanly
> passion and the error of the demons" (Waddell 1936:214).

A contemporary desert father of significant stature within and beyond
the Coptic Church is Abuna Matta el-Meskeen. The advice he gives
to his incoming novices about monastic asceticism resonates with the
hagiographical spirit:

> If you are a new monk, rejoicing in your vocation, your com-
> munity and your new life, notice that all the factors that con-
> tribute towards death of the self and self-renunciation, and help
> the gradual destruction of self-will and the passions, factors such
> as the bearing of injustice, insults and scorn, the disregard of
> your wishes, contempt for your ideas, opinions and basic needs,
> the suffering of pain and disease which you face during your
> lifetime, these very factors kindle the divine love and serve as
> fuel to a fire. The gates of the divine love are opened wide to
> the monk who intends to put to death his self and deny his own
> will, for out of the death of the self arises the power of love, for
> the Lord reveals Himself only in the hearts of those who
> surrender themselves to Him wholly and completely. *"If anyone
> would be my disciple, let him deny himself and take up his cross and
> follow Me."* (Matta el-Meskeen 1982:4)

Of the convergence of conflicting forces which meet in the ascetic
work of the monk, Abuna Matta el-Meskeen perceives not so much

demonic oppression, but the opposite, that is, an encounter with Christ:

> Hence, when a man enters into monasticism, a fierce struggle between the self and Christ begins. Far from being an open, visible or tangible conflict, it is subtle and formidable, often only perceived by man after he commits serious offenses against Christ. Then he wakes up to find that the self is actually engaged in conflict with Him, seeking to annihilate His presence and get rid of His Person altogether (Matta el-Meskeen 1982:4).

Contemporary with, and a peer of Abuna Matta el-Meskeen, is Pope Shenouda III who quotes the hagiography to the effect that monastic prayer is confrontational with devils:

> He is not comfortable as long as we have any relation with God knowing that this endangers his kingdom. Here are some wonderful words from (the Paradise of Monks), "When the bell rings in the middle of the night for prayers, *it does not only awake the monks to pray, but the devils are also aroused* to fight monks and prevent them from praying. . . ." So, St. Evagrius said, "When you begin a holy prayer, be ready for whatever may befall you."
>
> Whenever we start spiritual practices, whether prayers, contemplation, hymns, spiritual reading, or kneeling down in worship, the devil does not stand tied up or merely watching, but he also works and he has certain wars which he fights with (Shenouda III 1989:14-15).

Not so much a contradiction, but a true sense of the multi-valenced nature of sacrifice is established by these ascetical readings. Outside of the biblical tradition of sacrifice, a strong Near-Eastern tradition prevailed wherein the violence done to a sacrificial victim, or action of the offerer thereof, was perceived as the expulsion of evil (Rogerson 1980:46). Cultic lives, like ritual acts, are eloquent because they compress into one the coherent symbolic sentiments which defy the systemization of words. Religion has a grammar of which language has no knowledge (cf. Evans-Prichard in Hubert & Mauss 1964:viii). Sacrifice is its most eloquent discourse.

Chapter XI

Conclusion

The Biblical record of animal sacrifice outlined above shows a continuous development which can be interpreted by the believer as moving toward the monastic mode of ascetic sacrifice which parallels it so closely. The later Old Testament period showed marked interest in the process of humans internalizing the sacrificial intentionality into a sense of social and individual contrition. In support of this idea, J. W. Rogerson cites Psalm 51:18-19 from the translation in his copy of the Bible (1980:52):

> Do good to Zion in thy good pleasure;
> > rebuild the walls of Jerusalem,
> Then wilt thou delight in right sacrifices,
> > in burnt offerings and whole burnt offerings;
> then bulls will be offered on thy altar.

Hence, sacrifice tends to become a social and behavioral activity as much as a religious rite (Rogerson 1980:52) in which the expiational merit of sacrifice seems to be ideally preserved. The so-called "Suf-

fering Servant" of Yahweh in the Book of Isaiah clearly is typified as
a sacrificial human offering who gains pardon for his people.

> But he was pierced for our offenses,
>   crushed for our sins.
> Upon him was the chastisement that
>   makes us whole,
>   by his stripes we were healed.
>
> Through his suffering, my servant shall
>   justify many,
>   and their guilt he shall bear.
>   Isaiah 53:5,11

As discussed above, New Testament writers regard Jesus as the fulfillment of this prophecy, thus making his sacrifice central to all human
sacrificial acts. The New Testament, therefore, preserves a sense of
behavioral and social virtue predicated upon the ritual ideal of
sacrifice:

> I urge you, therefore, brothers, by the mercies of God, to offer
> your bodies as a living sacrifice, holy and pleasing to God, your
> spiritual worship.   Romans 12:1

In the chapter on the history and origins of Coptic monasticism, it
was noted that the Copts deemed the desert ascetic life as the perfect
embodiment of the biblical sacrificial mandate. Karl Rahner, one of
the great theologians of twentieth-century Catholicism, makes the following commentary on asceticism, which has much bearing on the
sacrificial role of the Coptic monk:

> [Asceticism] gives up . . . personal values such as marriage, and
> the freedom to develop one's personality by disposing of material
> possessions that make for independence.
>   Asceticism in this sense . . . cannot be deduced from the
> mere natural order. Nor does the natural law even suggest it.
> Values of intrinsic worth should not be given up in the natural
> order except under the pressure of circumstances. To give them
> up in this order would be impossible ontologically and perverse
> ethically (Rahner 1983:237).

It is a simple fact that the evangelical counsels [i.e., poverty, chastity and obedience] create new dangers. (One would be forced to draw some painful false conclusions if one wished to interpret the "heroic deeds" and "excesses" that have occurred in the history of Christianity in this way. We cannot explain the radicalism and immensity of the penance found in the lives of the saints by appealing to a motive of self-discipline; nor can it be explained by "pious folly" or "influences of a general, historical, spiritual nature" which really have nothing to do with Christianity.) . . . Christian asceticism, as an essential part of Christianity itself, must necessarily partake of the scandal of Christianity [i.e., the Cross] and its separation from the world. . . . The renunciation of values that, from an earthly point of view, are unrenounceable, is the *only possible* representation . . . for the eschatological-transcendent God. . . . The revelation of such a [renunciation] . . . is necessarily an intrusion into the isolation that the world would like to preserve; it is a rupture in which the world, even insofar as it is willed and governed by God, is reduced to a thing of only secondary importance--to something provisional, and our existential focal point is placed outside of it (Rahner 1983:238-39).

Coptic monasticism turns back the threat of forces in the world which work to make the Coptic community contingent and secondary. The sacrificial life in the monastery provides a symbolic affirmation of the Copts which is so strong that the symbol becomes absolute and the world which threatens the Copts is, itself, made provisional. Monastic sacrifice provides an experience of symbols so profound as to counterbalance the Coptic experience of ethnic desperation which is otherwise so pervasive. As Rahner states:

Asceticism, therefore, as the free sacrifice of values that should not be given up from an earthly point of view, is the only way in which our confession of the eschatological-transcendent God can "appear" in a palpable way (1983:239).

Word and logical argumentation cannot carry the weight of this message. Discursive dissuasion, on the other hand, is hardly sufficient to refute the gesture of asceticism, once it is culturally perceived.

Otherwise, the Copts could not have remained intact this many centuries in such adverse conditions.

> We should not imagine that we can fool anyone in this matter.
> [Rahner is a celibate priest.] We are carefully scrutinized. A full
> measure of asceticism will be required [of us] to win the trust of
> the modern man (Rahner 1983:240-41).

Monasticism, as the Copts practice it, then, is hardly a private life style of religious devotion. The institution has profound cultural ramifications inasmuch as it provides a compelling cultural framework in which a beleaguered people can find survival. The sacrifice of monastic asceticism, moreover, breaks the oppressive symbolic aspects of the social bondage which otherwise defeats the Copts, and provides for them a central religious value and operation by which the discordant elements of their lives are given order and meaning.

The monastic foundation of Coptic cultural life explains the remarkable pacifity of the Copts through recent decades of Islamization in Egypt, as well as the earlier epochs of minority tensions through a host of shifting regimes. But it also explains the rarest of all events in Egyptian social history: Coptic violence. For the most plausible reason for the Copts to riot, or publicly protest, is not their marginalization in civil service; it is not their denial of due process in the courts; it is not their progressive alienation from marketplace advantages. It is not the occasional looting of their shops, the burning of their churches, nor the bombing of their cars, nor even the forced conversion of their daughters "kidnapped" into mixed marriages. It is the disrespect shown to the institution of the monastery, especially at its most vulnerable symbolic core, that can release remarkably visible displays of Coptic abreaction. (The "mono" of "monastery," or "monk," infers the singleness of chaste celibacy.)

In June 2001, a popular Egyptian weekly, *Al Nabaa Al Watany*, published a libelous report alleging that a monk living in Deir el Muharraq regularly used the monastery for sexual trysts. Sexually explicit photographs accompanied the article. Coptic prelates and monastic spokesmen vigorously denied the charge that such improprieties had occurred in the monastery, and asserted that the man in question, a certain Adel Saadallah Gabriel, had been "defrocked" and expelled from el Muharraq at least five years before the alleged incidents occurred. Nevertheless, media fascination with the story and widespread reports on the consequences of the initial newspaper articles locked Egyptians, both Coptic and Muslim, into a protracted and intense focus on the story.

Coptic crowds gathered in city centers and town plazas, chanting angry demands that the newspaper (and its sister publication, *Ahker Khabar*, which also ran the story) be shut down and the editors punished. Riots broke out, leading to displays of violence, vandalism, threats and fires which required police intervention. Leading Copts, ecclesiastical, civil, and corporate, courageously spoke out to the media against the slanderous accounts. Copts took the matter to the courts with an array of high-profile and expensive lawyers. Such behavior is astonishing for the Copts who never, otherwise, risk the possibility of violent reprisals for strong public protests. However, in this case, the central icon of Coptic culture had been defaced.

Part of the power of the monastic symbol is the expected permanence of the monastic state of life. News that the former monk had been expelled from the monastery and subsequently excommunicated hardly penetrated the mythos of enduring monastic holiness. Many Copts, and presumably Moslems as well, do not temper the perception they have of monks with the possibility of their defection, yet alone their gross corruption. To ostentatiously publicize such a story strikes at the heart of the Coptic community, and tears the fabric of both Coptic and Egyptian society. Egyptian President Hosni Mubarak denounced the newspaper for failing to respect social and religious values. "We in Egypt respect the beliefs of every citizen and we have to protect the country's unity for the interests of its citizens . . . and we should never allow anyone to sew the seeds of sedition," Mubarak said during a meeting with members of his ruling party (Mubarak 2001:2). At the ensuing trial of the newspaper's editor, a lawyer representing the Copts declared that this article could have turned the Nile River into a river of blood.

The Catholic Church, especially in North America, might sympathize with the Copts in their anguish over such scandalous reports. But Western Catholicism is not in the precarious, minority position of the Orthodox Christians in Egypt. Fortunately for the Copts, the abusive behavior appeared to be somewhat safely contextualized in the end. Some punishments were meted out, and public officials sided with the Copts against sectarian abuse in the media. But the restoration of equilibrium did not occur without a flash of revelation of the otherwise secret, core value of Coptic culture: the power of monastic sacrifice in the desert.

My purpose in presenting this study will be fulfilled if the reader comes to appreciate the cultural value of monasticism in its unique expression in Coptic Egypt. The mystical, spiritual and contemplative aspects of monastic life may be compelling enough in their own right to merit exhaustive study, but the interior spirituality of a soul must be associated with the cultural context of the human person who embraces it. Anthropologists should be able to locate and describe that cultural context, and this study is one ethnographic moment in that effort.

The life of a monk may be the object of psychological analysis as well. Social scientists may ponder the emotional status of ascetics, solitaries and contemplatives. The kinds of men who become monks, and the kinds of men monks become is worthy of psychological investigation and has already been the subject of serious studies. However, this study has not emphasized individual psychological motivation, except in so far as it reveals broad communal social dynamics. Monasticism is a social segment as an institution among institutions and, indeed, for the Copts, as the heart of their institutions, it has been the primary focus here.

Historians have also treated monasticism in general, and Coptic monasticism in particular, with its own special tools of diachronic analyses. If they are ecclesiastical historians, the emergence of Coptic monasticism cannot help but be entirely contextualized by the complex theological drama which unfolded in the Patristic period. Coptic monasticism was framed by discussions of the formative ecumenical councils of the early Church, and by the hagiographical narratives which caused the emergence of monasticism in Egypt to become seminal for its pan-Christian Mediterranean expansion.

The study of Coptic monasticism in this regard is one of the most solid and imposing efforts of philological and intellectual labor in the

West. But the anthropoligical explication of monasticism, Coptic or otherwise, must be tangential to this effort. Our concern is synchronic more than diachronic; cosmological not theological, and cultural-personality, not hagiography. That is to say, we considered the monastery as a vital segment of a contemporary society, more than as the consequences of past historical forces. We explored the Coptic worldview as undergirded by its monasteries without reference to the legitimacy of its metaphysical ideology, and we reflected on the monk as a central player, more than on the religious meaning of his heroic holiness or virtue. The enormous corpus of historical data relevant to the desert fathers is for us more the object of our cultural excavation than our theological synthesis.

A work on Coptic monasticism naturally falls first into the hands of competent historians, theologians or, perhaps, pastoral psychologists for their analysis. Nevertheless, the proper context for the best appreciation of this study, anthropology, is eminently useful in laying bare a function of monastic institution and symbol which the other disciplines may well overlook. As J. Tambiah would have it, "world-renouncing" religions have enormous effects on worldly institutional processes (cf. Tambiah 1976). Monasticism, in its profound distancing from the world, especially desert monasticism as in Egypt, actually exhibits this world-renouncing, sacrificial modality which is utterly formative of, and preservative of, the Coptic culture and society.

Monastic desert separation from secular society is compounded for the Copts by the Islamic overlaying of public social life. As we have observed, the desert setting is enhanced in its cosmological function of sacrifice by its pilgrimage facility whereby the lay Copts can, in numbers, express and consolidate socially, out-of doors, their communal affiliation in the same place in which that affiliation is symbolically, powerfully, reinforced by sacrificial rites and gestures.

We considered the symbolic power of the desert setting itself, which not only removes a monk from his immediate communal context and makes him, instead, a "public" symbol for his society, but which is filled with every kind of power and ideological association for the Copt, and perhaps for most peoples cross-culturally. From the Arab bedouin to the Hebrew patriarchs, from the mountain-top visions of Mohammed to the Essenian community at Qumran; from

Amerindian vision-quests to aboriginal dream-time myths; from Hindu ascetics to Buddhist contemplatives, the desert remains the vast, empty, and mysterious place on which the potent, complex forces of cultural symbols can be projected. Here, cosmic dramas are played out, and whoever passes through it or, better yet, whoever lives in it, is the culture-affirming hero of his people.

We have seen how the monastic symbol generates the monastic persona, and orders the monastery's daily routine. The culture-affirming, sacrificial function compels the monks both to communal prayers and personal discipline, to their occasional pastoral services and even to their personal diet. A certain choreography overtakes the monks in all these regards, or, as we have said, a social "poetics." Ultimately, that poetry is most fully expressed in a liturgical regimen. Monastic prayer forms, culminating in the Coptic Kodes orients the interior life of the monk to the larger Church, and the whole monastery to Coptic society. In the last analysis, the liturgical choreography of the monk roots the monastery into the discourse hidden in the sacrificial gestures peculiar to the God the Copts worship on a Cross.

Monastic worship places the desert on a geographical continuum with Eden and the courts of heaven on one side, against the demonic temptations proximate to the gates of hell on the other. The former glories are intimated by the exercise of moral virtues (which strengthen the bonds of Coptic society) and the latter are engaged both by the moral weaknesses within and by the forces of persecution outside which undermine the integrity of Coptic society. But the monk has the capacity to animate the moral good and to exorcise the morally dubious, suitably demonized in such a way that the society he renounces is, in fact, renewed.

Epilogue

Ethiopian Monasticism

Ethiopian Christianity owes much of its formative history to Coptic monks who missionized Nilotic Africa in the early Middle Ages as Coptic Christianity spread southward through the Sudan into Ethiopia. Monastic life followed it, and monks from Ethiopia and Egypt have been in continuous communication ever since (cf. Meinardus 1965:19,161). As already noted, Ethiopian monks can still be found in Coptic monasteries even today. Moreover, the Coptic patriarch of Alexandria was also the head of the Ethiopian Church until the 1950s. Both churches shared the stigma of being "monophysite" in theological outlook, although in recent years Catholic and Orthodox bishops have tended to relegate the problem to discrepancies in terminology, rather than to theological differences. Both Churches were formed in relative estrangement from other Christian bodies, and bonded to each other.

The Ethiopian monasteries shared a common hagiographical tradition with the Copts well into the Arab period. The secular history and social conditions of Ethiopia have little else in common with the situation in Egypt. The Ethiopian Church has not had to survive under centuries of occupation and persecution and, until recent times, its monasteries have not had to symbolically repudiate a foreign economic or political system.

Monasteries in Ethiopia have functioned culturally and sociologically according to the Coptic model. In the absence of an external pole of symbolic resistance, the monasteries of Ethiopia have been aligned with segmental divisions within their own plural African society. To these segmental divisions, they have added their own religious values.

Steven Kaplan notes that the thirteenth century rise of the Solomonic Dynasty encroached on the power of the older noble families. Many of these men took to the monasteries where a limited freedom from royal control was tolerated by the Christian monarch. But the noble monks soon became land-owning abbots, who, as such, somewhat reentered the world of regional economics and politics. Kaplan notes how these abbots were able to maximize their resistance to the throne by the employment of non-political and anti-secular symbols, accomplishing worldly ends under the cover of otherworldly interests (cf. Kaplan 1984:1-10). The quote below, cited by Kaplan from Peter Brown (1971:91-92), makes this point well.

> The life of a holy man is marked by so many histrionic feats of self-mortification that it is easy at first sight to miss the deep social significance of asceticism as a long drawn out ritual of dissociation--of becoming the total stranger. For the society around him, the holy man is the one man who can stand outside the ties of family and of economic interests; whose attitude toward food itself rejected all ties of solidarity to kin and village that, in the present societies of the Near East, had always been expressed by the gesture of eating (Kaplan 1984:77).

Kaplan notes that the monk's "dissociation" from his society is dramatized by ascetic feats. These "histrionic feats" endow the monk with a special status which enables him to act effectively in ways that others, caught up in "the ties of family and economic interests" cannot. Economic and political loss translates into symbolic gain by the aura of monastic sacrifice. Symbolic authority and credibility serve to position the monk or the monastery as a balance of power between opposing forces: forces which impinge on the welfare of the society which sponsors the monastic life.

> If a common theme can be said to run through these numerous and diverse [Ethiopian hagiographic] episodes, it is the important mediatory role ascribed to the holy men. Repeatedly, the holy men intervened between men and demonic, divine, or natural forces. They protected mankind from demons, illness and wild beasts. They intervened with a distant God on behalf of their followers and disciples. They served as arbiters in disputes between husbands and wives, friends and neighbors. Born into human society, they attained and maintained a position some-what outside and above it, which enabled them to fulfill a variety of vital mediatory functions (Kaplan 1984:70).

We might expect significant similarities of outlook between the two Churches given their long, shared history of cultural and political interaction, their common hierarchies, the endurance of a common marginalization from Mediterranean Christendom and Near-Eastern Islam, and a common litany of saints. Many Westerners still refer to Christian Ethiopians as "Copts," in recognition of these common-alities. Nevertheless, serious and profound differences exist between the two Churches and peoples. Ethiopian Christians prefer not to be considered as "Copts."

Since environments influence history and cultures, the Ethiopian Orthodox religion is, therefore, notably different from that of the Copts. Egypt lies entirely within the Sahara Desert, drawing its life almost wholly from the river which bisects it. Ethiopia, by contrast, is given to yearly seasonal rains. The great bulk of silt and water in the Nile originates in its northern highlands, the very heart of the nation's Christian population. After arguing strongly about the value of the desert to the sacrificial idiom of Coptic monasticism, I began to wonder about the role of the diverse environment in the religion of Ethiopia.

Ethiopian Christians have been free of the Coptic patriarch's authority for over forty years, but the independent mentality of their Church is much older. The Ethiopians sought a greater degree of canonical independence for centuries precisely because their cultural and religious perspectives had little in common with the political agenda of the distant Alexandrian patriarch. The formal canonical subordination of the Ethiopian hierarchy to the Coptic Church held its place until the 1950s, long after the Churches ceased cooperative interrelations.

Ethiopia has its own peculiar medieval history of warring kingdoms, overreaching emperors, foreign armies, rising monasteries with their influential abbots, and growing merchant classes--all analogous to the Near East and Europe. It even had a "Jewish problem" similar to that of Spain and North Africa. Egypt could not exercise control over Ethiopia comparable to the colonial influences of Europe over Africa, nor could the Coptic Church succeed in keeping Ethiopian Christianity in a missionary status. My concern was that while Ethiopian Christianity was profoundly monastic in its institutional infrastructure, the Ethiopians might have symbolically invested their monastery with values contrary to the Egyptian model in intentional reaction-formation. For instance, some blending of native East African kinship values offers a plausible symbolic resource for Ethiopian monasticism, in contrast to the desert fathers of the Copts.

If monasticism in Ethiopia did not have the sacrificial meaning I found in Egypt, then perhaps the sacrificial mode of monastic symbolism is less essential to its function universally than I had believed. After all, monasticism in Ethiopia is exhibited by the Christian segment of the population which now, and historically, had need to define itself in contrast to other groups in the region, just as in Egypt. This need for the preservation of cultural integrity in the midst of challenging cultural boundary issues is exactly the setting I suggested is served by the monastic sacrificial symbol. And since the Ethiopians draw upon the biblical, liturgical, and sacramental tradition common to the Coptic, Orthodox, and Catholic religions, they follow the sacrificial system in the establishment of their cultural institutions. By comparing the Ethiopian monastery to that of the Copts, I hoped to determine that sacrificial asceticism is a universal feature of monasticism.

In the mid-1980s, Ethiopia was inaccessible for the kind of cultural investigations I needed to do. Civil wars, Marxist coups, famines and Islamic insurgencies rendered it closed to my visitation. By the 1990s, however, a degree of stability had settled in, so in late December 1997 through early January 1998, I took the opportunity to tour Ethiopia in order to answer these questions about the religion and monasticism of the country's large Christian population. I wanted to explore the current relationship between Ethiopian and Egyptian monasticism, especially to determine if the latter-day Ethiopian monastic symbol functions in ways similar to that of the sacrificial symbol in Coptic Egypt. Both religious groups share notable similarities which would make analogous symbolism possible.

Fortunately, I was able to engage the services of an Ethiopian deacon to serve as my informant, translator, and guide. I had first met him in 1986 when he was an Ethiopian refugee, a seminarian in the Coptic theologate in Cairo, and a retreatant in a monastery in which I was living to conduct my field study. Happily, he was well connected to Ethiopian ecclesiastical concerns, and was amenable to my academic interests.

The Issue of Numbers

As I began my research, I found one particularly troubling difference between Ethiopian monasticism, and that of the Coptic, Eastern Orthodox and Catholic Churches: the sheer number of monks and monasteries claimed by the Ethiopian Church. The number of monasteries was regularly cited as exceeding eight hundred, with monks in excess of tens of thousands throughout Ethiopia! The Christian population of the nation presently hovers at about twenty-six million souls, so the number of monks would approximate a whole percentage point of the population. Certainly, there were times in Coptic history when comparatively large numbers of Christian Egyptians took to the desert, so much so that one commentator considered monasticism in Egypt as demographic "suicide" (Butcher 1897:1,191). But these numbers of monks represented a fairly organized ethno-religious response to special cultural pressures. The Ethiopian case is not so clear. While, certainly, the Christians there are now living under a variety of pressures, the historical situation in which such high numbers of monks emerged was one of long duration of religious stability in which Christian emperors ruled a pluralistic religious society politically dominated by Christian tribal groups. To put the matter in relative terms, the number of monks in Coptic, Catholic and Orthodox Churches combined worldwide would be far less than that claimed by the Ethiopians alone. Can monasticism be a sacrificial symbol in such an environment with such numbers?

In the West, counting monks is a fairly simple procedure. Records are regularly updated there, and canonical registries and censuses are rigorously maintained. Numbering monks in Egypt is more difficult because records there are fewer and not readily accessible. Still, one can count the growing number of monasteries--a dozen or so for men and almost as many for women. By multiplying them by the average number of monks they house, one can arrive at a fair estimation of the total number, at least within range. In Ethiopia, the number of monasteries is itself a vagary, subject to wide differences of opinion. There, few records are kept and none are available for inspection. Most confusing of all to the foreign observer is the plethora of "monks" who do not live in any special institutional setting at all.

In my travels there, I met them everywhere: widowers who live in their grandchildren's homes; bachelors who assist in the local church liturgies; single, semi-professional men and women whose incomes are largely dispersed on charities, to name a few. All of them wear fairly secular garments, but these are over-wrapped in a loose, orange sarong. These people are called "monks," the same word used for those who live in enclosed monasteries, or ascetics who live in caves. (Ethiopians term both men and women monastics as "monks.") Many live in their ancestral villages and in the burgeoning cities amid their extended families. They work in the secular economy. Ethiopians regard the enclosed monastic community, the distant ascetic and the remote hermit as a special subcategory of monasticism, but the broadest application of the term "monk" applies to a special class of celibates outside the two-tier system of religious and laity, so common to other Churches. The assignment of the monastic title to a widespread group of unmarried, yet recognizably chaste, prayerful and committed laity must be part of the reason that Ethiopia can boast of so many "monks."

Following upon this discovery, I also came to realize the fact that not every "monastery," so named by the Ethiopians, qualifies as a religious or ecclesiastical institution. The place where a monk lives alone is regarded as his "monastery," and even more so, if two or more live together. Places where monks gather for prayers are considered as "monasteries," especially buildings in the compounds of rural churches. Over and above all this, Ethiopia has a superabundance of monasteries which are similar to those of Western observers, in addition to those which range along a spectrum downward to their less formal application of the term. For all these reasons, counting monks and monasteries in Ethiopia is a virtual impossibility.

What, then, of monasticism's symbolic role? If it is a way of life which melds into the laity at one end, and an institution of religious exclusivity on the other, can it really be a sign of sacrifice? According to Hubert and Mauss, the ritual designation of sacrifice requires the separation of both victim and sacrificers from their secular society (cf. 1964:28-29).

Grim History

In a certain sense, the Christians in Ethiopia are especially entitled to accentuate the sacrificial aspects of their religion. For the last century, they have readily perceived their lot as that of the victims of global forces. European colonial expeditions from England and Italy and political intrigue from France and Germany created internal divisions, intertribal conflicts and anti-colonial wars. Ottoman and Arab slave trading ravaged the nation during intermittent periods of political instability. Ethiopia became a target for Fascism when Mussolini invaded and conquered much of the nation in 1936. The inactivity of the League of Nations made the conquest possible, and the failure of the United Nations to reconstruct the nation after its liberation by the British in 1941 left the country vulnerable to additional internal conflicts. In fact, Haile Selassie's greatest acquisition from Europe was an influx of military hardware which only prompted him to exercise exaggerated authoritarian rule, and supply factions in the country's diverse military apparatus the wherewithal for civil war.

The Eritrea and Tigre provinces, in fact, waged such wars from the 1950s to the 1990s. Communist powers in the Soviet Union, China, and even Albania, sponsored these conflicts and indoctrinated several generations of Ethiopian intellectuals with Marxist ideology. Western corporate interests opened huge markets for Ethiopian lumber and other cash crops at the same time. Even while the worst of the famine was occurring, the production of coffee, tobacco and cotton was increased for cheap Western consumption. This profited Ethiopians little, and devastated the forest buffer to the Sahara which, in turn, created the ecological conditions for the southern sprawl of the desert into the Ethiopian highland agricultural regions. A spiral of draught, famine and more civil unrest followed. Forces which ultimately unseated the Solomonic Dynasty, the world's oldest monarchy, established the brutal dictatorship of Mengistu Haile Mariam.

Iranian, Saudi Arabian, Sudanese, Libyan and other Islamic groups regularly donate considerable capital to Muslim cells in Ethiopia in order to sponsor conversions and build new mosques. One goal seems to be to marginalize the Christian tribes and to erode the number of Christians in their ranks in order to establish a formal Islamic state. Even if this occurs, Ethiopia would still be caught in the cross-interests of these rival Islamic camps. Further wars might still be waged on Ethiopian soil because of foreign competition. Meanwhile, Evangelical, Pentecostal, Mormon and other sectarian Western religious movements are being sponsored in Ethiopia as an area of missionary enterprise. Their relative success further weakens the Ethiopian Orthodox Church, and renders its members ineffective in presenting a unified response to Islamic insurgence.

In short, just about every major movement of the past century has crushed Ethiopia: colonialism, Fascism, imperialism, ethnic factionalism, totalitarianism, Communism, capitalism, Islamism and fundamentalism. Nevertheless, in a nation saturated with the presence of monasticism, and religiously oriented to ritual sacrifice, both tribal and ecclesiastical, I found little evidence that the Ethiopians equate their plight with victimhood. The Ethiopians apparently do not espouse an identity predicated primarily on their oppressed status. The long, dynastic history of the nation prior to modern times, the general failure of colonial forces to long occupy the countryside without revolts, the spectacle of ancient empires and medieval cities in her archaeological remains all conspire to give the Christian tribal peoples of Ethiopia a cultural charter which precludes the status of sacrificial victim.

This realization compelled me to seriously question my thesis about the concept of monasticism as sacrifice for Ethiopian Christians. Nevertheless, I realize that monasticism has rooted itself into many cultures in which victimhood is not an ingrained category of self-perception. Even where peoples are possessed of a consciousness of ascendance and invulnerability, monasticism can flourish as an icon of sacrifice because suffering is an essential, even if secondary, component of any viable culture. Dealing with tensions of injustice, boundary erosion, political strife, economic failure, generational transition, and cycles of epidemics is commonplace in the history of every people and nation. The monastic impulse is one powerful and fairly pervasive response to these misfortunes. But are all monastic movements sacrificial? Ethiopia was a test case.

Asceticism

I decided to concentrate my primary investigation on the monks and monasteries of Ethiopia which are separated geographically from secular, social commerce. While the Ethiopians call people "monks" who live celibate lives among the laity, they too recognize a distinctive religious quality in the sequestered monastic soul. In Ethiopia, such souls are separated from "the world" by barriers of water, such as the monasteries on islands in Lake Tana, or by steep cliffs as in the case of Debre Domo near Eritrea. They are separated by barren wilderness as that of Kidus Gelawdros in the Gonder Province, or by thick walls such as that of Debre Libanos outside of Addis Ababa. The monks in these monasteries espouse an otherworldly aspect to their lives and invest themselves substantially in that effort. The Christian faithful properly regard their vocations as sacred and accord them special respect.

Ethiopians visit their monasteries for blessings and for special needs and spiritual favors. Much as in Egypt, Christians in Ethiopia may seek discernment, healing, fertility, forgiveness, success, deliverance, or peace by a pilgrimage to the monastery. They expect to see the persuasive reality of holy and ascetical lives at the end of their journey. Such a sight is part of the blessing they expect to receive. Invariably, they find that the monks respond to their needs.

Ethiopian monks practice considerable asceticism. In one monastery, the abbot proudly served me the bread which was freshly baked in the bakery I had just inspected. At first bite, I was immediately aware of a grating, gritty residue in the dough. Seeing my distaste, the abbot explained that charcoal from the earthen oven pit is generously mixed with the dough in every batch so that the monks may never enjoy a simple meal for its own sake. Rather, they are always "praying the cross" in every mouthful of food. "Besides," he said, "people must not presume to enter monasteries to get good food."

In another monastery I met several monks who have neither cell nor cave in which to dwell. Without any earthly possessions to speak of, they rest upon the ground for part of the day when it is warm, and pray by night, while walking to diminish the effects of the cool night air. In yet another monastery, I encountered scores of monks who lodge in rock overhangs, canyon fissures, earthen holes or shallow caves. The relatively constant temperature throughout the year grants Ethiopian monks a greater use of the outdoors than the desert heat and cold affords the Egyptian monks. Likewise, the Ethiopian monk is given to long vigils, sleepless nights of prayer, protracted psalmody in common, a spartan vegetarian diet, difficult fasts and a regimen of silence, work, and abject poverty. He commits volumes of prayers and hymns to memory and typically responds generously to the demands of pilgrims and guests. He must submit to the will of the spiritual father of the monastery, especially in the early years of his formation, and often intercedes long hours before God for the welfare of his Church.

In all these aspects, the Ethiopian and the Egyptian monk are similar. Since both monastic types follow the liturgical rites of a Eucharistic tradition in which the sacrificial work of Christ is represented to them daily for the world's redemption, both demonstrate a sufficient mentality of redemptive asceticism to validate a sacrificial value to their monastic vocation. The monk in Ethiopia, as in Egypt, sees his life as an extension of, or parallel to, the sacrificial ritual of his priest. In Egypt, such an intuition undergirds the viability of a monastic vocation. It grants the power of personal perseverance, and casts it against the backdrop of a cosmic drama which can make the burden and tedium of it seem well worthwhile. The Ethiopian monastic life has all the elements of this dynamic, symbolic association. But does the Ethiopian monk associate his asceticism and social persona with a cultic or ritual sacrifice for the benefit of his people?

The Ark of the Covenant

Perhaps the most famous and definitive aspect of the Ethiopian Church is the extraordinary emphasis placed upon the "Tabot," the "Ark of the Covenant." Westerners know the Ark to be a Hebrew religious object from remote Old Testament times. Later Jews seem to have forgotten it, and Christians have rarely referred to it. Yet, the Ark of the Covenant is the centerpiece of the religious imagination and ecclesiastical rites and architecture of the Ethiopian Church. The native Christians hold firmly, as an article of faith, that the Ark of the Covenant, the box constructed by Moses during the Exodus which contains the tablets of the Ten Commandments, has come to rest in Ethiopia in a monastery shrine which is guarded by a holy monk.

The possibility of such an historic biblical relic ending up in the highlands of East Africa is not the concern here. Graham Hancock has produced a colorful journalistic account of one possible scenario of this eventuality, one which is open to criticism in a number of ways (cf. Hancock 1992). However, the *meaning* of the Ark to the Christians of Ethiopia is important to this discussion. The Tabot is the jewel of the Ethiopian religion whose setting is a gated shrine within the enclosure of a walled monastery. Its guardian is a monk who is selected from the monastery which surrounds the shrine. This emblem of Ethiopian faith is protected by monks, not by armies nor political parties, nor distinguished lineage, nor the wealthy elite. The association of the Ark with monasticism is profound in Ethiopia. The biblical record has conditioned the Ethiopians' view of their religious treasure, and the biblical associations with the Ark reinforce its applicability as a sign of monastic sacrifice.

The Book of Exodus records the material elements and physical proportions of the Ark. It was to be a box constructed of durable acacia wood plated with pure gold. With seeming contradiction to one of the commandments to be stored in the box, two "graven images" of cherubim angels were to be mounted on top, hollowing out a place where God himself was to dwell for the purpose of communicating with his ministers (Exodus 25:10-22).

The Ark was not just a container of the "Law" (Covenant) which bound Israel to God, but more notably, it was the place of divine abiding, the "footstool" of the Deity, and thus it was also called the "Ark of God." The Israelites regarded it as "God's throne" in the world. Its mere presence made the sanctuary of Moses, the so-called "meeting tent," holy. In the center of the tent, as later in the Temple of Solomon, the Ark constituted the "Holy of Holies." Just to have it, Israel would deem itself to be validated as God's people and, therefore, the Israelites would become tempted to think of themselves as invincible (Joshua 6).

During a certain period in Israel's history, the Ark was absolutely central to the religion of the Hebrews. From it, God spoke to Moses and directed the priests of each successive generation. Joshua conquered Canaan and leveled Jericho by its power. David validated his kingship by dancing before the Ark, and Solomon sealed his dynastic royal power by building the temple as a fitting dwelling for it.

The glories and the miracles associated with the Ark are numerous. Important in biblical literature and in the Ethiopian perspective is the extraordinary degree of separation from profane exposure which the Ark must be accorded. From its beginning, the Ark was outfitted with rings along its side so that it could be transported by poles. The "meeting tent" in which it was housed was always constructed "outside the camp" due to its great sacredness. A curtain was always drawn around it. Only the high priest could look upon the Ark, and only on rare occasions. The merest secular approach, no matter how slight or well-intended it was, doomed the interloper to instant death (2 Samuel 5:6-7).

Today in Axum, the Ethiopian "City of the Ark," no one can gain access to the monastery to see the Ark except its monk caretaker who is not permitted outside the shrine wherein it is supposedly hidden. Abba Welde Giorgis, the monk who currently guards the Ark, told me that even Haile Selassie was not allowed to see it, nor was Queen Elizabeth when she visited the nation decades ago. Even the Ethiopian patriarch is forbidden to see it. "I would tremble if I were to see it," the guardian explained to me; "it is too holy and very dangerous." Several monks volunteered, "Because of its presence in Ethiopia, we have never become the colony of any other nation." This sentiment matches biblical Hebrew attitudes regarding the Ark.

If the extraordinary and singular mission of Moses brought the Ark of the Covenant to Israel, and only the high priests of the Tribe of Levi were permitted access to it, then the Ethiopian investment of the Ark into the hands of monks is a powerful testimony to the credentials which they enjoy in Ethiopia, at least those monks who live apart. Living apart, separated from secularity is essential to the possibility of ritual sacrifice. The monastic capability of receiving the Ark into its midst demonstrates that, at bottom, the Ethiopian monastery is a ritually separate sphere.

To further illustrate the point, if somehow any other Church gained possession of what is considered to be the Ark of God, it would be in the hands of the hierarchs of that Church. Monks, who are not members of the hierarchy, would not be considered the proper guardians of such a sign. Rather, the Ark would be claimed as an additional mark of the legitimacy of the hierarchy which obtained possession of it. The Ethiopians have not done this. Monasticism enjoys a special status among them, resistant to its subordination to ecclesiastical political structures. Perhaps this is because Christianity became rooted in Ethiopia before a clergy was canonically constituted, and the Ethiopians have never lost their extra-institutional sense of the ethnic Church. Or perhaps it is the distinctively African esteem for the "holy man," which sets the monastery apart for such an honor.

One other aspect of the Ark is worth noting. The Ark was the center of ritual sacrificial worship by which Israel was reconciled with God, and through which God was pleased to bless his people. On the top of the Ark, between the unfurled wings of the Cherubim, was a raised platform of gold called the "propitiatory" or the "mercy seat." There, God rested in the midst of the nation. Once a year, the high priest would sprinkle the blood of animal sacrifices over the propitiatory, and then over the altar outside the Holy of Holies (Leviticus 16). That blood which was then sprinkled over the assembly from the altar would render God and his people "one blood." The union of blood, of course, is the kinship principle which unites all tribal peoples. Through a special use of the Ark, Israel performed sacrificial rites by which God was made tribal, clan and family "blood." The Day of Atonement was, and still is, the highest holy day of Jewry which commemorates this blood-sealed union.

For the Ethiopian Christian, the Eucharistic Liturgy is an equivalent rite. The blood of Christ makes the people "one blood" with God. Now every Ethiopian church houses a concealed replica of the Ark in its sanctuary. All Ethiopian Liturgies are conducted in immediate proximity to these "arks," thereby making each church an extension of the monastic shrine in Axum, and every sanctuary an extension of the ark it contains. Sacrifice operates on every ritual and monastic stage. Sacrifice unites bloody rites to sacramental forms and to monastic practices. Though the rite of sacrifice is performed in Ethiopia with different emphases and imagery than it is in Egypt, its fundamental role is important to both Christian communities.

The foregoing treatment of the Coptic monk examined the interassociations of the monk and the Cross, the Mass and sacrifice. It emphasized the Coptic intuition that the monk himself is an embodiment of the liturgical rites of sacrifice and an elaboration of Christ's sacrificial work. A similar association is apparent in the Ethiopian context, but the Ethiopians have developed their own unique linkage of monk and sacrifice. The relationship of the Ark to their culture and its profound connection to monasticism give the Ethiopian ideal of monastic sacrifice its own emphasis. Ultimately, each monk is himself the bearer of a great mystery, a "covenant box" wherein resides the heritage of his people's religious identity. And just like the Ark, the presence of God is perceived to abide over the monk: the divine presence through which the monk reconciles his people by his blameless, pure, and separated life.

Notes

Chapter 1

[1]Talal Asad has produced a fine study of medieval Latin monasticism from an anthropological perspective, one which acknowledges its sacrificial role in close association with Christ's cross (1993:110). However, his work emphasizes more the construction of a monastic sense of the self given to collective subordination and obedience (1993:165-66) rather than the cultural function of sacrifice.

[2]A similar economic process may occur at the opposite end of the occupational spectrum. A very high percentage of urban refuse collectors are Copts who live in the most abject poverty. The garbage collected by these Copts is suitable fodder only for pigs which are animals forbidden for consumption in Islam. Hence, the Copts exploit another occupational zone left to them, which, though despicable to the Arab society, is economically fostered and culturally tolerated to a large degree.

[3]The number of monasteries for men is growing in Egypt. "Officially" established adiora numbered eleven in 1987, but several more were on the threshold of being canonically approved. Monasteries for women have also been on the increase in recent years. (For a study of monasticism of women in Egypt, see *Contemporary Coptic Nuns*, by Pieternella van Doorn-Harder, University of South Carolina Press, 1995.)

Chapter 2

[1]For individual treatments of Old Testament sacrifice in an anthropological perspective, see Gray 1925; Leach 1976; Davies 1977; and Douglas 1978.

[2]Although Girard's extraordinary insights into sacrifice, human and animal, do not include any analysis of monastic asceticism, he allows that the applications of his theories to Christianity may further elaborate them (cf. 1977:262-73). At any rate, any reader of Girard, as of 1977, will note the ready parallels between his analysis and the view taken in this account. (His later works reflect on Christianity and its mode of sacrifice in a highly nuanced and strangely apologetic manner that would move the present discussion far afield of its primary concerns. See J. Bottum 1996: 42-45.)

Chapter 3

[1]The Gospel of St. Matthew reports that Joseph and Mary took the infant Jesus into Egypt to avoid the persecution of Herod in Judea. Coptic hagiography provides much detail as to where they stopped: at wells, caves, holy trees, and desert tombs, which often became future monastery sites. (cf. Meinardus 1986:20-59). Rather cleverly, the exile into Egypt is said by the Copts to undo the harm that Egypt did to Israel in her slavery. A more contemporary Coptic application of the story refers to the Holy Family as "the first Palestinian refugees," a reference which they hope will show that their religion can make them palatable to the state after all.

[2]A somewhat more detailed description of monastic sites and cultural ramifications is found in a later chapter, although in one respect, no one is more illuminating than Otto Meinardus. His various works on the Coptic monasteries are largely descriptive of architectural features and historical building sequences. He has collected an enormous amount of data of interest to "Coptology" per se, but with little synthetic reflection as to larger religious or cultural issues.

[3]In this respect, secular Western society may not be as irreligious as it first appears. Non-believers and would-be believers are often deeply impressed by the spirituality of at least some full-time religious specialists. On the level of non-scientific analysis, at least, admiration is a means of communicating religious sensibility and identity.

Chapter 4

[1]The Church of Egypt was among the first in the outer provinces of the Roman Empire to seek autonomy from the imperial ecclesiastical

center. As shall be seen, the basis for this massive ecclesiastical division had to be postulated in terms of a fundamental theological dispute, else the antagonists would be exposed as politicizing the nature of Church.

The monophysite controversy concerned the theological understanding of Christ's human and divine aspects. The "great Church" proclaimed "two natures in one person;" the "monophysites" held the belief of "one nature in Christ."

²*RB* stands for *The Rule of St. Benedict*, the canon of Western monastic institutions. The study of this Rule has been a preoccupation of Western monks for centuries. Hence, modern Benedictines feel free to title a resource book on the subject by their commonly used abbreviation which is attached to its date of completion. As it is the monastic custom to conceal personal authorship in such texts, the books are cited solely by their title. *RB 1980*, then, is the title of a commentary on the Rule of St. Benedict compiled in 1980 by a group of American Benedictine monks, and subsequently published in 1981.

³The "Pax Deorum" was a Roman imperial convention whereby all the gods of the peoples living in the Empire would be considered as co-existing in one divine court.

⁴The "Therapeutae" were members of a faintly remembered, but undoubtedly significant, religious movement in pre-Christian Egypt. They espoused a strict moral code which separated them from the corruption of secular Romanized society. They wore distinctive white garments, practiced ritual bathing, and may have demonstrated lives of celibacy for protracted periods. In these ways, they exhibited features of an Egyptian psyche anticipating its later Christian propensity to monasticism.

Chapter 5

¹ The Mameluks were members of a military force (originally comprised of slaves) which seized power in Egypt around A.D. 1250 and ruled until A.D. 1517.

²Congenital blindness, or that induced by poor diet, poor sanitation and disease, is fairly common throughout the Third World and in Egypt. This childhood affliction is interpreted by the Copts as a divine invitation to cultivate the ear for religious music. A blind boy is therefore strongly encouraged to begin the process of sacred musical formation early in life until he has memorized the tomes of Coptic liturgical hymnody.

³The term *"feddan"* refers to a measure of land in Egypt, equivalent to about 1.25 acres.

Chapter 9

[1]Not to be confused with the *liturgical* designation "Shayel Saleeb," meaning "cross-carrier."

[2]Needless to say, I survived this grueling experience. I realized later, after entering the cave, that the journey was actually intended to save my life since the temperature in the cave was dramatically cooler than that on the floor of the desert. It also had an abundant supply of cool water with which the old monk drenched me until my body temperature went back down to normal. The water had been collected from a network of fine grooves carved in the surface rocks by monks of the founder's epoch. The rare rains of the North Sahara were thereby saved in collecting basins built into the cave's inner chambers, and scarcely subject to evaporation.

I remained in the cave for several days until the heat wave passed, then made the trek down the mountain and across the desert back to the monastery.

Chapter 10

[1]The Biblical fascination with the number "forty" may ultimately derive from this fact: e.g., forty days of Noah's flood; forty years of the Exodus; forty days given by Jonah for Nineveh to repent; and the forty days of Jesus' fasting and prayer on the mountain.

[2]According to Meinardus, the month of Nasi has six days if the following year is a leap year (1989:xiv).

Glossary

Coptic and Liturgical Terms

abuna. "My father" - title used to address a Coptic priest or monk.

abuna robeyta. Coptic monk overseer in charge of a work area in the monastery; "father controller."

Adama Kadeed. "A new Adam."

adiora. Monasteries (plural of "deir").

El Adra. The Virgin Mary.

Agbeya. Coptic prayer book of the Liturgical Hours.

akh. Title of "brother" given to novice monks, as well as the lay employees of the monastery.

anba. Title of a Coptic bishop or male saint, often used for an early monastic founder.

Anno Martyrium (A.M.) "Year of the Martyrs." Persecution of the Copts by Diocletian in A.D. 284 is considered as "Year 1" in the Coptic calendar.

arif. Blind cantor.

barakah. Blessing(s).

dahiah. Sacrifices performed by the Coptic laity, e.g., fasting, prayers, spiritual offerings, and other good works.

deir. Coptic monastery (plural: "adiora").

feddan. Measure of land in Egypt, about 1.25 acres.

fellaheen. Egyptian peasants; field laborers.

fule. Falafel beans.

galabeya. Long, flowing, beltless garment worm by Egyptian peasants; also the black habit of the Coptic monks.

galalib. Plural form of "galabeya."

Gibt. Egyptian word for the Copts; derived from "gypt" of the word "Egypt."

hagiography. Stories, maxims and exhortations of the early desert monks; considered to be the spiritual foundation of Coptic monasticism, social life and lore.

haikal. Altar or sanctuary in a Coptic church.

hegoumenos. Spiritual father of a Coptic monastery who may also be the abbot.

hezan. Leather girdle (belt) worn by Coptic monks.

horarium. (Latin) Daily schedule of the monks.

kalaswa. Black cotton cap worn by Coptic monks.

kellia. Strip of desert in the Wadi Natroun which housed thousands of monks' cells at one time.

Kodes. Eucharistic Liturgy (Mass) presided over by a priest-monk in a Coptic monastery.

kommos. Spiritual father of the Coptic monks; shortened form for the word "hegoumenos."

kommos-raeese. Head of a Coptic monastery, distinct from the spiritual father.

labesa saleeb. "Cross-bearer" - title given to the monks by the Copts.

laura. Cluster of scattered monks' cells in the desert with a church and a "tower of refuge" standing in the middle; was enclosed in a defensive wall during the 9th and 10th centuries.

laurae. Plural of "laura."

Maglis Milli. Community Councils instituted by the Egyptian government in 1873 to replace the Coptic Millets.

Melkites. Egyptian Christians associated with the Church in Rome who had a foreign-supported patriarch in Alexandria.

Meri Girgus. Saint George.

metanoia. Profound bows; prostrations.

Millets. Coptic units of local self-government instituted in Egypt by the Ottomans.

moazuf. Lay employee of a Coptic monastery.

monachos (Greek). State of "aloneness" - origin of the word "monk."

mozafeen. Lay employees - plural of "moazuf."

mulid. Coptic festival, usually held in honor of the patron saint of a monastery.

owshia. Liturgical prayer which distinguishes each of the three Coptic seasons.

raheb. Fear of God; feeling of dread.

raeese-deir. Kommos in charge of a Coptic deir; abbot of a Coptic monastery, as distinguished from the spiritual father.

Scete, Scetes, Shiet. "Measure of the heart"; "scales of the heart"; used in reference to the desert of the Wadi Natroun.

Sha'ria. Koranic code of justice.

Shayel Saleeb. "Cross-carrier"; Coptic *liturgical* name for a monk.

sitar. "The veil"; name given to the eighth prayer prayed by the Coptic monk before going to sleep.

stit. Early morning star; refers to the star Sirius of the constellation of Canis Majoris.

Theotokos. "God-bearer"; Mother of God.

Umma Coptya. "Coptic Nation." A short-lived militant group born out of Coptic frustration.

uskof. Coptic bishop.

uskof-hegoumenos. Bishop-abbot of a Coptic monastery.

waqf. Land, buildings and monies given to monasteries as religious endowments.

zabihah. Total sacrifice of a Coptic monk, likened to the offering on an altar.

Bibliography

Cited and Consulted Works

Abbott, Nabia.
    1937   *The Monasteries of the Fayum.* The Oriental Institute of the
            University of Chicago. Studies in Ancient Oriental Civiliza-
            tion, no. 16. Chicago: University of Chicago Press. (Reprinted
            from the *American Journal of Semitic Languages and Literatures*
            53:13-33, 73-96, 158-79.)
Abdel-Massih, Ernest T., Mikhail M. Melika, and Roufail S. Michail.
    1982   *The Divine Liturgy of St. Basil the Great.* Text in English,
            Coptic and Arabic. Troy, Mich.: St. Mark Coptic Orthodox
            Church.
Adams, Charles C.
    1968   *Islam and Modernism in Egypt: A Study of the Modern Reform
            Movement Inaugurated by Mu hammad Abduh.* New York:
            Russell & Russell; reprint of the 1933 ed., Oxford University
            Press, London.
Ahmed, Imam.
    1986   "Apparition of Virgin Mary Startles Cairo Neighborhood."
            Middle East Times (March 18-24).

Alexander, Kelly D., Jr.
  2002   *Ark of the Covenant: Simplified Information for Lay-Persons.*
          Lanham, Md: University Press of America.
Ansari, Hamied.
  1984   "Sectarian Conflict in Egypt and the Political Expediency of
          Religion." *The Middle East Journal* 38 (3): 397-418.
Arens, W.
  1986   *The Original Sin: Incest and Its Meaning.* New York and Ox-
          ford: Oxford University Press.
Armstrong, A. H. and E. J. Barbara Fry.
  1963   *Re-discovering Eastern Christendom.* London: Darton, Longman
          & Todd.
Asad, Talal.
  1993   *Genealogies of Religion: Discipline and Reasons of Power in
          Christianity and Islam.* Baltimore and London: The Johns Hop-
          kins University Press.
  1996   *The Idea of an Anthropology of Islam.* Occasional Paper Series,
          Center for Contemporary Arab Studies. Washington, D.C.,
          Georgetown University. Reprint of the 1986 ed.
Assad, Maurice.
  1972   "The Coptic Church and Social Change in Egypt. *International
          Review of Mission* 61 (242): 117-129.
Athanasius, Saint, Patriarch of Alexandria.
  1950   *The Life of Saint Antony.* Newly translated and annotated by
          Robert T. Meyer. Ancient Christian Writers: The Works of the
          Fathers in Translation, no. 10. Westminster, Md.: Newman
          Press.
Athanasius, Anba, Bishop of Beni-Suef and Bahnasa.
  n.d.   *The Copts through the Ages.* 7th ed. Cairo: Arab Republic of
          Egypt, Ministry of Information, State Information Service. Al-
          Ahram Press.
Atiya, Aziz S.
  1968   *History of Eastern Christianity.* First American ed. Notre Dame,
          Ind.: University of Notre Dame Press. Originally published in
          1967 by Methuen & Co., London.
  1979   *The Copts and Christian Civilization.* Salt Lake City: Published
          by the University of Utah Press for the Frederick William Rey-
          nolds Association.
Atiya, Aziz, S., ed.
  1991   *The Coptic Encyclopedia.* 8 vols. New York, Toronto, and Ox-
          ford: Macmillan.

Attwater, Donald.
1937   *The Dissident Eastern Churches*. Religion and Culture Series. Milwaukee, Wis.: Bruce Publishing Co.
1942   *The Liturgy of the Copts*. London: Orate Fratres.
Ayrout, Henry Habib.
1963   *The Egyptian Peasant*. Translated from the French by John Alden Williams. New English translation with revisions by the author. Boston: Beacon Press. First English edition published in Cairo in 1945 under title *The Fellaheen*.
Baal, J. van.
1976   "Offering, Sacrifice and Gift." *Numen* 23 (Fasc. 3): 161-78. Originally read at the 13th Congress of the International Association for the History of Religions, Lancaster, August 1975.
Baer, Gabriel.
1962   *A History of Landownership in Modern Egypt, 1800-1950*. Middle Eastern Monographs, 4. Issued under the auspices of the Royal Institute of International Affairs. London and New York: Oxford University Press.
1964   *Egyptian Guilds in Modern Times*. Oriental Notes and Studies, no. 8. Jerusalem: Israel Oriental Society.
1969   *Studies in the Social History of Modern Egypt*. Center for Middle Eastern Studies. Publications, no. 4. Chicago and London: University of Chicago Press.
Bahr, S.
1979   "Copts in the Economic Life of Egypt." Master's thesis (in Arabic). Cairo: University of Cairo.
Bailie, Gil.
1995   *Violence Unveiled: Humanity at the Crossroads*. New York: Crossroad.
Banton, Michael P., ed.
1966   *Anthropological Approaches to the Study of Religion*. A.S.A. Monograph 3. London: Tavistock Publications.
Barclay, Harold B.
1982   "Egypt: Struggling with Secularization." In *Religions and Societies: Asia and the Middle East*, edited by Carlo Caldarola, 119-146. Religion and Society 22. Berlin and New York: Mouton Publishers.
Barrington-Ward, S. and M. F. C. Bourdillon.
1980   "Postscript: A Place for Sacrifice in Modern Christianity?" In *Sacrifice*, edited by M. F. C. Bourdillon and Meyer Fortes, 127-133. London and New York: Published by Academic Press for

the Royal Anthropological Institute of Great Britain and
Ireland.

Bat Ye'or.
1985   *The Dhimmi: Jews and Christians under Islam*. Rev. and enlarged
        English ed.; translated from the French by David Maisel (text),
        Paul Fenton (document section), and David Littman. Ruther-
        ford, N.J.: Fairleigh Dickinson University Press; London and
        Toronto: Associated University Presses.

Bates, M. Seale.
1946   "Religious Liberty in Moslem Lands." *The Moslem World* (Jan-
        uary): 54-56.

Beattie, J. H. M.
1980   "On Understanding Sacrifice." In *Sacrifice*, edited by M. F. C.
        Bourdillon and Meyer Fortes, 29-44. London and New York:
        Published by Academic Press for the Royal Anthropological
        Institute of Great Britain and Ireland.

Beidelman, T. O.
1974   *W. Robertson Smith and the Sociological Study of Religion*. Chi-
        cago and London: University of Chicago Press.
1987   "Sacrifice and Sacred Rule in Africa." Review of *Sacrifice in
        Africa, a Structuralist Approach*, by Luc de Heusch. *American
        Ethnologist* 14 (3): 542-51.

Bell, H. Idris, ed.
1924   *Jews and Christians in Egypt: The Jewish Troubles in Alexandria
        and the Athanasian Controversy*, illustrated by texts from Greek
        papyri in the British Museum . . . with three Coptic texts
        edited by W. E. Crum. London: Humphrey Milford, Oxford
        University Press.

Benedict, Saint, Abbot of Monte Cassino.
1981   *RB 1980: The Rule of St. Benedict in Latin and English, with
        Notes*. Edited by Timothy Fry, et al. Collegeville, Minn.: Litur-
        gical Press.

Berger, Morroe.
1957   *Bureaucracy and Society in Modern Egypt*. Princeton Oriental
        Studies: Social Science, no. 1. Princeton, N.J.: Princeton Uni-
        versity Press.
1970   *Islam in Egypt Today: Social and Political Aspects of Popular
        Religion*. Cambridge: Cambridge University Press.

Berger, Peter L.
1967   *The Sacred Canopy: Elements of a Sociological Theory of Religion*.
        Garden City, N.Y.: Doubleday & Co.

Berger, Peter L. and Thomas Luckmann.
1966   *The Social Construction of Reality: A Treatise in the Sociology of Knowledge*. Garden City, N.Y.: Doubleday & Co.

Betts, Robert Brenton.
1978   *Christians in the Arab East: A Political Study*. Rev. ed. Athens: Lycabettus Press.

Bidney, David.
1962   "The Concept of Value in Modern Anthropology." In *Anthropology Today: Selections*, edited by Sol Tax, 436-53. Chicago and London: University of Chicago Press.

Blackman, Winifred S.
1921   "Some Modern Egyptian Graveside Ceremonies." *Discovery* 2:207-12.
1924   "Some Modern Egyptian Saints. II. Coptic Saints." *Discovery* 5:67a-71a.
1968   *The Fellahin of Upper Egypt: Their Religious, Social and Industrial Life with Special Reference to Survivals from Ancient Times*. London: Frank Cass & Co. Reprint of the 1927 ed.

Bolle, Kees W.
1983   "A World of Sacrifice." *History of Religions* 23 (1): 37-63.

Bosworth, C. E.
1972   "Christian and Jewish Religious Dignitaries in Mamluk Egypt and Syria: Qalqashandi's Information on Their Hierarchy, Titulature, and Appointment." *International Journal of Middle East Studies* 3 (1): 59-74; 3 (2): 199-216.

Bottum, J.
1996   "Girard Among the Girardians: Review Essay." Review of *Violence Unveiled* by Gil Bailie. *First Things* 61 (March): 42-45.

Bourdillon, M. F. C.
1980   "Introduction." In *Sacrifice*, edited by M. F. C. Bourdillon and Meyer Fortes, 1-27. London and New York: Published by Academic Press for the Royal Anthropological Institute of Great Britain and Ireland.

Bourdillon, M. F. C. and Meyer Fortes, eds.
1980   *Sacrifice*. Based on the proceedings of a Conference on Sacrifice held at Cumberland Lodge, Windsor, February 23-25, 1979. London and New York: Published by Academic Press for the Royal Anthropological Institute of Great Britain and Ireland.

Bouyer, Louis.
1955   *The Meaning of the Monastic Life*. Translated from the French by Kathleen Pond. New York: P. J. Kenedy & Sons.

Bowie, Leland.
    1977   "The Copts, the Wafd, and Religious Issues in Egyptian Poli-
            tics." *The Muslim World* 67 (2): 106-26.
Bramblett, Claud A.
    1994   *Patterns of Primate Behavior.* 2d ed. Prospect Heights, Ill.:
            Waveland Press.
Brown, Peter.
    1971   "The Rise and Function of the Holy Man in Late Antiquity."
            The Journal of Roman Studies 61:80-101.
    1972   *Religion and Society in the Age of Saint Augustine.* New York:
            Harper & Row.
    1988   *The Body and Society: Men, Women and Sexual Renunciation in
            Early Christianity.* Lectures on the History of Religions; n.s.,
            no. 13. New York: Columbia University Press.
Brown, Raymond E.
    1977   *The Birth of the Messiah: A Commentary on the Infancy Narra-
            tives in Matthew and Luke.* Garden City, N.Y.: Doubleday &
            Co.
Brown, Raymond E., Joseph A. Fitzmyer and Roland E. Murphy, eds.
    1968   *The Jerome Biblical Commentary.* 2 vols in 1. Englewood Cliffs,
            N.J.: Prentice-Hall.
Budge, E. A. Wallis, trans.
    1893   *The Nile, Notes for Travellers in Egypt.* 3d ed. London: T. Cook.
    1910   *Coptic Homilies in the Dialect of Upper Egypt from the Papyrus
            Codex Oriental 5001 in the British Museum.* Vol. 1 of *Coptic
            Texts.* London: British Museum.
    1912   *Coptic Biblical Texts in the Dialect of Upper Egypt.* Vol. 2 of
            Coptic Texts. London: British Museum.
    1913   *Coptic Apocrypha in the Dialect of Upper Egypt.* Vol. 3 of *Coptic
            Texts.* London: British Museum.
    1914   *Coptic Martyrdoms, etc., in the Dialect of Upper Egypt.* Vol. 4 of
            Coptic Texts. London: British Museum.
    1972   *The Paradise or Garden of the Holy Fathers; Being Histories of the
            Anchorites, Recluses, Monks, Coenobites and Ascetic Fathers of the
            Deserts of Egypt between A.D. 250 and circa A.D. 400.* Compiled
            by Athanasius, Archbishop of Alexandria; Palladius, Bishop of
            Helenopolis; Saint Jerome, and Others. Now translated out of
            the Syriac with notes & introd. by E. A. Wallis Budge. 2 vols.
            Research & Source Works Series; Philosophy & Religious

Monographs 112. New York: Burt Franklin. Reprint of the 1907 ed. which was a 1904 rev. translation of *The Book of Paradise* compiled by Anan-Isho in the seventh century.

Burkitt, F. C.
n.d.   "The Monasteries of the Wadi 'n-Natrun." Review of *The Monasteries of the Wadi 'n-Natrun*, by H. G. Evelyn White. Parts 1-3. *Journal of Theological Studies* 28:320-25; 34:188-92; 36:105-107.

Burmester, O. H. E.
1954   *A Guide to the Monasteries of the Wadi 'N-Natrun.* Cairo: Société d'Archéologie Copte.
1954   "Rite of the Initiation into Monasticism." *Eastern Churches Quarterly* 11:217-29.
1967   *The Egyptian or Coptic Church: A Detailed Description of Her Liturgical Services and the Rites and Ceremonies Observed in the Administration of Her Sacraments.* Cairo: Société d'Archéologie Copte.

Burmester, O. H. E., trans. and ed.
1960   *The Rite of Consecration of the Patriarch of Alexandria.* Text according to MS. 253 Lit., Coptic Museum. Cairo: Société d'Archéologie Copte.

Butcher, E. L.
1897   *The Story of the Church of Egypt: Being an Outline of the History of the Egyptians Under Their Successive Masters from the Roman Conquest Until Now.* 2 vols. London: Smith, Elder & Co.
1911   "In the House of Bondage: A Short Sketch of Coptic History." In *Copts and Moslems under British Control*, by Kyriakos Mikhail, 1-13. London: Smith, Elder & Co.

Bute, John Patrick, trans.
1908   *The Coptic Morning Service for the Lord's Day.* Translated into English by John, Marquis of Bute. London: Cope & Fenwick.

Butler, Alfred J.
1911   "Copts and Muslims in Egypt." London: Excerpt from vol. 70, no. 415 of *The Nineteenth Century and After.* 13 pages.
1970   *The Ancient Coptic Churches of Egypt.* 2 vols. Oxford: Clarendon Press. Reprint of the 1884 ed. with a new appendix.

Caldarola, Carlo, ed.

1982   *Religions and Societies: Asia and the Middle East.* Religion and Society 22. Berlin and New York: Mouton Publishers.

Campbell-Jones, Suzanne.

1979   *In Habit: An Anthropological Study of Working Nuns.* London and Boston: Faber & Faber.

1980   "Ritual in Performance and Interpretation: The Mass in a Convent Setting." In *Sacrifice*, edited by M. F. C. Bourdillon and Meyer Fortes, 89-106. London and New York: Published by Academic Press for the Royal Anthropological Institute of Great Britain and Ireland.

Carter, B. L.

1983   "On Spreading the Gospel to Egyptians Sitting in Darkness: The Political Problem of Missionaries in Egypt in the 1930s." *Middle Eastern Studies* 19 (October): 18-36.

1988   *The Copts in Egyptian Politics, 1918-1952.* Cairo: American University in Cairo Press. Originally published in 1986 by Croon Helm, London.

Chauleur, Sylvestre.

1960   *Histoire des coptes d'Égypte.* Paris: La Colombe.

Chitham, E. J.

1986   *The Coptic Community in Egypt: Spatial and Social Change.* Centre for Middle Eastern and Islamic Studies. Occasional Papers Series no. 32. Durham, Eng.: University of Durham.

Chitty, Derwas J.

1966   *The Desert a City: An Introduction to the Study of Egyptian and Palestinian Monasticism under the Christian Empire.* Oxford: Basil Blackwell.

Christian, William A.

1972   *Person and God in a Spanish Valley.* Studies in Social Discontinuity. New York and London: Seminar Press.

Cirlot, J. E.

1991   *A Dictionary of Symbols.* Translated from the Spanish by Jack Sage. 2d ed. New York: Dorset Press. Originally published in 1971 by Routledge.

Coser, Lewis A.

1974   *Greedy Institutions: Patterns of Undivided Commitment.* New

York: Free Press; London: Macmillan.

Crum, W. E.
1932   "A Nubian Prince in an Egyptian Monastery." Reprinted from
        Studies Presented to F. LI. Griffith, 137-48. London: Egypt
        Exploration Society; Humphrey Milford, Oxford University
        Press.

Curzon, Robert.
1955   *Visits to Monasteries in the Levant*. Ithaca, N.Y.: Cornell Uni-
        versity Press. Originally published in London in 1849. Reprint
        of the 1865 ed.

Daniel-Rops, H.
1959   *The Church in the Dark Ages*. Vol. 2 of *History of the Church of
        Christ*. Translated from the French by Audrey Butler. London:
        J. M. Dent & Sons; New York: E. P. Dutton & Co.

Daoud, Marcos.
1975   *The Coptic Orthodox Church: Church Sacraments*. Cairo: Dar el
        Alam el Arabi.

Davies, Douglas.
1977   "An Interpretation of Sacrifice in Leviticus." *Zeitschrift für die
        alttestamentliche Wissenschaft* 89:387-99.

Davis, Leo Donald.
1987   *The First Seven Ecumenical Councils (325-787)* Wilmington, Del.:
        Michael Glazier.

De Waal Malefijt, Annemarie.
1968   *Religion and Culture: An Introduction to Anthropology of Reli-
        gion*. New York and London: Macmillan.
1974   *Images of Man: A History of Anthropological Thought*. New
        York: Alfred A. Knopf.

Doorn-Harder, Nelly van and Kari Vogt, eds.
1997   *Between Desert and City: The Coptic Orthodox Church Today*.
        Oslo: Institute for Comparative Research in Human Culture.

Doorn-Harder, Pieternella van.
1995   *Contemporary Coptic Nuns*. Studies in Comparative Religion.
        Columbia, S.C.: University of South Carolina Press.

Douglas, Mary.
1966   *Purity and Danger: An Analysis of Concepts of Pollution and
        Taboo*. London: Routledge & Kegan Paul.

1970   *Natural Symbols: Explorations in Cosmology*. First American ed. New York: Pantheon Books. Originally published by Barrie & Rockliff: Cresset Press, London.

1978   *Cultural Bias*. Royal Anthropological Institute of Great Britain and Ireland. Occasional Paper, no. 35. London: Royal Anthropological Institute.

Duby, Georges.

1967   *The Making of the Christian West, 980-1140*. Translated from the French by Stuart Gilbert. Geneva: Éditions d'Art Albert Skira.

Durkheim, Emile.

1965   *The Elementary Forms of the Religious Life*. Translated from the French by Joseph Ward Swain. New York: Free Press. Originally published in 1915 by Allen & Unwin, London.

Evans-Pritchard, E. E.

1940   *The Nuer, a Description of the Modes of Livelihood and Political Institutions of a Nilotic People*. Oxford: Clarendon Press.

1962   *Nuer Religion*. Oxford: Clarendon Press. Reprint of the 1956 ed.

1964   Foreword to *Sacrifice: Its Nature and Function*, by Henri Hubert and Marcel Mauss. Chicago and London: University of Chicago Press.

1974   Foreword to *W. Robertson Smith and the Sociological Study of Religion*, by T. O. Beidelman. Chicago and London: University of Chicago Press.

Evelyn White, Hugh G.

1973   *The History of the Monasteries of Nitria and of Scetis*, edited by Walter Hauser. Part II of *The Monasteries of the Wadi 'N Natrun*. New York: Arno Press. Reprint of the *Publications of the Metropolitan Museum of Art*. Egyptian Expedition, vols. 2, 4 and 8. New York: Metropolitan Museum of Art, 1932.

Evetts, B. T. A., ed. and trans.

1888   *The Rites of the Coptic Church: The Order of Baptism and the Order of Matrimony According to the Use of the Coptic Church*. Translated from Coptic MSS. London: David Nutt.

1948   *History of the Patriarchs of the Coptic Church of Alexandria*. Attributed to Severus, Bishop of Ashmunen, et al. 4 vols. Published in parts in vols. 1, 5 and 10 of *Patrologia Orientalis*. Arabic text edited, translated and annotated by B. Evetts. Paris: Firmin-Didot and Co. Reprint of the 1904-14 ed.

1969   *The Churches & Monasteries of Egypt and Some Neighbouring Countries.* Attributed to Abu Salih, the Armenian. Translated from the original Arabic with added notes by Alfred J. Butler. London: Butler & Tanner. Reprint of the 1895 ed. published by Clarendon Press, Oxford.

Fakhouri, Hani.
1972   *Kafr el-Elow: An Egyptian Village in Transition.* Case Studies in Cultural Anthropology. New York and London: Holt, Rinehart and Winston.

Farag, Rofail Farag.
1964   *Sociological and Moral Studies in the Field of Coptic Monasticism.* Supplement 1 to the Annual of Leeds University Oriental Society. Leiden: E. J. Brill.

Farag, Youssef.
1983   *al-Qibt; Les Coptes; The Copts; Die Kopten.* Text in Arabic, French, English and German. Hamburg: European Coptic Union.

Fedden, Henry.
1937   "A Study of the Monastery of St. Antony in the Eastern Desert." University of Egypt. Faculty of Arts. *Bulletin* 5:1-60.

Ferrar, W. I.
1919-20 "Egyptian Monasticism." *Church Quarterly Review* 89:233-46.

Firth, Raymond.
1961   *Elements of Social Organization.* 3d ed. Josiah Mason Lectures delivered at the University of Birmingham in 1947. London: Watts & Co.

1963   "Offering and Sacrifice: Problems of Organization." *The Journal of the Royal Anthropological Institute of Great Britain and Ireland* 93 (1-2): 12-24.

1973   *Symbols, Public and Private.* Symbol, Myth, and Ritual Series. Ithica, N.Y.: Cornell University Press.

Foley, Rolla.
1953   *Song of the Arab: The Religious Ceremonies, Shrines and Folk Music of the Holy Land Christian Arab.* New York: Macmillan.

Foucault, Michael.
1988   *Technologies of the Self: A Seminar with Michael Foucault.* Amherst: University of Massachusetts Press.

Frend, W. H. C.
1969   "Christianity in the Middle East: Survey down to A. D. 1800." In *Judaism and Christianity.* Vol. 1 of *Religion in the Middle East: Three Religions in Concord and Conflict,* edited by A. J.

Arberry, 239-96. Cambridge: Cambridge University Press.

1972   *The Rise of the Monophysite Movement: Chapters in the History of the Church in the Fifth and Sixth Centuries.* Cambridge: Cambridge University Press.

1985   *Saints and Sinners in the Early Church: Differing and Conflicting Traditions in the First Six Centuries.* Theology and Life Series, vol. 11. Wilmington, Del.: Michael Glazier.

Gabriel, Alfons.
1969   "The Geography of the Sahara." In *Sahara*, edited by Christopher Kruger, in collaboration with Alfons Gabriel, et al., 10-65. New York: G. P. Putnam's Sons.

Gaselee, Stephen.
1932   "The Psychology of the Monks of the Egyptian Desert." *Philosopher* 10:73-81.

Geertz, Clifford.
1966   "Religion as a Cultural System." In *Anthropological Approaches to the Study of Religion*, edited by Michael Banton, 1-46. A.S.A. Monograph 3. London: Tavistock Publications.

1968   *Islam Observed: Religious Development in Morocco and Indonesia.* New Haven, Conn. and London: Yale University Press.

Gellner, Ernest.
1981   *Muslim Society.* Vol. 32 of the Cambridge Studies in Social Anthropology. London and New York: Cambridge University Press.

Gilmore, David D.
1990   *Manhood in the Making: Cultural Concepts of Masculinity.* New Haven, Conn. and London: Yale University Press.

Gilsenan, Michael.
1973   *Saint and Sufi in Modern Egypt: An Essay in the Sociology of Religion.* Oxford Monographs on Social Anthropology. Oxford: Clarendon Press.

Girard, Rene.
1977   *Violence and the Sacred.* Translated from the French by Patrick Gregory. Baltimore, Md. and London: Johns Hopkins University Press.

1995   Foreword to *Violence Unveiled: Humanity at the Crossroads*, by Gil Bailie. New York: Crossroad.

Goffman, Erving.
1959   *The Presentation of Self in Everyday Life.* Garden City, N.Y.: Doubleday & Co.

1961   *Asylums: Essays on the Social Situation of Mental Patients and Other Inmates*. Garden City, N.Y.: Doubleday & Co.

Gorst, Eldon.
1970   "Egypt in 1904." Appendix 3 in *England and Egypt*, by Alfred Milner, 404-22. New York: Howard Fertig. Reprint of the 1920 (13th) ed., Edward Arnold, London.

Gray, G. B.
1925   *Sacrifice in the Old Testament: Its Theory and Practice*. Oxford: Clarendon Press.

Gregorius, Anba, Bishop for Higher Theological Studies, Coptic Culture and Scientific Research, Cairo.
1975   "Baptism and Chrismation According to the Rite of the Coptic Orthodox Church." *Bulletin de la Société d'Archéologie Copte* 21:19-32.
1982   "Christianity, the Coptic Religion and Ethnic Minorities in Egypt." *GeoJournal* 6 (1): 57-62.

Grimes, Ronald L.
1982   *Beginnings in Ritual Studies*. Lanham, Md., New York and London: University Press of America.

Habashi, Labib and Zaki Tawudrus.
1939   *Fi Sahra' al-'Arab wa al-'Adyira al-Sharqiya* (On the Arab Desert and the Eastern Monasteries). Cairo: Egyptian Archaeological Society.

Hancock, Graham.
1992   *The Sign and the Seal: A Quest for the Lost Ark of the Covenant*. London: Macmillan.

Hanna, Shenouda.
1963   *Who Are the Copts?* 3d ed. Cairo: Costa Tsoumas & Co.

Hardy, Edward R.
1952   *Christian Egypt: Church and People: Christianity and Nationalism in the Patriarchate of Alexandria*. New York: Oxford University Press.

Heikal, Mohamed.
1983   *Autumn of Fury: The Assassination of Sadat*. First American ed. New York: Random House. Also published by Andre Deutsch, London.

Herzfeld, Michael.
1985   *The Poetics of Manhood: Contest and Identity in a Cretan Mountain Village*. Princeton, N.J.: Princeton University Press.

Heusch, Luc de.
1985   *Sacrifice in Africa: A Structuralist Approach*. Translated from the

author's French MS by Linda O'Brien and Alice Morton. African Systems of Thought. Bloomington, Ind.: Indiana University Press.

Heyworth-Dunne, J.
1950   *Religious and Political Trends in Modern Egypt.* His Near and Middle East Monographs, no. 1. Washington, D.C.

Hopkins, Keith.
1980   "Brother-Sister Marriage in Roman Egypt." *Comparative Studies in Society and History* 22:303-54.

Horner, Norman A.
1989   *A Guide to Christian Churches in the Middle East: Present-day Christianity in the Middle East and North Africa.* Elkhart, Ind.: Mission Focus. Originally published in 1974 as *Rediscovering Christianity Where it Began: A Survey of Contemporary Churches in the Middle East and Ethiopia* by the Near East Council of Churches, Beirut.

Hourani, Albert Habib.
1947   *Minorities in the Arab World.* London and New York: Oxford University Press.

Hubert, Henri and Marcel Mauss.
1964   *Sacrifice: Its Nature and Function.* Translated from the 1898 French ed. by W. D. Halls. Chicago and London: University of Chicago Press.

Ibrahim, Fouad N.
1982   "Social and Economic Geographical Analysis of the Egyptian Copts." *GeoJournal* 6 (1): 63-67.

Ibrahim, Ibrahim A.
1979   "Salama Musa: An Essay on Cultural Alienation." *Middle Eastern Studies* 15:346-57.

Ishak, Fayek M., trans.
1973   *A Complete Translation of the Coptic Orthodox Mass and the Liturgy of St. Basil.* Toronto, Ont.: Coptic Orthodox Church, Diocese of North America.

Jackson, Michael.
1982   *Allegories of the Wilderness: Ethics and Ambiguity in Kuranko Narratives.* African Systems of Thought. Bloomington, Ind.: Indiana University Press.

Joseph, Suad, and Barbara L. K. Pillsbury, eds.
1978   *Muslim-Christian Conflicts: Economic, Political, and Social Origins.* Boulder, Colo.: Westview Press.

Kamil, Jill.
  1987   *Coptic Egypt: History and Guide*. Plans and maps by Hassan
           Ibrahim. Cairo: American University in Cairo Press.
Kamil, Murad.
  1968   *Coptic Egypt*. Cairo: Printed by Le Scribe Égyptien.
Kammerer, Winifred, comp.
  1950   *A Coptic Bibliography*. Compiled by Winifred Kammerer with
           the collaboration of Elinor Mullett Husselman and Louise A.
           Shier. University of Michigan. General Library Publications,
           no. 7. Ann Arbor: University of Michigan Press.
Kaplan, Steven.
  1984   *The Monastic Holy Man and the Christianization of Early Solo-
           monic Ethiopia*. Studien zur Kulturkunde. Vol. 73. Wiesbaden:
           Franz Steiner Verlag.
Karas, Shawky F.
  1986   *The Copts Since the Arab Invasion: Strangers in Their Land*.
           Jersey City, N.J.: American, Canadian and Australian C. Cop-
           tic Associations.
Karl Baedeker (Firm)
  1929   *Egypt and the Sudan: Handbook for Travellers*. 8th rev. ed.
           Leipzig: Karl Baedeker.
Kepel, Gilles.
  1985   *Muslim Extremism in Egypt: The Prophet and Pharaoh*. Trans-
           lated from the French by Jon Rothschild. Berkeley and Los
           Angeles: University of California Press.
King, Archdale A.
  1947-48 *The Rites of Eastern Christendom*. 2 vols. Rome: Catholic Book
           Agency.
Kluckhohn, Clyde.
  1972   "Myths and Rituals: A General Theory," In *Reader in Compara-
           tive Religion: An Anthropological Approach*, 3d ed. Edited by
           William A. Lessa and Evon Z. Vogt, 93-105. New York:
           Harper & Row. Reprinted with minor abridgements from the
           Harvard Theological Review 35 (January 1942): 45-79.
Knowles, David.
  1969   *Christian Monasticism*. New York and Toronto: McGraw-Hill
           Book Co.
Lacarrière, Jacques.
  1964   *Men Possessed by God: The Story of the Desert Monks of Ancient
           Christendom*. Translated from the French by Roy Monkcom.
           Garden City, N.Y.: Doubleday & Co.

Lambdin, Thomas O.
  1983   *Introduction to Sahidic Coptic.* Macon, Ga.: Mercer University
          Press.
Lane, Edward William.
  1973   *An Account of the Manners and Customs of the Modern Egyp-
          tians.* Facsimile of the 1860 (5th) ed., edited by Edward Stanley
          Poole. With a new introd. by Jon Manchip White. New York:
          Dover Publications.
  1906   *The Story of Cairo.* London: J. M. Dent & Co.
  1968   *A History of Egypt in the Middle Ages.* London: Frank Cass &
          Co. Reprint of the 1925 (4th) ed.
Lane-Poole, Stanley.
  1968   *A History of Egypt in the Middle Ages.* London: Frank Cass &
          Co. Reprint of the 1925 (4th) ed.
Leach, Edmund.
  1967   *Genesis As Myth and Other Essays.* New York: Cambridge Uni-
          versity Press.
  1972   "The Structure of Symbolism." In *The Interpretation of Ritual:
          Essays in Honour of A. I. Richards,* edited by J. S. La Fontaine,
          239-75. London: Tavistock Publications.
  1974   *Claude Levi-Strauss.* Rev. ed. New York: Viking Press. Origin-
          ally published in 1970.
  1976   *Culture & Communication, the Logic by Which Symbols Are
          Connected: An Introduction to the Use of Structuralist Analysis
          in Social Anthropology.* Themes in the Social Sciences. London
          and New York: Cambridge University Press.
Leach, Edmund and D. Alan Aycock.
  1983   *Structuralist Interpretations of Biblical Myth.* London and New
          York: Published for the Royal Anthropological Institute of
          Great Britain and Ireland by Cambridge University Press.
Leeder, S. H.
  1973   *Modern Sons of the Pharaohs.* New York: Arno Press. Reprint
          of the 1918 ed. published by Hodder and Stoughton under title:
          *Modern Sons of the Pharaohs: A Study of the Manners and Cus-
          toms of the Copts of Egypt.*
Leroy, Jules.
  1963   *Monks and Monasteries of the Near East.* Translated from the
          French by Peter Collin. London: George G. Harrap & Co.
Levi-Strauss, Claude.
  1945   "French Sociology." Chapter 17 of *Twentieth Century Sociology,*
          edited by Georges Gurvitch and Wilbert E. Moore, 503-37.

New York: Philosophical Library.

1963   "The Structural Study of Myth." In vol. 1 of *Structural Anthropology*, 206-31. Translated from the French by Claire Jacobson and Brooke Grundfest Schoepf. New York and London: Basic Books.

Levy, Reuben.

1962   *The Social Structure of Islam*. Cambridge: Cambridge University Press. Originally published as *The Sociology of Islam*, 1957.

Liesel, Nikolaus.

1963   *The Eucharistic Liturgies of the Eastern Churches*. Translated from the German by David Heimann. Collegeville, Minn.: Liturgical Press.

Little, Tom.

1958   *Egypt*. Nations of the Modern World Series. New York: Frederick A. Praeger.

Loisy, Alfred Firmin.

1962   *The Birth of the Christian Religion* and *The Origins of the New Testament*. 2 vols in 1. Authorized translation from the French by L. P. Jacks. New Hyde Park, N.Y.: University Books.

Mackean, W. H.

1920   *Christian Monasticism in Egypt to the Close of the Fourth Century*. London: Society for Promoting Christian Knowledge. New York: Macmillan.

Malan, Solomon C., trans.

1872   *The Divine Liturgy of Saint Mark the Evangelist*. Translated from an old Coptic MS, and compared with the printed copy of that same liturgy as arranged by St. Cyril. Vol. 1 of *Original Documents of the Coptic Church*. London: David Nutt.

1873   *The Calendar of the Coptic Church*. Translated from an Arabic MS, with notes. Vol. 2 of *Original Documents of the Coptic Church*. London: David Nutt.

1873   *A Short History of the Copts and of Their Church*. Translated from the Arabic of Taqi-ed-Din el-Maqrizi. Vol. 3 of *Original Documents of the Coptic Church*. London: David Nutt.

Malaty, Tadrous Y.

1986a   *The Coptic Orthodox Church As an Ascetic Church*. Preparatory ed. Text in English and Arabic. Alexandria: St. George Coptic Orthodox Church.

1986b   *The Coptic Orthodox Church As a Church of Erudition & Theology*. Preparatory ed. Text in English and Arabic. Alexandria: St. George Coptic Orthodox Church.

1986c   *Christ in the Eucharist*. The Orthodox Concept, 2. Alexandria: St. George Coptic Orthodox Church.

1987   *Introduction to the Coptic Orthodox Church*. Preparatory ed. Ottawa, Ont.: St. Mary Coptic Orthodox Church.

Malinowski, Bronislaw.
1954   *Magic, Science and Religion and Other Essays*. Garden City, N.Y.: Doubleday & Co.

Martin, M.
1973   "The Coptic-Muslim Conflict in Egypt: Modernization of Society and Religious Renovation." In *Tensions in the Middle East.* CEMAM Reports 1:31-51.

al Masri, Iris Habib.
1958   "A Historical Survey of the Convents for Women in Egypt Up to the Present Day." *Bulletin de la Société d'Archéologie Copte* 14:63-111.

1977   *Introduction to the Coptic Church*. Cairo: Dar el Alam el Arabi.

1978   *The Story of the Copts: The True Story of Christianity in Egypt.* Book 1: *From the Foundation of the Church by Saint Mark to the Arab Conquest.* Cairo: Middle East Council of Churches.

1982   *The Story of the Copts*. Book 2: *From the Arab Conquest to the Abba Shenouda III.* Newberry Spring, Calif.: St. Anthony Coptic Orthodox Monastery.

1987   *The Story of the Copts*. Book 3: *Grandeur and Servitude: From the Reign of the Mamlukes to the End of Ismail's Rule.* Calif.: Coptic Bishopric for African Affairs.

Matta el-Meskeen, Abuna.
1982   *Rules for Ascetic Life*. Desert of Scete: Monastery of St. Macarius Press.

1984   *Coptic Monasticism & The Monastery of St. Macarius: A Short History.* Scetis: Monastery of St. Macarius.

1988   *The Coptic Calendar*. Desert of Scete: Monastery of St. Macarius Press.

McKinnon, Michael (Producer/Director)
1995   *Nile: River of Gods*. Bethesda, Md.: Discovery Communications. Video.

Meinardus, Otto F. A.
1965   *Christian Egypt, Ancient and Modern.* Cairo: Cahiers d'Histoire Égyptienne.

1966-67 "Mystical Phenomena Among the Copts." Parts 1-2. *Ostkirchliche Studien* 15:143-53; 16:289-307.

1969   "The Coptic Church in Egypt." In *Judaism and Christianity*. Vol. 1 of *Religion in the Middle East: Three Religions in Concord and Conflict*, edited by A. J. Arberry, 423-53. Cambridge: Cambridge University Press.

1970a   *Christian Egypt, Faith and Life*. Cairo: American University in Cairo Press.

1970b   "Notes on Some Non-Byzantine Monasteries and Churches in the East." *Eastern Churches Review* (Spring): 50-58.

1986   *The Holy Family in Egypt*. Cairo: American University in Cairo Press. Originally published as *In the Steps of the Holy Family from Bethlehem to Upper Egypt*. Cairo: Dar al-Maaref, 1963.

1989   *Monks and Monasteries of the Egyptian Deserts*. Rev. ed. Cairo: American University in Cairo Press. Originally published in 1961.

Merton, Thomas.

1973   *The Asian Journal of Thomas Merton*. Edited from his original notebooks by Naomi Burton, Patrick Hart & James Laughlin. New York: New Directions.

1977   *The Monastic Journey*. Edited by Patrick Hart. Mission, Kans.: Sheed Andrews and McMeel.

Middleton, J. Henry.

1882   "The Copts of Egypt and Their Churches." *The Academy* 22: 248-49; 266-67; 285-86; 318-19.

Middleton, John.

1964   *Lugbara Religion: Ritual and Authority Among an East African People*. London and New York: Published for the International African Institute by Oxford University Press. Reprint of the 1960 ed.

Mikhail, Kyriakos.

1911   *Copts and Moslems under British Control: A Collection of Facts and a Résumé of Authoritative Opinions on the Coptic Question*. London: Smith, Elder & Co.

Milner, Alfred.

1970   *England in Egypt*. New York: Howard Fertig. Reprint of the 1920 (13th) ed., Edward Arnold, London. First published in 1892.

Mohler, James A.

1971   *The Heresy of Monasticism. The Christian Monks: Types and Antitypes, an Historical Survey*. Staten Island, N.Y.: Alba House.

Morenz, Siegfried.

1973   *Egyptian Religion*. Translated from the German by Ann E.

Keep. London: Methuen & Co.

Morrison, Stanley Andrew.
1954   *Middle East Tensions: Political, Social, and Religious.* New York: Harper. First published as *Middle East Survey: The Political, Social, and Religious Problems.* London: SCM Press.

Morton, H. V.
1945   *Through Lands of the Bible.* 3d ed. London: Methuen & Co.

Mosharrafa, Moustafa M.
1947-48 *Cultural Survey of Modern Egypt.* 2 vols. London and New York: Longmans, Green.

Moubarac, Youakim.
1977   *Recherches sur la pensée chrétienne et l'Islam dans les temps modernes et à l'époque contemporaine.* Beirut: Université Libanaise.

Mubarak, Hosni
2001   Cited in "Egypt delays trial of editor charged over monk story," *Jordon Times* (June 25, 2001). Quoted from the Internet article: http://www.jordanembassyus.org/06252001003.htm, page 2.

Naguib, Selim.
1981   *Les Copts: Chrétiens d'Égypte face à l'Islam.* Montreal and Jersey City, N.J.: Associations Copte Américaine et Canadienne.

Neame, A.
1972   "The Christian Dilemma in Egypt and Lebanon." *The New Middle East* 51:19-22.

Needham, Rodney.
1972   *Belief, Language, and Experience.* Chicago: University of Chicago Press.
1985   *Exemplars.* Berkeley and Los Angeles: University of California Press.

New York Times.
1985   "Coptic Pope Welcomed by Hundreds in Cairo." (January 4).

O'Leary, De Lacy.
1911   *The Daily Office and Theotokia of the Coptic Church.* London: Simpkin, Marshall, Hamilton, Kent.
1937   *The Saints of Egypt.* London: Society for Promoting Christian Knowledge. New York: Macmillan.

Otto, Rudolf.
1950   *The Idea of the Holy: An Inquiry into the Non-Rational Factor in the Idea of the Divine and Its Relation to the Rational.* 2d ed. Translated by John W. Harvey. London and New York:

Oxford University Press.

Palladius, Bishop of Aspuna.
1964   *Palladius: The Lausiac History.* Translated and annotated by
        Robert T. Meyer. Ancient Christian Writers: The Works of the
        Fathers in Translation, no. 34. New York: Newman Press.

Pankhurst, Richard.
1990   *A social History of Ethiopia: The Northern and Central Highlands
        from Early Medieval Times to the Rise of Emperor Tewodros II.*
        Addis Ababa: Institute of Ethiopian Studies, Addis Ababa Uni-
        versity.

Pearson, Birger A. & James E. Goehring, eds.
1986   *The Roots of Egyptian Christianity.* Studies in Antiquity and
        Christianity. Philadelphia: Fortress Press.

Pennington, J. D.
1982   "The Copts in Modern Egypt." *Middle Eastern Studies* 18 (2):
        158-79.

Piddocke, Stuart.
1968   "The Potlatch System of the Southern Kwakiutl: A New
        Perspective." In *Economic Anthropology: Readings in Theory and
        Analysis,* edited by Edward E. LeClair, Jr., and Harold K.
        Schneider, 283-99. New York: Holt Rinehart and Winston.

Polanyi, Karl.
1971   *Primitive, Archaic, and Modern Economics: The Essays of Karl
        Polanyi.* Edited by George Dalton. Boston: Beacon Press.

Polk, William R.
1991   *The Arab World Today.* 5th ed. Cambridge, Mass. and London:
        Harvard University Press. First ed. published in 1965 as *The
        United States and the Arab World.*

Radcliffe-Brown, A. R.
1958   "The Comparative Method in Social Anthropology." Chapter
        5 of *Method in Social Anthropology: Selected Essays,* edited by M.
        N. Srinivas, 108-29. Chicago: University of Chicago Press.

Rahner, Karl.
1983   *The Practice of Faith: A Handbook of Contemporary Spirituality.*
        New York: Crossroad. Originally published as *Praxis des
        Glaubens: Geistliches Lesebuch,* edited by Karl Lehmann and
        Albert Raffelt. Verlag Herder Freiburg im Breisgau, 1982.

Rappaport, Roy A.
1971   "Ritual Regulation of Environmental Relations Among a New
        Guinea People." In *Melanesia: Readings on a Culture Area,*
        edited by L. L. Langness and John C. Weschler, 68-82. New

enl. ed. Scranton and London: Chandler Publishing Co. Reprinted from *Ethnology*, 1967 (6): 17-30.

Reidhead, Van A.
  1993   "Structure and Anti-Structure in Monasticism and Anthropology: Epistemological Parallels and Adaptive Models." *Anthropology of Consciousness* 4 (2): 9-22.

Rifaat, Mohammed.
  1947   *The Awakening of Modern Egypt*. London and New York: Longmans, Green.

Robertson Smith, William.
  1927   *Lectures on the Religion of the Semites: The Fundamental Institutions*. 3d ed. New York: Macmillan; London: A. & C. Black.

Rogerson, J. W.
  1980   "Sacrifice in the Old Testament: Problems of Method and Approach." In *Sacrifice*, by M. F. C. Bourdillon and Meyer Fortes, 45-59. London and New York: Published by Academic Press for the Royal Anthropological Institute of Great Britain and Ireland.

Rohlfs, Gerhard.
  1985   *Drei Monate in der libyschen Wüste*, mit einer Einleitung von Frank Bliss. Bonn: Politischer Arbeitskreis Schulen. Originally published in 1875 by T. Fischer, Cassel.

Roncaglia, Martiniano.
  1966   *Histoire de l'église copte*. Vol 1 of *Histoire de l'église en Orient*. Beyrouth: Dar al-Kalima.

Rugh, Andrea B.
  1984   *Family in Contemporary Egypt*. Contemporary Issues in the Middle East. Syracuse, N.Y.: Syracuse University Press.

Sadat, Jehan.
  1987   *A Woman of Egypt*. New York: Simon and Schuster.

Samaan, Makram and Soheir Sukkary.
  1978   "The Copts and Muslims of Egypt." In *Muslim-Christian Conflicts*, edited by Joseph Suad and Barbara L. K. Pillsbury, 129-155. Boulder, Colo.: Westview Press.

Saraya, Osama.
  1987   "Isolation of Copts." *Middle East Times* (April): 7,19-25.

Séguy, Jean.
  1954   Le monachisme copte. Cairo: Institut copte.

Seikaly, S.
  1970   "Coptic Communal Reform: 1860-1914." *Middle Eastern Studies* 6 (3): 247-75.

Shari'ati, Ali.
  1979   *On the Sociology of Islam.* Lectures by Ali Shari'ati. Translated
          from the Persian by Hamid Algar. Berkeley: Mizan Press.
Shaw, Stanford J., trans.
  1964   *Ottoman Egypt in the Age of the French Revolution*, by Huseyn
          Efendi. Translated from the original Arabic with notes. Har-
          vard Middle Eastern Monographs, no. 11. Center for Middle
          Eastern Studies. Cambridge, Mass.: Harvard University Press.
Shenouda III, Coptic Patriarch of Alexandria.
  1989   *Diabolic Wars.* Translated by Wedad Abbas. Cairo: Printed for
          the Coptic Orthodox Patriarchate by the Nuber Printing
          House.
Shoukri, M.
  1962   *Monasteries of the Wadi Natrun* (in Arabic). Cairo.
Sicard, Claude.
  1780   *Lettres édifiantes et curieuses.* Vol. 5 of *Mémoires du Levant.*
          Paris: J. G. Merigot. (Arabic translation located in the Library
          of the Société d'Archéologie Copte, Cairo.)
Simaika, Marcus.
  1897   "Some Social Coptic Customs." *Archaeological Journal* 54:225-
          238.
Sobhy, Georgy.
  1923   "Customs and Superstitions of the Egyptians Connected with
          Pregnancy and Childbirth." *Ancient Egypt* 9-16.
  1935   "Notes on the Ethnology of the Copts Considered from the
          Point of View of Their Descendance from the Ancient Egyp-
          tians." *Bulletin de la Société d'Archéologie Copte* 1:43-49.
  1943   "Education in Egypt During the Christian Period and Amongst
          the Copts." *Bulletin de la Société d'Archéologie Copte* 9:103-22.
Sozomen, Hermias.
  1855   *The Ecclesiastical History of Sozomen, Comprising a History of the
          Church from A.D. 324 to A.D. 440.* Translated from the Greek
          with a memoir of the author. London: Henry G. Bohn.
Stark, Werner.
  1970   *Types of Religious Man.* Vol. 4 of *The Sociology of Religion: A
          Study of Christendom.* First American ed. New York: Fordham
          University Press. Originally published in 1969 by Routledge
          & Kegan Paul, London.

Steiner, Franz.
  1956   *Taboo*. With a Preface by E. E. Evans-Pritchard. New York:
          Philosophical Library.
Suro, Roberto.
  1986   "Coptic Dusk in Cairo: The Faithful and the Wary." *The New
          York Times* (April 26): 2.
Taft, Robert.
  1985   "A Pilgrimage to the Origins of Religious Life: The Fathers of
          the Desert Today." *The American Benedictine Review* 36 (2):
          113-42.
Tambiah, S. J.
  1976   *World Conqueror and World Renouncer*. London and New
          York: Cambridge University Press.
Thévenot, Jean de.
  1687   *The Travels of Monsieur de Thévenot into the Levant*. Translated
          from the French by Archibald Lovell. 3 vols. in 1. London:
          Printed by H. Clark for H. Faithorne, et al.
Tugwell, Simon.
  1985   *Ways of Imperfection: An Exploration of Christian Spirituality*.
          Springfield, Ill.: Templegate Publishers.
Turner, Victor.
  1967   *The Forest of Symbols: Aspects of Ndembu Ritual*. Ithaca, N.Y.:
          Cornell University Press.
  1968   *The Drums of Affliction: A Study of Religious Processes Among
          the Ndembu of Zambia*. Oxford: Clarendon Press and the Inter-
          national African Institute.
  1969   *The Ritual Process: Structure and Anti-Structure*. Chicago: Aldine
          Publishing Co.
  1974   *Dramas, Fields, and Metaphors: Symbolic Action in Human
          Society*. Ithaca, N.Y. and London: Cornell University Press.
  1975   *Revelation and Divination in Ndembu Ritual*. Ithica, N.Y. and
          London: Cornell University Press.
  1979   *Process, Performance and Pilgrimage: A Study in Comparative
          Symbology*. Ranchi Anthropology Series, 1. New Delhi: Con-
          cept Publishing Co.
Turner, Victor, ed.
  1982   *Celebration: Studies in Festivity and Ritual*. Published on the
          occasion of an exhibition of the same name organized by the
          Office of Folklife Programs of the Smithsonian Institution at
          the Renwick Gallery, Spring 1982. Washington, D.C.: Smith-
          sonian Institution Press.

Turner, Victor and Edith Turner.

    1978   *Image and Pilgrimage in Christian Culture: Anthropological Perspectives.* Lectures on the History of Religions, n.s., no. 11. New York: Columbia University Press.

Tylor, Edward Burnett.

    1958a   *The Origins of Culture.* New York: Harper & Row. Originally published as Chapters 1-10 of *Primitive Culture* by John Murray, London.

    1958b   *Religion in Primitive Culture.* New York: Harper & Brothers Publishers. Originally published as Chapters 11-19 of *Primitive Culture* by John Murray, London.

Van Baaren, Th. P.

    1964   "Theoretical Speculations on Sacrifice." *Numen* 11:1-12.

Van Gennep, Arnold.

    1960   *The Rites of Passage.* Translated by Monika B. Vizedom and Gabrielle L. Caffee. London: Routledge & Kegan Paul.

Van Loon, Gertrud.

    1990   "The Sacrifice by Abraham and the Sacrifice by Jephthah in Coptic Art." In *Coptic Art and Culture,* edited by H. Hondelink, 43-51. Cairo: Shouhdy Publishing House.

Vaux, Roland de.

    1964   *Studies in Old Testament Sacrifice.* Cardiff: University of Wales Press.

    1975-76   *Case Studies on Human Rights and Fundamental Freedoms: A World Survey.* Assisted by Winifred Crum Ewing, et al. 5 vols. The Hague: Published for the Foundation of Plural Societies by Nijhoff.

Volbach, Wolfgang Friedrich.

    1929   "Die Koptischen Kloster in der Nitrischen Wüste." *Atlantis* 1:566-69.

Vucinich, Wayne S.

    1965   *The Ottoman Empire: Its Record and Legacy.* Princeton, N.J. and London: D. Van Nostrand Co.

Waddell, Helen, trans.

    1936   *The Desert Fathers.* Translated from the Latin with an introd. New York: Henry Holt and Co.

Wadle, Steven J.

    1980   "Christian Survival in an Islamic Nation: A Study of the Copts of Egypt." Master's thesis. Fort Wayne, Ind.: Concordia Theological Seminary.

Wakin, Edward.
   1961   "The Copts in Egypt." *Middle Eastern Affairs* 12 (7): 198-208.
   1963   *A Lonely Minority: The Modern Story of Egypt's Copts.* New York: William Morrow & Co.
Ward, Benedicta, trans.
   1975   *The Sayings of the Desert Fathers: The Alphabetical Collection.* Translated from the Greek. Cistercian Studies, 59. London: A. R. Mowbray & Co.; Kalamazoo, Mich.: Cistercian Publications.
Warriner, Doreen.
   1948   *Land and Poverty in the Middle East.* London and New York: Royal Institute of International Affairs.
Weber, Max.
   1947   *Max Weber: The Theory of Social and Economic Organization.* Translated by A. M. Henderson and Talcott Parsons; edited with an introd. by Talcott Parsons. Glencoe, Ill.: Free Press.
   1963   *The Sociology of Religion.* Translated from the 4th German ed. by Ephraim Fischoff. Boston: Beacon Press.
   1968   *Max Weber on Charisma and Institution Building: Selected Papers.* Edited with an introd. by S. N. Eisenstadt. Chicago and London: University of Chicago Press.
Wellard, James.
   1970   *Desert Pilgrimage. Journeys to the Egyptian and Sinai Deserts: Completing the Third of the Trilogy of Saharan Expeditions.* London: Hutchinson.
Westermarck, Edward.
   1916   *The Moorish Conception of Holiness (Baraka).* Helsinki: Akademiska Bokhandeln.
   1924-26 *The Origin and Development of the Moral Ideas.* 2 vols. London: Macmillan. Reprint of the 1912-17 (2d) ed.
Wilkinson, John Gardner.
   1981   *Modern Egypt and Thebes: Being a Description of Egypt, Including the Information Required for Travellers in That Country.* 2 vols. Wiesbaden: LRT-Verlag. Originally published in 1843 by J. Murray, London.
William, Archbishop of Tyre.
   1943   *A History of Deeds Done Beyond the Sea.* Translated and annotated by Emily Atwater Babcock and A. C. Krey. 2 vols. Records of Civilization: Sources and Studies. New York: Columbia

University Press. Originally published circa 1185 as *Historia Rerum in Partibus Transmarinis Gestarium.*

Wolf, Eric R.
1969   "Society and Symbols in Latin Europe and in the Islamic Near East: Some Comparisons." *Anthropology Quarterly* 42 (3): 287-301.

Woolley, Reginald, trans.
1930   *Coptic Offices.* Translations of Christian Literature. Series 3: Liturgical Texts. London, Society for Promoting Christian Knowledge. New York and Toronto: Macmillan.

Workman, Herbert B.
1913   *The Evolution of the Monastic Ideal from the Earliest Times down to the Coming of the Friars: A Second Chapter in the History of Christian Renunciation.* London: Charles H. Kelly.

Worrell, William Hoyt.
1945   *A Short Account of the Copts.* Henry Russell Lecture for 1941-1942. Ann Arbor, Mich.: University of Michigan Press.

Wray, Raymond Matthew.
2002   "On the Trail of the Ark." *Crisis* 20 (July/August): 14-23.

Würmseer, Notker.
1924   "Vom Sinn des Mönchtums." *Benediktinische Monatschrift zur Pflege religiösen und geistigen Lebens* 6:107-12.

Yamagata, Takao.
1983   *Coptic Monasteries at Wadi al Natrun in Egypt: From the Field Notes on the Coptic Monks' Life.* Studia Culturae Islamicae, no. 20. Tokyo: Institute for the Study of Languages and Cultures of Asia and Africa, Tokyo University of Foreign Studies.

Yanni, Mina K., ed.
1981   *The Agpeya: The Coptic Orthodox Prayer Book of the Hours.* Brooklyn, N.Y.: Coptic Orthodox Church of St. George.

Yinger, J. Milton.
1970   *The Scientific Study of Religion.* London and New York: Macmillan.

Author Index

In the entries citing a note, the page reference enclosed in parentheses indicates the origin of the note in the text.

Subject Index

Abd el-Masih, Abuna
  Ethiopian hermit living in Egypt, 84, 85
  Coptic monastic reform, influenced by, 85
alpha-beta analogy
  behavior affected by, 155
  lesson of, 151
  spiritual worldview of, 152
Ali, Mohammed, Mameluk ruler
  Egypt, gained control of, in A.D. 1805, 78
  Egypt, turned Westward because of reforms, 78
  Copts obtained bureaucratic positions under, 81
anchorites, Egyptian
  St. Pola, earliest, 5
  desert-based, solitary monasticism, initiated by, 64
angels
  monks lead into the desert by, 40

angels (*continued*)
  monks directed to favorable sites for new monasteries by, 46
  people, especially children, accompanied by, 152
  mozafeen, questions about, 104
Anno Martyrium (A.M.)
  See "Year of the Martyrs"
Antonius el Suriani, Abuna
  consecrated as bishop by Pope Kyrillos VI, 91
  See also Shenouda III, Pope
Antony, Saint
  "father of monasticism," 58
  biography of, 58
  meeting with St. Pola, 58, 61
  founder of eremitical monasticism, 64, 65
  Hellenized Church of Alexandria, associated with, 62
Ark of God
  See Ark of the Covenant

Kyrillos VI, Pope (*continued*)
  Abuna Matta's followers ordered
    back to the monastery by, 91
  See also Mina el Muttawahad el
    Baramous, Abuna

Libyan Desert
  source of water reserves for mon-
    asteries in Wadi Natroun, 46
"liminality"
  concept of, 29
  desert, zone of, 37, 175
  Hebrew temple, burning of oil
    lamps in, a sign of, 30
  monastery, a place of, 30
Liturgical Hours
  "eighth hour," 150, 155
  Evening Prayer, practice of, 149
  laity, also the prayer of, 155
  number of, 148
  participation of monks in Passion
    of Christ, 31, 163, 164, 173

Maglis Milli (Community Councils)
  authority of, obstructed, 80
  Butros Pasha Ghali, establishment
    of, 80, 82
  Coptic Congress, members of, 82
  Millets, replacement for, 80
  purpose of, 80
Mameluks
  ruling power in Egypt, period of,
    217n5:1(77)
marriage
  between different religions for-
    bidden in Egypt, 154
  brother-sister marriage
    heritage from pharaonic times,
      74
    social adaptation to foreign
      domination, as, 74
    strategy to protect inheri-
      tances and family estates, 73-
      74

marriage (*continued*)
  Christian women forced into
    Muslim religion by, 154, 196
martyrdom
  Islamic view of, 95
  Coptic view of, 95
  Diocletian's reign, in, 60-61, 178
  self-ascribed virtue of the Coptic
    Church, 67
  monasticism, equated with, 68, 95
  price of ethnic solidarity before
    A.D. 313, 68
Mary, Saint, Virgin Mother of God
  apparitions of, 112, 152, 182
  fast days of, 147, 184
  feast days of, 181, 182, 183
Mass, Catholic
  re-enactment of Christ's death and
    resurrection, 26
  ethical superiority of, over other
    rituals, 19, 23
Mass, Coptic
  See Kodes
Matta el-Meskeen, Abuna
  monks led from Deir el Suriani to
    the Wadi Rayan by, 43, 91
  Deir Abu Maqar, appointed as
    abbot of, 92
  1,000 feddan of farmland received
    from Sadat by, 95
Melkites
  "king's people," 72
  Church of Rome, associated with,
    72
  separate, foreign-supported patri-
    arch retained in Alexandria by,
    72
  Coptic patriarchs forced out into
    the desert by, 72
  Alexandria handed over to the
    Arabs by, 76
Millet system
  Coptic nation, framework of, 79
  Copts, rights under, 79